Contemporary
European
Architects

Volume VI

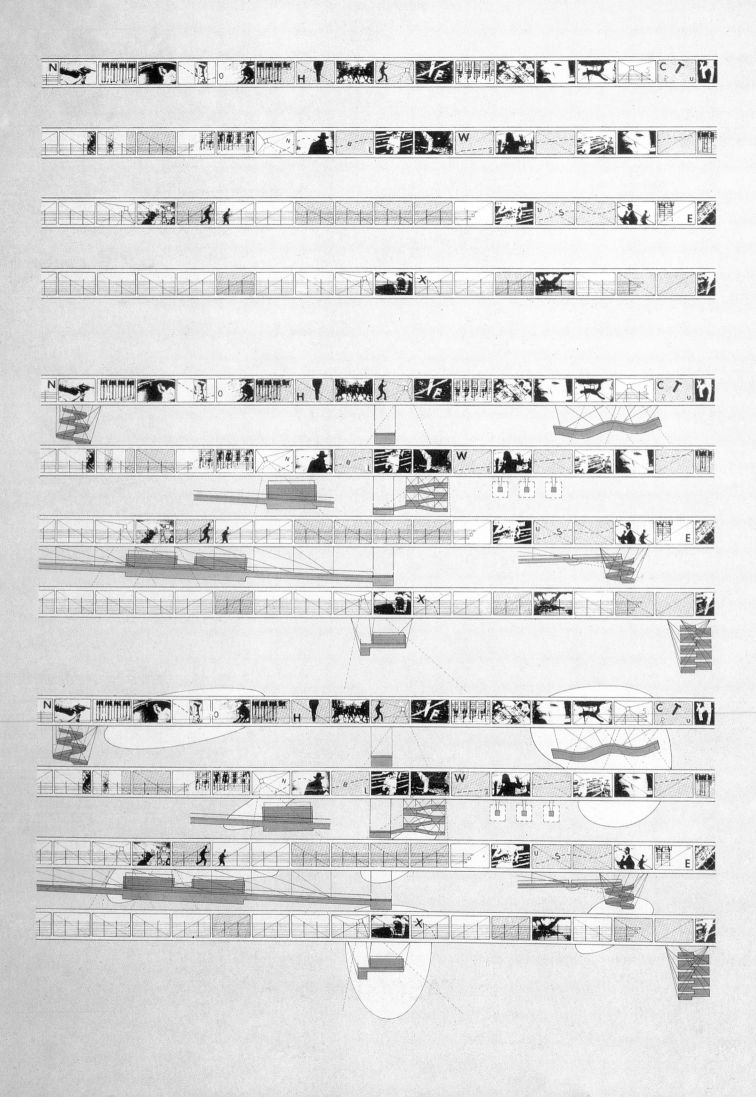

Philip Jodidio

Contemporary **European** Architects

Volume VI

KÖLN LISBOA LONDON NEW YORK PARIS TOKYO

Page 2 | Seite 2
Bernard Tschumi, Le Fresnoy National Studio for
Contemporary Arts, Tourcoing, France, 1991–97.

Bernard Tschumi, Medien- und Kulturzentrum Le
Fresnoy, Tourcoing, Frankreich, 1991–97.

Bernard Tschumi, Le Fresnoy, Studio national des
Arts Contemporains, Tourcoing, France, 1991–97.
© Bernard Tschumi Architects

© 1998 Benedikt Taschen Verlag GmbH
Hohenzollernring 53, D-50672 Köln

Edited by Christine Fellhauer, Cologne
Design: Sylvie Chesnay, Paris
Cover Design: Catinka Keul, Cologne
French translation: Jacques Bosser, Paris
German translation: Alexander Sahm,
Frankfurt am Main

Printed in Italy
ISBN 3-8228-7432-9

Contents | Inhalt | Sommaire

Exceptions to the Rule
European Architects as the century draws to a close

Ausnahmen von der Regel
Europäische Architekten im ausgehenden 20. Jahrhundert

Exeptions à la règle
L'architecture européenne au moment où le siècle s'achève

The vitality of contemporary architecture in Western Europe as the century draws to a close provides ample justification for optimism. Although economic considerations have given architects many reasons for concern about their professional future, on the whole a rising awareness of the importance of the quality of the built environment has led to a very high number of innovative projects. The time of seemingly unlimited resources is no more than a distant memory for most practicing architects. Costs must be controlled, but so too must the environmental impact of construction. These facts, rather than impoverishing the creativity of architecture, seem to have stimulated a large variety of new solutions. Then too, architects have learned to be more respectful of the existing built environment. Modernity and historical context have been brought much more into symbiosis in Europe than they were at the height of the Modernist style, which on the contrary sought very often to impose itself as a new order. The day-to-day living experience of most Europeans places them at a crossroads between tradition and rapidly evolving current events. A fundamental factor in the viability of today's architecture has been its capacity to evolve toward an acceptance of the past, even as new forms and solutions emerge. Technological progress and the widespread use of computer-aided design have also played an important role in remaking architecture.

The projects selected for publication in this book are intended to give a broad overview of the complex variety of the work of contemporary European architects. There is no dominant style today, even if a pared-down simplicity reminiscent of Minimalist art of the 1970s seems to have come to the forefront in terms of what is fashionable. The aesthetics of architectural design seem more and more often to be dictated not by predetermined stylistic conventions, but by the factors that influence a given site or a given program. This does not mean that architects no longer make "personal statements," but many have realized that building in today's Europe requires a tolerance and an openness that are ill suited to a dogmatic approach. To each rule there are exceptions. Today's architecture is more than anything else the sum of those exceptions.

Die Vitalität der zeitgenössischen Architektur in Westeuropa bietet heute, da sich das Jahrhundert seinem Ende nähert, reichlich Anlaß zum Optimismus. Obwohl ökonomische Überlegungen den Architekten durchaus Gründe geliefert haben, sich Sorgen über ihre berufliche Zukunft zu machen, kann insgesamt doch gesagt werden, daß das Bewußtsein dafür, wie wichtig die Qualität des gebauten Umfeldes ist, wächst und zu einer beträchtlichen Zahl innovativer Projekte geführt hat. Die Ära scheinbar unbegrenzter Ressourcen ist freilich für die meisten heutigen Architekten längst Vergangenheit. Kosten müssen unter Kontrolle gehalten werden, und das gleiche gilt für die ökologischen Auswirkungen eines Baus. Indes hat dieser Umstand nicht etwa den Niedergang der Kreativität in der Architektur gezeigt, sondern im Gegenteil eine bemerkenswerte Vielfalt an neuen Lösungen angeregt. Hinzu kommt, daß mittlerweile viele Architekten den bereits bestehenden Bausituationen mehr Respekt zollen. Historischer Kontext und Moderne sind inzwischen in Europa eine weitaus engere Symbiose eingegangen, als das zur Blütezeit der Moderne der Fall war, die ja stärker danach trachtete, sich selbst als neue Ordnung zu etablieren. Ihre Alltagserfahrung stellt die meisten Europäer an einen Scheideweg von Tradition und dem schnell veränderlichen Ereignis des Augenblicks. Als entscheidend für die Lebensfähigkeit der heutigen Architektur hat sich ihr Vermögen entpuppt, die Vergangenheit zunehmend zu akzeptieren, selbst dann, wenn sich neue Formen und Lösungen herausbilden. Auch der technologische Fortschritt und die Verbreitung des Computer Aided Design (CAD) haben eine wichtige Rolle beim Wandel der Architektur gespielt.

Die Projekte, die für das vorliegende Buch ausgewählt worden sind, sollen eine Übersicht über die komplexe Vielfalt der Arbeit zeitgenössischer europäischer Architekten vermitteln. Einen dominierenden Stil gibt es momentan nicht, wenn auch eine aufs Wesentliche reduzierte Einfachheit, die fern an die Minimal Art der 70er Jahre erinnert, gerade besonders im Trend zu sein scheint. Die ästhetische Beschaffenheit eines architektonischen Entwurfs dürfte mittlerweile weniger von festgeschriebenen

En cette fin de siècle, la vitalité de l'architecture contemporaine en Europe occidentale fournit ample matière à l'optimisme. Bien que le contexte économique ait récemment donné aux architectes de multiples raisons de s'inquiéter pour leur avenir, on constate une prise de conscience grandissante de l'importance de la qualité du bâti qui entraîne la réalisation d'un nombre très élevé de projets novateurs. L'époque des investissements illimités n'est plus qu'un souvenir lointain pour la plupart des praticiens. Loin d'avoir appauvri l'architecture, cette situation nouvelle a stimulé d'innombrables réactions positives. Les architectes semblent davantage avoir appris à respecter le contexte. En Europe, la modernité et le cadre historique paraissent former une symbiose beaucoup plus forte qu'à la grande époque du modernisme, qui cherchait à imposer un ordre nouveau. La vie quotidienne des Européens est soumise à la confrontation permanente de la tradition et d'une évolution rapide. L'un des facteurs fondamentaux de la viabilité de l'architecture contemporaine est sa capacité à évoluer vers une acceptation du passé, alors même qu'apparaissent de nouvelles formes et solutions. Le progrès technologique et l'utilisation de plus en plus répandue de la conception assistée par ordinateur jouent également un rôle important dans ce refaçonnage de l'architecture.

La sélection des projets présentés dans cet ouvrage se propose de fournir un panorama général de la variété complexe des interventions des architectes européens. On ne repère plus de style dominant, même si une certaine simplicité épurée, qui rappelle l'art minimaliste des années 70, semble être très à la mode. L'esthétique de la conception architecturale paraît de plus en plus souvent dictée non pas par des conventions stylistiques prédéterminées, mais par les facteurs liés au site ou au programme. Ceci ne signifie pas pour autant que les architectes aient renoncé à toute prise de position personnelle, mais que beaucoup d'entre eux ont réalisé que construire en Europe aujourd'hui requiert une tolérance et une ouverture qui ne conviennent guère à une approche dogmatique. Chaque règle connaît ses exceptions. L'architecture actuelle est d'abord la somme de ces exceptions.

Big and Modern

The French architects Jean-Paul Morel and Philippe Chaix have achieved a certain notoriety through a mastery of dynamic modern forms, often executed on a large scale. Such is the case with their "Avancée," a spectacular wedge-shaped building that forms the entrance to the enormous Renault Technocenter, located in Guyancourt, near Paris. Inspired by similar centers created by Chrysler in Detroit or BMW in Munich, the French auto maker began work on a 350 hectare complex of research and design buildings in 1993. Due to be completed quite soon, the Technocentre will include some 350,000 square meters of floor space for 6,500 persons whose mission is to "conceive more and more sophisticated models faster and at a lower cost." Laid out on the 54 meter grid established by project lead architects Valode & Pistre, the 74,000 square meter Avancée houses a variety of functions including the research and design teams. As it is situated at the entrance to the complex, it contains an entrance hall, as well as a 380 seat conference center, three restaurants, and spaces for the presentation of vehicles. The 295 meter long wedge rises up from a large basin, creating what the architects term a "fifth facade" as seen from the air. Despite the unexpected form of the building, it is a classic "post and beam" design with a prefabricated aluminum chassis and cast-in-place concrete roof elements. Made for reasons of cost, the selection of these materials is echoed in the flexible aeration system, which allows many windows to be opened as opposed to imposing air conditioning.

Chaix & Morel are one of a number of successful French offices such as Architecture Studio or Valode & Pistre that have brought a measure of design quality to industrial or administrative buildings that would otherwise have been architecturally undistinguished. A 74,000 square meter building for an auto maker, at that situated in the midst of an industrial park, naturally requires that certain compromises be made in the architecture. The trick is to produce a result that has a symbolic impact and a real presence, a result that Chaix & Morel have achieved in Guyancourt.

stilistischen Konventionen diktiert sein, als vielmehr von solchen Faktoren, die einen gegebenen Ort oder ein bestehendes Programm beeinflussen und definieren. Das heißt freilich nicht, es würden nicht länger »persönliche Aussagen« getroffen; vielmehr haben zahlreiche Architekten realisiert, daß es, um heute in Europa zu bauen, einer Toleranz und Offenheit bedarf, die mit einer dogmatischen Festlegung unvereinbar ist. Bei jeder Regel gibt es Ausnahmen. Mehr als alles andere ist die Architektur von heute die Summe solcher Ausnahmen.

Groß und modern

Die französischen Architekten Jean-Paul Morel und Philippe Chaix sind berühmt für ihren meisterhaften Umgang mit dynamischen modernen Formen, die sie häufig in großem Maßstab verwirklicht haben. Das gilt auch für ihr Projekt Avancée, einen spektakulären keilförmigen Bau, der den Eingang zu dem gigantischen Technologiezentrum von Renault in Guyancourt, nahe Paris, bildet. Inspiriert durch bereits bestehende ähnliche Zentren, etwa von Chrysler in Detroit oder von BMW in München, begann der französische Automobilkonzern im Jahre 1993 mit der Erschließung eines 350 Hektar großen Geländes, auf dem er Gebäude für Forschungs- und Entwicklungszwecke errichten ließ. Das demnächst fertiggestellte Technologiezentrum wird rund 350 000 m² Gesamtfläche für 6 500 Beschäftigte bieten, deren Aufgabe es sein soll, »immer hochwertigere Modelle in kürzerer Zeit und zu geringeren Kosten zu konzipieren«. Gebaut ist das Avancée auf der Grundlage eines Rasters von 54 m Seitenlänge, das von den mit der Projektleitung betreuten Architekten Valode & Pistre entwickelt wurde. Es hat eine Nutzfläche von 74 000 m² und erfüllt eine Vielzahl von Funktionen; so sind unter anderem darin auch die Forschungs- und Entwicklungsteams untergebracht. Da von dort aus die Gesamtanlage erschlossen wird, gibt es eine Eingangshalle, ein Konferenzzentrum mit 380 Sitzen, drei Restaurants und Flächen für die Präsentation von Fahrzeugen. Ein Blick aus der Vogelperspektive auf den aus einem großen Becken aufsteigenden 295 m langen Keil verdeutlicht, was die Architekten als eine »fünfte Fassade«

Grand et Moderne

Les architectes français Jean-Paul Morel et Philippe Chaix ont acquis une certaine notoriété par leur maîtrise des formes modernes dynamiques, souvent mises en œuvre pour des projets à très grande échelle. C'est le cas de leur Avancée, spectaculaire bâtiment en forme de coin qui constitue l'entrée de l'énorme Technocentre Renault à Guyancourt, près de Paris. Inspiré de centres similaires créés par Chrysler à Detroit ou BMW à Munich, le constructeur automobile français a entamé le chantier de ce complexe de recherche et de design en 1993 sur 350 hectares. Achevé prochainement, le Technocentre comptera 350 000 m² d'installations, où travailleront 6 500 personnes pour «concevoir plus rapidement des modèles de plus en plus sophistiqués et à moindre coût». Sur la trame orthogonale de 54 m de côté établie par les architectes en chef du projet, Valode & Pistre, cette «Avancée» de 74 000 m² abrite diverses fonctions, dont les équipes de recherche et de design. Située à l'entrée du complexe, elle contient un hall d'entrée, une salle de conférence de 380 places, trois restaurants et des espaces pour la présentation des véhicules. Ce triangle de 295 m de long s'élève au-dessus d'un vaste bassin, et dessine ce que les architectes appellent «une cinquième façade», lorsqu'il est vu de l'avion. En dépit de sa forme inhabituelle, il s'agit d'une construction classique en poteaux et poutres, avec châssis en aluminium préfabriqués et éléments de toit en béton coulés sur place. La recherche d'économie dans les matériaux sélectionnés se retrouve dans un système d'aération souple qui autorise l'ouverture des fenêtres, et évite les contraintes de l'air conditionné.

Les architectes Chaix et Morel font partie de ces agences françaises renommées (comme Architecture Studio ou Valode & Pistre), qui ont insufflé une réelle qualité dans la réalisation d'immeubles industriels ou administratifs, qui, sans elles, risquaient de tomber dans l'anonymat. Un bâtiment de 74 000 m², édifié par exemple pour un constructeur automobile en pleine zone industrielle, nécessite naturellement un certain nombre de compromis architecturaux. Si la difficulté reste d'aboutir à un résultat qui exerce un impact symbolique et possède une

Although it is by no means as vast as the Renault project, the Archeological Museum in Saint-Romain-en-Gal, also by Chaix & Morel, is on a large scale. Its 12,000 square meters of floor space are divided in two buildings, which are connected by a glass bridge. The first, a concrete building that sits in traditional fashion on the ground, contains a bookshop, cafeteria, temporary exhibition space, an amphitheater, offices, storage areas, and a 2,300 square meter restoration laboratory for mosaics. Located across the Rhone River from the French city of Vienne, this museum is quite literally on the site of a former Roman settlement, the Colonia Iulia Viennensium, which to date has yielded no fewer than 250 mosaics. The second building designed by Chaix & Morel for the permanent collections is more unexpected than the first. Set up on four rows of six pillars, it is located directly above an archeological dig. Made of metal and glass, it offers ample views out onto the 7 hectare site, which has been classified by French authorities as an historic monument. Built with an ample 181.5 million franc budget provided by the region and the central government, following a 1988 competition won by Chaix & Morel, this museum bears witness to the ambitious cultural plans of France in the 1980s. Few current projects are on the scale of this structure. Despite the fact that its design was undertaken some years ago, the building's basic volumetric simplicity sets it firmly in the spirit of the times.

Jo Coenen, who was born in 1949 in Heerlen, is perhaps best known for his Netherlands Architecture Institute, located in Rotterdam not far from the Kunsthal by Rem Koolhaas. In 1989, he was called on to help to rethink the urban layout of southern Tilburg. Located in North Brabant Province, this 200 year old town with a population of 165,000 began an industrial growth centered on textiles, machinery, leather goods, and dyes after 1860. The collapse of its textile business in the 1960s left Tilburg with vacant factory complexes located in the city center. Although attention was given to the construction of housing, the city center was neglected, a fact that is still evident in its awkward spaces and often unattractive modern architecture. It is on a highly visible and symbolic site, opposite the town hall, on the

bezeichnen. Entgegen seiner überraschenden Form handelt es sich um eine klassische »Stützen und Träger«-Konstruktion mit einer vorgefertigten Aluminiumfassade und vor Ort gegossenen Dachelementen aus Beton. Die aus Kostengründen erfolgte Wahl der Materialien findet ihr Echo in dem flexiblen Belüftungssystem, welches das Öffnen zahlreicher Fenster erlaubt und somit vielerorts die Installation teurer Klimaanlagen überflüssig macht.

Chaix & Morel zählen, wie auch Architecture Studio oder Valode & Pistre, zu jenen erfolgreichen französischen Büros, denen es gelungen ist, Industrie- und Verwaltungsbauten zu architektonischer Qualität zu verhelfen – Gebäudetypen also, deren Architektur sonst eher vernachlässigt wird. Natürlich macht ein 74 000 m² großer Bau für einen Automobilkonzern inmitten eines Industriegeländes so manchen architektonischen Kompromiß unabdingbar. Die Kunst besteht somit darin, einen Baukomplex zu schaffen, der sowohl eine symbolische Wirkung als auch wirkliche Präsenz erzielt – eine schwierige Aufgabe, die Chaix & Morel in Guyancourt zweifellos gemeistert haben.

Auch das ebenfalls von Chaix & Morel entworfene Archäologische Museum in Saint-Roman-en-Gal kann, selbst wenn es lange nicht die Ausmaße des Renault-Projekts hat, durchaus als weitläufig bezeichnet werden. Seine 12 000 m² Nutzfläche verteilen sich auf zwei Gebäude, die durch eine gläserne Brücke miteinander verbunden sind. Das erste, ein auf Bodenniveau errichteter Betonbau, nimmt eine Buchhandlung, eine Cafeteria, Ausstellungsräume, ein Amphitheater, Büros, Magazine und eine 2 300 m² große Restaurierungswerkstatt von Mosaiken auf. Das von der Stadt Vienne durch die Rhône getrennte Museum befindet sich auf dem Gelände einer ehemaligen römischen Siedlung, der Colonia Iulia Viennensium, wo bislang nicht weniger als 250 Mosaiken gefunden worden sind. Der zweite Bauteil, den die Architekten der ständigen Sammlung vorbehalten haben, ist ungewöhnlicher als der erste. Er ruht auf vier Reihen von jeweils sechs Pfeilern und steht unmittelbar über einer archäologischen Grabungsstätte. Der Bau aus Glas und Metall eröffnet einen hervorragenden Blick auf das 7 Hektar

authentique présence, Chaix et Morel ont certainement réussi à la résoudre à Guyancourt.

En rien aussi vaste que le projet Renault, le Musée archéologique de Saint-Romain-en-Gal, toujours de Chaix & Morel, reste cependant d'une échelle généreuse. Situé en face de Vienne, sur l'autre rive du Rhône, ce musée se trouve pratiquement au-dessus d'une ancienne colonie romaine, la Colonia Iulia Viennensium, qui, à ce jour, n'a révélé pas moins de 250 mosaïques. Ses 12 000 m² de surface utile sont répartis en deux bâtiments reliés par une passerelle en verre. Le premier, une construction en béton implantée de manière traditionnelle, contient un espace pour les expositions temporaires, une librairie, une cafétéria, un auditorium en amphithéâtre, des bureaux, des réserves et 2 300 m² de laboratoires pour la restauration des mosaïques. Le second bâtiment, destiné aux collections permanentes, est plus inattendu. Posé sur quatre rangées de six piliers, il s'élève directement au-dessus d'une fouille archéologique. En métal et en verre, il offre de multiples points de vue sur ce site archéologique de 7 hectares, classé Monument historique. Construit pour un confortable budget de 181,5 millions de F, apporté par la Région et l'État, à l'issue d'un concours remporté par les deux architectes en 1988, ce musée témoigne de l'ambition des projets culturels français des années 80. Peu de réalisations actuelles sont à l'échelle de celui-ci. Bien qu'il date de quelques années déjà, sa simplicité volumétrique participe de l'esprit du temps.

Jo Coenen, né en 1949 à Heerlen, est surtout connu pour l'Institut néerlandais d'architecture qu'il a construit à Rotterdam, non loin de la Kunsthal de Rem Koolhaas. En 1989, il a été appelé à contribuer à une réflexion sur l'urbanisme de Tilburg-Sud. Cette ville ancienne du Brabant-Septentrional compte 165 000 habitants. Son essor industriel dans les textiles, les machines-outils, la maroquinerie et les teintures date de 1860. L'effondrement de l'industrie textile au cours des années 60 a laissé en plein centre ville un important ensemble d'usines désaffectées. Les efforts d'urbanisme ont longtemps porté sur la construction de logements et le centre a été négligé, ce que

grounds of a former monastery garden that Jo Coenen has recently completed the new conservatory, ballet academy, and concert hall. The most visible volume, on the street side, contains the 840-seat concert hall and conservatory. Pedestrians can walk through this complex easily since much of it is lifted up to the first floor level, to reach the long straight ballet academy, which faces a large green park space. Indeed, the permeability and the transparency of the structure belie its substantial volume and make it fit into the town in a friendly way. Its direct proximity to the existing municipal theater accentuates the idea that culture, rather than industry, is now at the heart of Tilburg. Aside from the collage of curving and rectilinear forms that Coenen has brought together here with some skill, the building stands out because of an unusual use of materials including large areas of dark stained wood.

The Commerzbank of Germany is one of the country's largest private sector banks with a staff of 30,000 and 1,000 domestic branch offices. These figures may explain why the bank called on Sir Norman Foster to build the tallest office building in Europe (298.74 meters with its aerial) for its headquarters. It is obvious too that the visibility of this structure, together with public knowledge of other Foster buildings, and in particular his Hongkong and Shanghai Banking Corporation Headquarters in Hongkong, contributed to the Commerzbank's choice of architect. Foster says that this is the "world's first ecological high rise tower – energy efficient and user friendly." Four-story gardens spiral around the gently curved triangular plan with its service cores placed in the corners. A central atrium serves as a "natural ventilation chimney." In terms of energy efficiency and user comfort, the decision to allow windows of the tower both inward and outward facing to be opened in each office is certainly a good one. An automatic system closes the windows under extreme climatic conditions, just as it can open them to allow cooling at night. As is often the case in Foster's buildings, the offices are column-free. Another frequent feature of his designs, a careful attention to the immediate environment of the building is also respected. Neighboring buildings have been restored, maintaining the

umfassende Gelände, das von den französischen Behörden als historisches Monument eingestuft worden ist. Das für großzügige – ein von der Region sowie der Regierung in Paris bereitgestelltes Budget – 181,5 Millionen Francs errichtete Museum, dessen Entwurf aus einem 1988 veranstalteten Wettbewerb hervorging, ist ein Zeugnis des kulturellen Ehrgeizes im Frankreich der 80er Jahre. Nur wenige Projekte der Gegenwart weisen eine diesem Bau vergleichbare Größenordnung auf. Obwohl der Entwurf bereits einige Jahre alt ist, verkörpert das Gebäude mit seiner schlichten Einfachheit den heutigen Zeitgeist.

Die Bekanntheit des 1949 in Heerlen geborenen Jo Coenen geht vermutlich am ehesten auf das Niederländische Architektur-Institut in Rotterdam zurück, das er ganz in der Nähe der Kunsthalle von Rem Koolhaas errichtet hat. Im Jahre 1989 wurde Coenen in den Beraterstab berufen, dem die Aufgabe zufiel, Ideen für eine stadtplanerische Umgestaltung des südlichen Teils der Stadt Tilburg zu entwickeln. In der im Nordbrabant gelegenen, rund 200 Jahre alten Stadt mit 165 000 Einwohnern hatte 1860 ein industrieller Aufstieg eingesetzt, dessen Grundlage die Herstellung von Textilien, Maschinen, Lederwaren und Farbstoffen war. 100 Jahre später hinterließ der Zusammenbruch der Textilindustrie in der Innenstadt von Tilburg zahlreiche leerstehende Fabrikkomplexe. Zwar wurde der Errichtung von Wohnungen Aufmerksamkeit beigemessen, das Stadtzentrum jedoch darüber vernachlässigt – ein Umstand, der sich auch heute noch an den schwierig zu bebauenden Freiflächen und einer größtenteils unattraktiven modernen Architektur ablesen läßt. Auf dem Gelände eines ehemaligen Klosters gegenüber dem Rathaus – an einem sehr auffälligen und symbolischen Ort – konnte Jo Coenen vor kurzem ein neues Konservatorium, eine Ballettakademie sowie eine Konzerthalle fertigstellen. Der auffälligste Baukörper des Ensembles nimmt auf der Seite zur Straße hin die Konzerthalle mit 840 Sitzen und das Konservatorium auf. Um die langgestreckte Ballettakademie zu erreichen, die sich zu einer großen Grünfläche hin öffnet, können Fußgänger diesen Bau mühelos passieren, da weite Teile der Räumlichkeiten durch eine Stelzenkonstruktion auf die Obergeschoß-

démontrent des espaces publics maladroits et une architecture moderne souvent sans attrait. C'est sur un terrain hautement symbolique et visible, à savoir un ancien jardin de couvent face à l'hôtel de ville, que Jo Coenen a récemment achevé le nouveau conservatoire, une académie de danse et une salle de concert. Le volume le plus remarquable – côté rue – contient la salle de 840 places et le conservatoire. Les piétons peuvent traverser l'ensemble – pour l'essentiel surélevé d'un niveau – pour gagner le long bâtiment rectiligne de l'académie de danse qui donne sur un vaste parc. Cette ouverture et cette transparence font oublier l'importance des volumes, et les intègrent de manière agréable à la ville. La proximité directe du théâtre municipal accentue l'idée que la culture, plus que l'industrie, a repris possession du cœur de Tilburg. Outre un talentueux «collage» de formes arrondies ou droites, le bâtiment est remarquable pour son recours à des matériaux peu classiques, dont de vastes surfaces de bois teinté de couleur foncée.

La Commerzbank est l'une des grandes banques allemandes privées. Elle emploie 30 000 personnes et compte, en Allemagne, 1 000 agences. Ces chiffres expliquent que l'établissement ait pu faire appel à Sir Norman Foster pour construire son nouveau siège social qui est le plus haut immeuble de bureaux d'Europe (298,74 m, les antennes comprises). Le caractère institutionnel de ce projet et la notoriété des réalisations de Foster, en particulier le siège social de la Hongkong and Shangai Banking Corporation à Hongkong, ont contribué au choix de l'architecte. Foster précise qu'il s'agit là «de la première tour de grande hauteur à caractère écologique et convivial». Quatre étages de jardins s'enroulent autour d'un plan en triangle aux côtés légèrement incurvés, les volumes techniques étant repoussés dans les angles. Un atrium central sert de «cheminée de ventilation naturelle». En termes d'efficacité énergétique et de confort des utilisateurs, la décision de permettre l'ouverture des fenêtres de chaque bureau aussi bien vers l'intérieur que vers l'extérieur a été judicieuse. Un système automatique les ferme lorsque les conditions climatiques se détériorent, ou les ouvrent pour faciliter le rafraîchissement de la tour pendant la

Jo Coenen, Kunstcluster, Tilburg, The Netherlands, 1992–96. Openings, both within the building and towards the immediate environment make this complex very "user friendly."

Jo Coenen, Kunstcluster, Tilburg, Niederlande, 1992–96. Da sich der Bau sowohl im Inneren als auch zur unmittelbaren Umgebung hin mehrfach öffnet, wirkt er sehr »benutzerfreundlich«.

Jo Coenen, Kunstcluster, Tilburg, Pays-Bas, 1992–96. De multiples ouvertures, aussi bien vers l'intérieur que vers l'environnement immédiat, rendent ce complexe très convivial.

height of the surrounding structures, and a winter garden with restaurants and exhibition spaces is open to the public. With enormous building projects underway across the globe, including the new Hong Kong Airport, or the rehabilitation of the Reichstag in Berlin, Sir Norman Foster has done much to prove that technology, ecological awareness, and user friendliness can go hand in hand. By bringing his expertise to projects such as that of the Commerzbank, he has shown that the quality of corporate architecture can be vastly improved.

The Deutsche Messe AG, which manages Hanover's permanent fair grounds, is nothing if not big and modern. It controls 27 halls, which contain more than 450,000 square meters of floor space. Every year it plans and organizes about 50 trade fairs and exhibitions, which attract 25,000 exhibitors, 2.3 million visitors, and 16,000 journalists from over 100 countries. The Hanover fair ground is to be the site of Expo 2000, whose theme is to be "Man, Nature and Technology." The Hall 26, a 220 by 115 meter structure whose roof takes the form of three 25 meter high waves of suspended steel, glass and wood, was completed in 1996. Its author, Thomas Herzog, was born in 1941 in Munich. He was the winner of the Bund Deutscher Architekten (BDA) Gold Medal in 1993 for his entire body of work. Herzog is known in Germany for his interest in the use of sun, light and heat to create innovative energy-efficient structures. His Youth Educational Center Guest House (Windberg, Germany, 1987–91), for example, was designed with particular attention to the temperatures required in each type of room, a factor that determined the layout of the building. Thomas Herzog's Design Center (Linz, Austria, 1989–94) is a spectacular 31,000 square meter exhibition hall, for which he was selected following an international competition, demonstrating his qualifications for the Hanover building. Both the Design Center in Linz and his new building have been compared to Paxton's 19th century Crystal Palace. It is interesting to note that the reference in the area of large exhibition spaces remains one of the first great iron and glass pavilions. Although excessive energy consumption was one reason for the retreat of very large glass-covered structures,

ebene erhoben worden sind. Tatsächlich täuscht die Durch-
lässigkeit und Transparenz des Gebäudes über sein doch erheb-
liches Volumen hinweg, weshalb es sich gut in die Stadt einfügt.
Die Nähe zum bereits bestehenden Stadttheater unterstreicht
noch den Gedanken, daß heute die Kultur und nicht länger die
Industrie das Herz von Tilburg darstellt. Neben der collagen-
haften Zusammenstellung gekrümmter und rechteckiger
Formen, die Coenen mit großem Geschick durchgeführt hat,
ist es vor allem der ungewöhnliche Einsatz von Materialien,
darunter große Flächen aus dunkel gefärbtem Holz, der den
Gebäudekomplex heraushebt.

Die Commerzbank gehört mit 30 000 Beschäftigten und
1 000 inländischen Geschäftsstellen zu Deutschlands großen
Privatbanken. Diese Zahlen mögen erklären, weshalb die Bank
Norman Foster beauftragte, für ihre Hauptzentrale das höchste
Bürogebäude Europas (298,74 m mit Antenne) zu errichten.
Ebenso offenkundig ist es, daß der Wunsch nach Sichtbarkeit des
Gebäudes sowie der Bekanntheitsgrad Fosters – insbesondere
aufgrund seines Entwurfs für die Hongkong and Shanghai
Banking Corporation in Hongkong – die Commerzbank bei der
Architektenwahl beeinflußten. Das Gebäude ist, so Foster, »der
erste ökologische Wolkenkratzer der Welt – energiesparend und
benutzerfreundlich«. Über vier Geschosse winden sich Gärten
spiralförmig um den sanft abgerundeten dreieckigen Grundriß,
dessen Versorgungskerne in die Ecken verlegt worden sind. Ein
zentrales Atrium dient als »natürlicher Luftkanal«. In Hinblick
auf die Energieeffizienz und den benutzerfreundlichen Komfort
war die Entscheidung zweifellos gerechtfertigt, daß die Fenster
aller Büros – sowohl der zum Atrium hin als auch der außen
gelegenen – geöffnet werden können. Ein automatisches System
schließt die Fenster bei extremen Klimabedingungen und öffnet
sie, um nachts für Abkühlung zu sorgen. Wie häufig bei den
Bauten Fosters sind die Büros stützenfrei. Auch läßt sich hier ein
weiteres Merkmal vieler seiner Projekte, nämlich die sorgfältige
Berücksichtigung der unmittelbar benachbarten Bebauung,
feststellen. Ein Wintergarten mit Restaurants und Ausstellungsflächen ist der Öffentlichkeit zugänglich. Mit zahlreichen

nuit. Comme souvent dans les bâtiments de Foster, les plateaux
de bureaux sont sans piliers. Autre caractéristique fréquente
dans ses réalisations: l'attention portée à l'environnement
immédiat. Ici, les immeubles voisins ont été restaurés pour
préserver la hauteur du bâti environnant, et un jardin d'hiver
avec restaurants et espaces d'exposition a été ouvert au public.
Avec de gigantesques projets en cours de réalisation dans le
monde entier – dont le nouvel aéroport de Hongkong ou la
réhabilitation du Reichstag à Berlin – Norman Foster a beaucoup fait pour montrer que technologie, conscience écologique
et convivialité peuvent aller de pair. En apportant son expertise
à des projets comme celui de la Commerzbank, il démontre
que la qualité de l'architecture institutionnelle est capable de
progrès importants.

La Deutsche Messe AG (Foire d'Allemagne), qui gère les
espaces d'exposition de Hanovre, est une énorme organisation. Elle contrôle 27 halls d'exposition représentant plus de
450 000 m². Chaque année, elle programme et organise environ
50 foires et expositions commerciales, qui attirent 25 000
exposants, 2,3 millions de visiteurs et 16 000 journalistes de
plus de 100 pays. Le parc des expositions de Hanovre sera le site
de l'Expo 2000 sur le thème «L'Homme, la nature et la technologie». Achevé en 1996, le hall 26 est une structure de 220 x 115 m,
dont le toit a pris la forme de trois vagues d'acier, de verre et de
bois de 25 m de haut. Son auteur, Thomas Herzog, est né en
1941 à Munich. En 1993, il a remporté la médaille d'or du Bund
Deutscher Architekten (BDA) pour l'ensemble de son œuvre.
Connu en Allemagne pour son intérêt quant à la chaleur et la
lumière solaires, il est à l'origine de constructions novatrices
énergétiquement rentables. Sa résidence pour élèves du Centre
d'éducation de la jeunesse de Windberg (Allemagne, 1987–91),
par exemple, a été conçue avec une attention particulière par
rapport à la température requise dans chaque type de pièce,
ce qui a déterminé le plan du bâtiment. Toujours de Herzog,
le Centre de design de Linz (Autriche, 1989–94), premier prix
d'un concours international, est un spectaculaire hall d'exposition de 31 000 m² qui a illustré d'avance ce que l'architecte allait

contemporary technology has come to grips with this problem and has begun a significant return to the forms that for many were the first historical proof that modern industrial techniques could create new building types. With his Hall 26, Thomas Herzog has given proof of his ability to create dramatic, airy spaces while taking into account the realities of energy consumption. By carefully studying computer simulations and wind tunnel tests, and taking into account natural air movements, Herzog + Partner succeeded in halving ventilation costs.

The work of architects such as Chaix & Morel, Jo Coenen, Norman Foster or Thomas Herzog on large buildings has done a great deal in recent years to show that design quality, energy efficiency or respect for an urban environment are fully compatible with the demands of cost effectiveness and practicality that have always been the primary concern of clients.

The neo-minimalists

One of the clearest trends to emerge in recent years is an apparent return to the clean, simple lines of the early Modern Movement. Dubbed "neo-Modern" by some, this radical simplification of architectural volumes may in fact have as much to do with the Minimal Art of the 1970s as it does with the origins of Modernism early in the twentieth century. At least this is how some architects, such as the Frenchman Dominique Perrault, perceive their own work. Perrault, whose most notable work is the Bibliothèque Nationale de France in Paris, insists on the fact that his work differs substantially from that of the Modernists for example because he digs into the earth in order to build. Le Corbusier, he points out, with seminal works such as the Villa Savoye, created buildings that sat lightly on the earth, as though they rejected all connection to nature.

Although Perrault and others of his generation have benefited from the fashionable aspect of their minimalist approach, it would be an exaggeration to say that their work is fundamentally innovative. Indeed, their originality is often a question of surfaces and materials, a play on opacity and transparency. The Lugano-based architect Mario Botta traces the origins of his own style to

laufenden Großprojekten in aller Welt, darunter der neue Flughafen für Hongkong und die Umgestaltung des Reichstagsgebäudes in Berlin, hat Norman Foster vielfach unter Beweis gestellt, daß Technologie, Umweltbewußtsein und benutzerfreundliches Bauen miteinander zu vereinbaren sind. Indem er seine Erfahrung in Projekte wie die Commerzbank einbrachte, hat er gezeigt, daß die architektonische Qualität von Verwaltungsbauten noch erheblich gesteigert werden kann.

Die Deutsche Messe AG, von der das Messegelände in Hannover verwaltet wird, erscheint geradezu als Verkörperung all dessen, was groß und modern ist. Sie verwaltet 27 Hallen, die insgesamt mehr als 450 000 m² Grundfläche beinhalten. Jedes Jahr plant und organisiert sie rund 50 Messen und Ausstellungen, die 25 000 Aussteller, 2,3 Millionen Besucher und 16 000 Journalisten aus mehr als 100 Ländern anziehen. Auf dem Messegelände in Hannover findet zudem die EXPO 2000 statt, deren Thema »Mensch, Natur und Technologie« ist. 1996 konnte die Halle 26 fertiggestellt werden, ein 220 x 115 m großer Bau, dessen Dach die Form von drei jeweils 25 m hohen Wellen aus Stahl, Glas und Holz erhielt. Architekt ist der 1941 in München geborene Thomas Herzog, dem 1993 für sein Gesamtwerk die Goldmedaille des Bundes Deutscher Architekten (BDA) verliehen wurde. In Deutschland ist er bekannt für sein Interesse am Einsatz von Sonne, Licht und Wärme bei der Schaffung innovativer energiesparender Gebäude. So richtete Herzog beispielsweise beim Entwurf des Wohnheims der Jugendbildungsstätte in Windberg (Deutschland, 1987–91) besondere Aufmerksamkeit auf die in den jeweiligen Räumen benötigten Temperaturen, woraus sich schließlich auch der Grundriß des Gebäudes ergab. Herzogs Design-Center in Linz (Österreich, 1989–94) – das Siegerprojekt eines internationalen Wettbewerbes – ist eine spektakuläre, 31 000 m² große Ausstellungshalle, mit der er seine Eignung für das Projekt in Hannover unter Beweis stellen konnte. Sowohl das Design-Center als auch die Messehalle sind mit Paxtons Kristallpalast aus dem 19. Jahrhundert verglichen worden. Es ist übrigens bemerkenswert, daß der am häufigsten erwähnte Referenzbau unter den großen Ausstellungshallen

faire pour Hanovre. Le Centre de design de Linz et le Hall 26 ont été comparés au Crystal Palace de Paxton. Il est intéressant de noter que la référence des grands halls d'exposition demeure l'une des premières grandes réalisations en verre et acier du XIXᵉ siècle. Si la consommation énergétique excessive de ces vastes structures en verre explique en grande partie leur déclin, la technologie contemporaine a permis de maîtriser ce défaut et de réutiliser des formes qui, pour beaucoup, sont la première preuve historique que les techniques industrielles modernes peuvent donner naissance à de nouveaux types de bâtiments. Avec ce Hall 26, Thomas Herzog a prouvé sa capacité à créer des espaces spectaculaires et aériens, tout en prenant en compte les réalités de la consommation énergétique. Grâce à une étude approfondie en soufflerie, à des simulations par ordinateur, et à l'intégration des mouvements naturels de l'air, Herzog et son associé ont réussi à diviser par deux les coûts de ventilation.

Au cours des années récentes, les travaux d'architectes comme Chaix & Morel, Coenen, Foster ou Herzog sur des constructions de vastes dimensions ont beaucoup contribué à démontrer que la qualité de conception, l'efficacité énergétique ou le respect de l'environnement urbain étaient pleinement compatibles avec les exigences financières et la praticité qui restent, comme toujours, parmi les premiers soucis des clients.

Les Néo-Minimalistes

L'une des tendances les plus nettes à faire son apparition au cours de ces dernières années est un retour aux lignes nettes et simples des débuts du modernisme. Baptisée néo-moderne par certains, cette simplification radicale des volumes architecturaux est peut-être plus proche de l'art minimaliste des années 70 que des origines du mouvement moderne. C'est du moins ainsi que certains architectes perçoivent leur travail, tel le Français Dominique Perrault. Celui-ci, dont l'œuvre la plus importante est la Bibliothèque Nationale de France à Paris, insiste sur ce qui différencie substantiellement ses réalisations de celles des modernistes, par exemple, la manière dont il creuse le sol pour construire, alors que Le Corbusier, dans ses œuvres majeures,

Thomas Herzog + Partner, Hall 26, Deutsche Messe, Hanover, Germany, 1994–96. A wave-like form intended to take advantage of natural light and ventilation.

Thomas Herzog + Partner, Messehalle 26, Deutsche Messe Hannover, Deutschland, 1994–96. Die Wellenform ist vorteilhaft für den Einfall von Tageslicht und natürliche Belüftung.

Thomas Herzog + Partner, Hall 26, Foire d'Allemagne, Hanovre, Allemagne, 1994–96. Une toiture en forme de vagues pour mieux bénéficier de la lumière et de la ventilation naturelles.

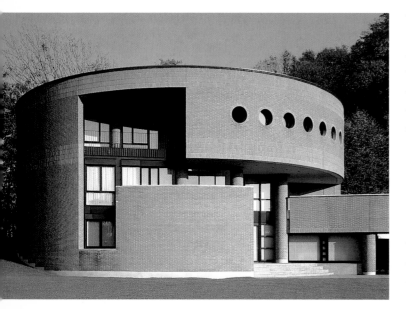

Mario Botta, Private House, Montagnola, Ticino, Switzerland, 1989/91–94. Strong geometric forms and brick cladding are typical of Botta's work.

Mario Botta, Privathaus, Montagnola, Tessin, Schweiz, 1989/91–94. Die streng geometrische Form und die Backsteinverblendung sind typisch für die Arbeiten Bottas.

Mario Botta, résidence privée, Montagnola, Tessin, Suisse, 1989/91–94. Géométries puissantes et parements de briques sont typique des œuvres de Botta.

the early influences of Le Corbusier or other figures such as Louis Kahn, and yet a defining characteristic of his work is certainly the powerful simplicity of his geometry. Circles or truncated cylinders are amongst his favorite forms, and he has very often called on brick as a primary cladding material. In its fundamental opacity, Botta's architecture does stand apart from the "neo-minimalists" who play in a different way on surfaces and the density of their materials. Botta's Private House (Montagnola, Ticino, Switzerland, 1989/91–94) published here is a reinforced concrete structure with brick facing. Its notched, semi-circular form may bear some comparison to Richard Meier's Grotta House (Harding Township, New Jersey, 1984–89). Indeed, the two architects share a common sense of the necessity to create an ordered architecture where strong lines define space, even beyond the limits of their own walls. The weight of Botta's architecture does however set it apart not only from Meier but also from the new minimalism despite its geometric volumes.

David Chipperfield, born in 1953 in London, is definitely in the forefront of a new, and quite fashionable generation of architects. Perhaps still best known for the crisp, clean lines of his boutiques for Issey Miyake, Joseph and Equipment in London, Paris, Tokyo and New York, he recently won the contract to rebuild Berlin's Neues Museum. This very large project involves the reconstruction of the war-damaged Neues Museum, which will house collections of Egyptian art, and the creation of links to the Altesmuseum and the Pergamonmuseum. A graduate of the Architectural Association in London, he worked in the offices of Norman Foster and Richard Rogers before establishing David Chipperfield Architects in 1984. His first major building to be completed in England, the River & Rowing Museum at Henley is situated in meadows on the south bank of the Thames. Intended to house a collection of rowing shells and boats, the Museum is built on an elevated concrete slab. Glass and English green oak are used to create shed-like forms, which recall not only the boat houses of Henley but also the more ephemeral tents that are put up each year at the time of the Henley Regatta. The idea of raising the platform above ground level on exposed

noch immer dieser faszinierende, zu den ersten Pavillons aus Eisen und Glas zählende Großbau ist. Einer der Gründe für den Rückgang solch großer gläserner Bauwerke war deren enormer Energieverbrauch, doch ist dieses Problem inzwischen von der modernen Technologie gelöst worden. Aus diesem Grund kehrt man nun nicht selten zu diesem Bautypus zurück, in dem viele den ersten historischen Beweis dafür sehen, daß die industrielle Technik sehr wohl imstande ist, neuartige Bauformen hervorzubringen. Mit der Messehalle von Thomas Herzog + Partner ist es gelungen, den Beleg zu erbringen, daß man dramatische, luftige Räume zu erschaffen vermag, ohne den Faktor Energieverbrauch dabei aus dem Auge zu verlieren. Durch die ausgiebige Beschäftigung mit Computersimulationen und Windkanaltests und die Berücksichtigung natürlicher Luftbewegungen ist es den Architekten gelungen, die Kosten für die Belüftung zu halbieren.

Die Arbeit von Architekten wie Chaix & Morel, Jo Coenen, Norman Foster und Thomas Herzog hat in den letzten Jahren viel dazu beigetragen zu zeigen, daß Entwurfsqualität, geringer Energieverbrauch und die Berücksichtigung des urbanen Umfeldes vereinbar sind mit der Notwendigkeit, kostengünstig und praktisch zu bauen – denn dies sind seit jeher die zwei größten Sorgen und Anforderungen von Seiten der Auftraggeber.

Die Neo-Minimalisten

Eine der Tendenzen, die sich in den letzten Jahren am deutlichsten herausgebildet haben, ist die scheinbare Rückkehr zur klaren und einfachen Linienführung der frühen Moderne. Die von einigen Kritikern als »Neo-Modernismus« bezeichnete, radikale Vereinfachung des architektonischen Baukörpers dürfte freilich mit der Minimal Art der 70er Jahre ebensoviel gemein haben wie mit den Ursprüngen der Moderne in den ersten Jahrzehnten des 20. Jahrhunderts. So zumindest sehen manche Architekten, wie beispielsweise der Franzose Dominique Perrault, das eigene Werk. Perrault, dessen wichtigste Arbeit die Bibliothèque Nationale in Paris ist, betont, daß seine Entwürfe sich wesentlich von denjenigen der Großmeister der Moderne unterscheiden, indem sie etwa in die Erde vordringen. Le Corbusier

suspendait ses constructions au-dessus du sol comme pour rejeter tout lien avec la nature.

Bien que Perrault et d'autres praticiens de sa génération aient bénéficié de l'aspect «à la mode» de ce minimalisme, il serait exagéré d'affirmer que leur œuvre est fondamentalement novatrice. En fait, leur originalité tient souvent à des surfaces, à des matériaux et à un jeu entre l'opacité et la transparence. Installé à Lugano, l'architecte Mario Botta aime à citer parmi ses sources l'influence des premières œuvres de Le Corbusier et d'autres grands maîtres, comme Louis Kahn, même si l'une des caractéristiques de son travail tient à la puissante simplicité de ses compositions géométriques. Cercles et cylindres tronqués font partie de son vocabulaire favori, et il aime à recouvrir de briques ses réalisations. Dans son opacité profonde, l'architecture de Botta se distingue d'un néo-minimalisme qui façonne de manière différente les surfaces et la densité des matériaux. La maison de Botta (Montagnola, Tessin, Suisse, 1989/91–94), présentée dans ce livre, est en béton armé paré de briques. Sa forme semi-circulaire n'est pas sans rappeler la Grotta House de Richard Meier (Harding Township, New Jersey, 1984–89). En fait, les deux architectes partagent le même sens de la nécessité d'une architecture ordonnée, dont les lignes fortement tracées définissent l'espace, même au-delà des limites de leurs murs. Le poids de la présence de l'architecture de Botta la distingue néanmoins à la fois de celle de Meier et des nouveaux minimalistes, malgré ses volumes géométriques.

David Chipperfield, né à Londres en 1953, se trouve certainement à l'avant-garde d'une nouvelle génération d'architectes passablement à la mode. Surtout connu pour l'instant par les lignes claires et tendues de ses boutiques pour Issey Miyake, Joseph et Équipement à Londres, Paris, Tokyo et New York, il a récemment remporté le contrat de la rénovation du Neues Museum à Berlin. Ce très vaste projet implique la reconstruction du musée endommagé pendant la guerre (qui abritera les collections égyptiennes) et la création de liaisons avec l'Altes Museum et le Pergamonmuseum. Diplômé de l'Architectural Association de Londres, il a travaillé dans les agences de Norman Foster et

concrete piles may also bring to mind certain traditional Japanese temple structures such as the Shosoin storehouse at Todaiji (Nara, 8th century). The careful detailing of the River & Rowing Museum, from the concrete to the woodwork and up to the stainless steel roofing, together with its clean lines, makes it an emblematic structure, which undoubtedly will have substantial influence on younger architects.

Dominique Perrault received what must be considered the commission of a lifetime when he won the competition to build the massive Bibliothèque Nationale de France in Paris. To his credit, despite the enormous political, intellectual and economic pressures that he was under, and despite the fact that he did change the form of his project in response to criticism (the four towers were lowered from a proposed height of 100 meters to 80 meters, and the base was enlarged), Perrault managed to complete a structure that is very close to his original plan. The kind of minimalism and rough elegance that he put to good use in Paris comes to the fore again in his surprising sports complex in Berlin, whose Velodrome was completed in 1997. Conceived in 1992, when Berlin was competing for the Olympic Games for the year 2000, the Velodrome appears as a shining disk, 140 meters in diameter. But rather than sitting on the earth as might be expected, this disk is all but buried, reaching down 17 meters below grade, and emerging only one meter above the surface. Within, the arena, with seating for 5,800 to 9,500 persons is set under a 115 meter clear span roof. Unexpectedly, given the radical simplicity of its exterior, the Velodrome makes something of a show of its spoked roof structure. Like a gigantic bicycle wheel, or the underside of some type of spacecraft, this defining technical element appears to float above the spectators, negating its 3,500 ton mass. The neighboring but as yet unfinished Olympic Swimming Pool complex is housed in a rectangular volume that also emerges from the earth in only a minimal way. The two shapes have been compared to silver lakes in the midst of an apple orchard. The architect has consciously sought to negate the monumental structures typically associated with the Olympic Games, and in particular those

habe, so Perrault, mit seinen Entwürfen – wie zum Beispiel der Villa Savoye – Bauten geschaffen, die scheinbar losgelöst vom Erdboden jede Verbindung mit der Natur verweigerten.

Perrault und andere Architekten seiner Generation profitierten vom modischen Aspekt ihrer minimalistischen Formensprache, doch wäre es eine Übertreibung zu sagen, ihr Werk sei wirklich innovativ. Ihre Originalität ist häufig eine Frage der Oberflächen und Materialien, ein Spiel mit Transparenz und Lichtundurchlässigkeit. Der in Lugano ansässige Mario Botta sieht die Wurzeln seines Stils im Einfluß des frühen Le Corbusier oder anderer Meister wie beispielsweise Louis Kahn. Dabei ist ein entscheidendes Merkmal seines Werks sicherlich die ausdrucksstrarke Schlichtheit der Geometrie. Kreise oder Zylinderstümpfe gehören zu seinen bevorzugten Formelementen, und häufig verwendet er Backstein als primäres Verkleidungsmaterial. In der ihr eigenen Opazität weicht Bottas Architektur von derjenigen der »Neo-Minimalisten« ab, die auf ganz andere Weise mit der Oberfläche und der Dichte der gebrauchten Materialien verfahren. Bei dem hier vorgestellten Privathaus Bottas (Montagnola, Tessin, Schweiz, 1989/91–94) handelt es sich um einen Stahlbetonbau mit Backsteinverblendung. Sein halbkreisförmiger, eingekerbter Grundriß legt den Vergleich mit Richard Meiers Grotta House (Harding Township, New Jersey, 1984–89) nahe. In der Tat teilen die beiden Architekten die Überzeugung von der Notwendigkeit einer geordneten Architektur, bei der eine strenge Linienführung den Raum definiert, auch noch jenseits der eigentlichen Umgrenzungsmauern. Allerdings unterscheidet ihr optisches Gewicht Bottas Bauten nicht nur von jenen Meiers, sondern trotz seiner Vorliebe für geometrische Baukörper auch von denen des neuen Minimalismus.

Der 1953 in London geborene David Chipperfield gehört zweifellos zur Avantgarde einer neuen, sehr erfolgreichen Architektengeneration. Seine bekanntesten Arbeiten sind bis heute seine von klarer Linienführung gekennzeichneten Boutiquen für Issey Miyake, Joseph und Equipment in London, Paris, Tokio und New York. Vor kurzem konnte Chipperfield den Wettbewerb für den Wiederaufbau des Neuen Museums in Berlin

de Richard Rogers avant de créer David Chipperfield Architects en 1984. Sa première réalisation d'importance en Grande-Bretagne est le River & Rowing Museum de Henley, situé en pleine campagne sur la rive sud de la Tamise. Ce musée, destiné à une collection de bateaux et de barques, est construit sur une dalle de béton surélevée. Le verre et le chêne anglais teinté en vert viennent habiller des structures qui rappellent les hangars à canots de Henley ou les tentes dressées chaque année à l'occasion des célèbres régates. L'idée de surélever la plate-forme sur des piliers fait également penser à certains bâtiments de temples traditionnels japonais, comme le Shosoin de Todaiji (Nara, VIIIe siècle). L'exécution soignée de ce musée et ses lignes nettes en font une structure emblématique qui exercera certainement une influence substantielle sur les jeunes architectes.

Dominique Perrault a reçu ce que l'on peut qualifier de commande de sa vie lorsqu'il a remporté le concours pour la nouvelle Bibliothèque nationale de France, édifiée à Paris. Il faut porter à son crédit que malgré les énormes pressions politiques, intellectuelles et économiques auxquelles il a été soumis, et la modification de la forme de son projet (les tours ont été abaissées de 100 à 80 m de haut et le socle a été élargi), Perrault a réussi à réaliser un bâtiment très proche de son plan d'origine. La sorte de minimalisme et d'élégance brute, dont il a fait si bon usage à Paris, est à nouveau en vedette à Berlin dans son surprenant complexe sportif, dont le vélodrome a été achevé en 1997. Conçu en 1992, lorsque Berlin avait déposé sa candidature pour les Jeux Olympiques de l'an 2000, le vélodrome est un disque brillant de 140 m de diamètre. Au lieu de reposer sur son terrain, comme on aurait pu s'y attendre, il est complètement enterré, descendant jusqu'à 17 m au-dessous du niveau du sol, dont il ne dépasse la surface que d'un mètre. À l'intérieur, l'arène, qui peut accueillir de 5 800 à 9 500 personnes, est protégée par un toit transparent sans piliers de 115 m de diamètre. De manière surprenante, étant donnée la simplicité radicale de son aspect extérieur, le vélodrome expose sa charpente rayonnante, ressemblant ainsi à une immense roue de vélo ou le dessous d'un vaisseau spatial. Elle donne l'impression de flotter au-dessus des

David Chipperfield, River & Rowing Museum, Henley-on-Thames, Great Britain, 1989/96–97. Forms intended to recall overturned boats, or the tents erected each year for the Henley Regatta.

David Chipperfield, Fluß- und Rudermuseum, Henley-on-Thames, Großbritannien, 1989/96–97. Die Form der Gebäude soll an umgedrehte Boote oder an die alljährlich bei der Henley-Regatta errichteten Zelte erinnern.

David Chipperfield, River & Rowing Museum, Henley-on-Thames, Grande-Bretagne, 1989/96–97. Ces formes rappellent les coques de bateaux retournées, ou les tentes dressées chaque année à l'occasion des régates de Henley.

Dominique Perrault, Velodrome and Olympic Swimming Pool, Berlin, Germany, 1993–98. The roof of the Velodrome seems to be the antithesis of the minimalism of the exterior of this building.

Dominique Perrault, Rad- und Schwimmsporthallen, Berlin, Deutschland, 1993–98. Die Dachkonstruktion des Velodroms erscheint wie eine Antithese zur minimalistischen Außengestalt des Gebäudes.

Dominique Perrault, vélodrome et piscine olympique, Berlin, Allemagne,1993–98. Le toit du vélodrome semble à l'antithèse du minimalisme extérieur de cette réalisation.

of 1936, which were of course held in Berlin. As important as the symbolism of this gesture may be, it should be noted that the largely buried design together with the use of thermal paning for the glass surfaces has permitted energy savings on the order of 60% compared with to an equivalent, more traditional configuration.

No school of architecture really is as coherent as critics would like it to be, but what we will call "neo-minimalism" certainly has to do with the use of simple geometric forms, careful detailing, and a play on transparency, opacity, and weightlessness. Terence Riley's 1996 "Light Construction" exhibition at the Museum of Modern Art in New York, which singled out the work of architects such as Peter Zumthor, Kazuyo Sejima or Ben van Berkel, may have defined the spirit of this movement as well as any published critique. It is clear that there is no direct connection between such disparate architects aside perhaps from their mutual awareness of each other's work. Rather the similarities that may emerge are indeed a question of the spirit of the times, a spirit that emerges with rather more strength in the main Western European countries, and perhaps in Japan, than it does for the moment in the United States, or in other areas. As Terence Riley wrote in the "Light Construction" catalogue, "In recent years a new architectural sensibility has emerged, one that not only reflects the distance of our culture from the machine aesthetic of the early twentieth century but marks a fundamental shift in emphasis after three decades when debate about architecture focused on issues of form. In projects notable for artistic and technical innovation, contemporary designers are investigating the nature and potential of architectural surfaces. They are concerned not only with their visual and material qualities but with the meanings they may convey. Influenced by aspects of our culture including electronic media and the computer, architects and artists are rethinking the interrelationships of architecture, visual perception and structure."[1]

Still deconstructing after all these years
If it can be said that an exhibition defines a movement in architecture, then a show that preceded "Light Construction" at the

für sich entscheiden. Das Projekt umfaßt die Rekonstruktion des kriegsbeschädigten Neuen Museums, das einmal die Sammlungen mit ägyptischer Kunst aufnehmen soll, und die Schaffung einer Anbindung an das Alte Museum sowie an das Pergamonmuseum. Bevor er 1984 das Büro David Chipperfield Architects gründete, hat der Absolvent der Architectural Association in London zunächst in den Büros von Norman Foster und Richard Rogers gearbeitet. Sein erster größerer Bau in England, das River & Rowing Museum in Henley-on-Thames, steht inmitten von Weideland am Südufer der Themse. Bei dem mit einer Sammlung von Ruderbooten ausgestatteten Museum handelt es sich um einen Pfahlbau aus Beton. Mit den verwendeten Materialien, Glas und englisches Eichenholz, wurde eine Grundform erzielt, die nicht nur an die Bootshäuser in Henley erinnert, sondern auch an jene eher kurzlebigen Zelte, die alljährlich um die Zeit der dortigen Regatta aufgestellt werden. Die Idee, den Bau mittels Pfeiler über Bodenniveau zu erheben, läßt auch an manche japanische Tempelbauten wie das Schatzhaus Shosoin des Todaiji-Tempel (Nara, 8. Jahrhundert) denken. Die sorgfältigen Detaillösungen – sei es der Beton oder das Holz oder auch das Dach aus Edelstahl – sowie seine klare Linienführung machen das River & Rowing Museum zu einem richtungsweisenden Bau, der zweifelsohne maßgeblichen Einfluß auf jüngere Architekten ausüben wird.

Für Dominique Perrault war es vielleicht der Auftrag seines Lebens, als er den Wettbewerb für den gewaltigen Neubau der Bibliothèque Nationale de France in Paris gewann. Trotz des enormen politischen, intellektuellen und finanziellen Drucks, dem er sich ausgesetzt sah, und trotz der Tatsache, daß er die Grundform infolge der geäußerten Kritik veränderte (die Höhe der vier Türme wurde von den ursprünglich vorgesehenen 100 m auf 80 m Höhe verringert und die Gebäudebasis vergrößert), gelang es Perrault, ein Bauwerk fertigzustellen, dessen Erscheinungsbild seinem ursprünglichen Entwurf sehr nahekommt. Der vorteilhaft gebrauchte Minimalismus und die kantige Eleganz der Nationalbibliothek tritt auch bei Perraults überraschendem Entwurf für einen Sportkomplex in Berlin hervor, von dem das

spectateurs, comme si elle niait son poids de 3 500 tonnes. Le complexe de la piscine olympique voisine – encore inachevé – est logé dans un volume rectangulaire qui émerge également du sol avec une discrétion toute minimaliste. Les deux formes ont été comparées à des lacs d'argent au milieu d'un verger. L'architecte a cherché à se différencier du type de structures monumentales généralement associées aux manifestations olympiques, et en particulier aux Jeux de 1936 qui s'étaient tenus à Berlin. Aussi important le symbolisme de ce geste soit-il, il faut noter par ailleurs que cet «ensevelissement» permet des économies d'énergie de l'ordre de 60% par rapport à une configuration plus traditionnelle. Aucune école d'architecture n'est en fait aussi cohérente que les critiques aimeraient qu'elle ne soit.

Ce que nous appelons «néo-minimalisme» est une pratique qui fait appel à des formes géométriques simples, à une exécution raffinée et un jeu entre transparence, opacité et légèreté. L'exposition organisée par Terence Riley («Light Construction») au Musée d'art moderne de New York en 1996, qui présentait les travaux d'architectes comme Peter Zumthor, Kazuyo Sejima ou Ben van Berkel, a sans doute plus contribué à définir l'esprit de ce mouvement que bien des articles de presse. Il est clair qu'il n'existe pas de connexion directe entre des architectes aussi divers, si ce n'est, peut-être, la conscience que chacun a des recherches des autres. Plutôt que des similarités qui relèvent de l'esprit du temps, c'est un esprit qui émerge avec une vigueur plus marquée dans les grands pays de l'Europe de l'Ouest, et peut-être au Japon, que pour l'instant aux États-Unis ou dans d'autres régions du monde. Comme l'écrit Terence Riley dans le catalogue de l'exposition «Light Construction»: «Au cours de ces dernières années, une nouvelle sensibilité architecturale a émergé, qui ne reflète pas seulement la distance de notre culture par rapport à l'esthétique mécaniste du début du XXe siècle, mais marque une évolution fondamentale après trois décennies de débats architecturaux concentrés sur des enjeux formels. Dans des projets notables pour leur nouveauté artistique et technique, les concepteurs contemporains explorent la nature et le potentiel des surfaces architecturales. Ils se préoccupent non

Museum of Modern Art must be cited here. "Deconstructivist Architecture," curated by Philip Johnson and Mark Wigley in 1988, brought together projects by Frank O. Gehry, Daniel Libeskind, Rem Koolhaas, Zaha Hadid, and Bernard Tschumi amongst others. Tschumi was cited at the time for his work on the Parc de la Villette in Paris. As much as any other building, his bright red garden structures, which did seem to harken back to the Constructivist designs of revolutionary Russia, defined the public view of the deconstructivist movement.

In a more fundamental definition, Mark Wigley wrote in the exhibition catalogue, "In each project, the traditional structure of parallel planes – stacked up horizontally from the ground plane within a regular form – is twisted. The frame is warped. Even the ground plane is warped. The interrogation of pure form pushes structure to its limits, but not beyond. The structure is shaken but does not collapse; it is just pushed to where it becomes unsettling."[2] Although Frank O. Gehry, with the spectacular sculptural forms of buildings like his Guggenheim Bilbao Museum in Spain, remains at the forefront of an effort to liberate architecture from its planar regularity, Bernard Tschumi, particularly in his role as Dean of the Columbia School of Architecture, has been a leading theoretician of what continues to be called Deconstructivism despite the varying goals of its supposed practitioners.

The Deconstructivist aesthetic has spread widely in Europe and in the United States. One recent building that espouses its shapes is the Museum of Modern Art or Arken in Copenhagen, by Søren Robert Lund. Set in a landscape of dunes and sailboats located to the south of the Danish capital it stands out boldly, recalling the angular shapes favored by such patently Deconstructivist architects as Zaha Hadid. Like another museum published in this volume, Renzo Piano's Science Museum in Amsterdam, the Arken takes on nautical references that are justified more by its environment than by its contents. The very name of the institution in Danish means "ark," an unexpected metaphor for an art museum. The museum café, looking out on Koge Bay, has an almost explicitly boat-like shape, which is

Velodrom 1997 vollendet wurde. Die 1992 – als Berlin sich für die Austragung der Olympischen Spiele im Jahre 2000 bewarb – konzipierte Radsporthalle bietet sich als glänzende Scheibe von 140 m Durchmesser dar. Wider Erwarten ragt diese Scheibe nicht in die Höhe, sondern ist fast vollständig, bis in 17 m Tiefe, in die Erde versenkt, so daß sie sich nur 1 m über Bodenniveau erhebt. Die Arena, die zwischen 5 800 und 9 500 Zuschauern Platz bietet, liegt unter einem stützenfreien Dach, das 115 m überspannt. Angesichts der radikalen Einfachheit der äußeren Gestalt ist man überrascht, wie effektvoll das Velodrom im Inneren seine gespeichte Dachstruktur präsentiert. Wie das gigantische Rad eines Fahrrads oder die Unterseite eines futuristischen Raumschiffs scheint dieses markante Element über den Zuschauern zu schweben und dabei sein Gewicht von immerhin 3 500 Tonnen zu verleugnen. Das benachbarte, noch im Bau befindliche olympische Schwimmstadion ist in einem rechteckigen Baukörper untergebracht, der das Bodenniveau ebenfalls nur minimal überragt. Die beiden Bauten sind als Silberseen inmitten eines Obstgartens bezeichnet worden. Ganz bewußt hat Perrault versucht, jene architektonische Monumentalität zu vermeiden, die gemeinhin mit Olympischen Spielen assoziiert wird, insbesondere mit jenen des Jahres 1936, die bekanntlich in Berlin stattfanden. So wichtig eine solche symbolische Geste ist, soll darüber auch nicht vergessen werden, daß die Eigenart des Entwurfs und der Einsatz von Spezialglas bei den großen Glasflächen dafür gesorgt haben, den Energieverbrauch im Vergleich zu herkömmlichen Bauten dieser Art um 60 % zu senken.

Keine architektonische Schule ist in Wirklichkeit so kohärent, wie es die Kritiker gerne hätten. Gleichwohl umschreiben wir mit der Bezeichnung »Neo-Minimalismus« im wesentlichen den Einsatz einfacher geometrischer Formen, eine sorgfältige Detailbehandlung und den spielerischen Umgang mit Transparenz, Opazität und scheinbarer Schwerelosigkeit. Die 1996 von Terence Riley im New Yorker Museum of Modern Art konzipierte Ausstellung »Light Construction«, die das Werk von Architekten wie Peter Zumthor, Kazuyo Sejima oder Ben van Berkel vorstellte, dürfte zur Definition des der minimalistischen Bewegung zu-

seulement de leurs qualités visuelles et matérielles, mais également des significations qu'elles peuvent véhiculer. Influencés par des aspects de notre culture, comme les médias électroniques ou l'ordinateur, les architectes et les artistes repensent les interrelations de l'architecture, de la perception visuelle et de la structure.»[1]

Déconstruire malgré tout

Si une exposition peut définir un mouvement architectural, c'est bien le cas de celle qui précéda «Light Construction», à savoir «Deconstructivist Architecture», qui avait réuni en 1988 sous la direction de Philip Johnson et de Mark Wigley un certain nombre de projets, dont ceux de Frank O. Gehry, Daniel Libeskind, Rem Koolhaas, Zaha Hadid et Bernard Tschumi. Tschumi était alors cité pour son travail sur le Parc de la Villette à Paris. Ces folies laquées d'un rouge éclatant, qui semblent renvoyer à des dessins constructivistes de la Russie révolutionnaire, ont beaucoup contribué à la perception publique du déconstructivisme. Dans une définition plus fondamentale, Mark Wigley écrivait dans le catalogue de l'exposition: «Dans chaque projet, la structure traditionnelle des plans parallèles – empilés horizontalement à partir du sol – et le cadre sont faussés. Même le plan du sol est faussé. Une interrogation de pure forme pousse la structure vers ses limites, mais sans les dépasser. La structure est ébranlée, mais n'est pas renversée; elle est juste poussée jusqu'au point où elle devient dérangeante.»[2] Bien que Frank O. Gehry – et l'on pense aux formes spectaculaires du Musée Guggenheim de Bilbao en Espagne – soit resté aux avant-postes des efforts de libération de l'architecture de sa rigueur géométrique, Bernard Tschumi, et en particulier en tant que doyen de la Columbia School of Architecture, est toujours le principal théoricien de ce que l'on persiste à appeler déconstructivisme, en dépit des différents objectifs de ses adeptes supposés.

L'esthétique déconstructiviste s'est largement répandue en Europe et aux États-Unis. Un bâtiment récent comme le Musée d'art moderne ou «l'Arken» à Copenhague, signé Søren Robert Lund, s'en inspire. Implanté dans un paysage de dunes et de

Søren Robert Lund, Arken Museum of Modern Art, Copenhagen, Denmark, 1988–96. Set amidst dunes, the museum makes frequent reference to nautical metaphors.

Søren Robert Lund, Arken-Museum für Moderne Kunst, Kopenhagen, Dänemark, 1988–96. Bei dem inmitten von Dünen errichteten Museum werden vielfach nautische Metaphern verwendet.

Søren Robert Lund, Musée d'art moderne de l'Arken, Copenhague, Danemark, 1988–96. Implanté au milieu de dunes, le musée se réfère fréquemment à des métaphores nautiques.

Søren Robert Lund, Arken Museum of Modern Art, Copenhagen, Denmark, 1988–96. Although it is in a decidedly "deconstructivist" style, this museum seeks a close relationship to its natural setting.

Søren Robert Lund, Arken-Museum für Moderne Kunst, Kopenhagen, Dänemark, 1988–96. Auch wenn sein Entwurf dem Stil des Dekonstruktivismus verpflichtet ist, steht das Museum in einer engen Verbindung zur Natur.

Søren Robert Lund, Musée d'art moderne de l'Arken, Copenhague, Danemark,1988–96. Bien que traité dans un style incontestablement déconstructiviste, ce musée entretient une relation étroite avec son cadre naturel.

reminiscent of other such references in contemporary architecture – for example, in a different style, Franklin Israel's Art Pavilion (Beverly Hills, California, 1991) with its lifeboat balcony. Although it is not to be suggested that the Arken is inspired by Frank O. Gehry's design for the Guggenheim Bilbao Museum, the two institutions do share the peculiarity of an enormous central gallery. In the case of the Arken, this space, called the "Art Axis", is no less than 150 meters long. By calling up images such as that of the Ark, the primordial vehicle of survival, does the architect mean to suggest a connection between art and the forces of nature? Or is architecture the issue here? Another response to this question may be offered by the 36 ton rough granite monolith that sits in the entrance hall of the museum. This gesture too has been seen before, as in the Banque de Luxembourg headquarters by Arquitectonica (Luxembourg, 1989–94), which has a 43 ton block of raw Normandy granite next to the main door. The Arken is intended to offer a wide variety of arts, ranging from theater to ballet or music as well as painting or sculpture. In this respect, it is a vehicle for cultural expression. By calling on the images of its environment or on the power of nature, Søren Robert Lund confers a feeling of permanence on the Arken. Neither architecture nor the arts have had much of that in recent times.

Bernard Tschumi, who has long gravitated around the main figures of contemporary architecture, has today become an active builder. Like Peter Eisenman, who established his presence in architectural theory before he actually put his ideas to the text on any substantial scale, Tschumi has a substantial reputation to live up to. One of his first completed works since the Parc de la Villette structures in Paris is the Le Fresnoy National Studio for Contemporary Arts (Tourcoing, France, 1991–97). Here, in a space of some 10,000 square meters, an international center for contemporary arts including a film school, exhibition and performance space, two movie theaters, research and production laboratories for sound, electronic images, film and video, administrative offices, housing and a bar/restaurant has been inserted into a partially preserved set of 1920s buildings, which

grundeliegenden Denkens ebensoviel beigetragen haben wie eine veröffentlichte Architekturkritik. Natürlich gibt es keine direkten Verbindungen zwischen so unterschiedlichen Architekten, sieht man einmal von der Tatsache ab, daß sie ihr Werk gegenseitig zur Kenntnis nehmen. Eventuell bestehende Ähnlichkeiten sind vielmehr ein Ergebnis des Zeitgeistes, eines Denkens, das gegenwärtig eher in den wichtigen westeuropäischen Ländern und vielleicht in Japan als in den USA oder anderswo zum Vorschein kommt. Terence Riley bemerkte im Ausstellungskatalog: »In den letzten Jahren ist eine neue architektonische Sensibilität zutage getreten, die nicht nur die Distanz unserer heutigen Kultur zur Maschinenästhetik des frühen 20. Jahrhunderts widerspiegelt, sondern auch nach einer drei Jahrzehnte lang primär auf Formprobleme konzentrierten Debatte eine Schwerpunktverschiebung markiert. Mit Projekten, die aufgrund künstlerischer und technischer Innovationen bemerkenswert sind, untersuchen die zeitgenössischen Architekten und Künstler die Natur und das Potential architektonischer Oberflächen. Dabei beschäftigen sie sich nicht nur mit deren visuellen und materialbezogenen Eigenschaften, sondern auch mit den Bedeutungen, die diese Oberflächen vermitteln können. Unter dem Einfluß bestimmter Aspekte unserer Kultur, darunter die elektronischen Medien und der Computer, überdenken sie die Wechselbeziehungen zwischen Architektur, visueller Wahrnehmung und Struktur.«[1]

Dekonstruktion, auch noch nach Jahren

Wenn eine Ausstellung eine architektonische Bewegung zu definieren vermag, muß an dieser Stelle eine genannt werden, die das Museum of Modern Art einige Jahre vor »Light Construction« präsentierte. Die von Philip Johnson und Mark Wigley 1988 konzipierte Ausstellung »Deconstructivist Architecture« zeigte unter anderem Werke von Frank O. Gehry, Daniel Libeskind, Rem Koolhaas, Zaha Hadid und Bernard Tschumi. Tschumi wurde damals im Zusammenhang mit seinen Entwürfen für den Parc de la Villette in Paris vorgestellt. Nicht zuletzt seine leuchtend roten Pavillons, die auf konstruktivistische Entwürfe des revolutionären Rußland zurückzugreifen schienen, bestimmten

voiliers au sud de la capitale danoise, il se dresse avec audace, rappelant les formes anguleuses de déconstructivistes aussi rigoureux que Zaha Hadid. De même qu'un autre musée présenté dans cet ouvrage, le Centre des Sciences et des Technologiques édifié à Amsterdam par Renzo Piano, l'Arken s'appuie sur des références nautiques qui se justifient plus par son environnement que par son contenu. En danois, le nom de l'institution signifie «arche», métaphore curieuse pour un musée d'art. Le café du musée, qui donne sur la baie de Koge, a la forme d'un navire, et rappelle d'autres références de l'architecture contemporaine, comme par exemple, dans un style différent, l'Art Pavilion de Franklin Israel (Beverly Hills, Californie, 1991) au balcon en forme de canot de sauvetage. Si l'on ne peut suggérer que l'Arken se soit inspiré du Musée Guggenheim de Bilbao de Frank O. Gehry, les deux institutions partagent la caractéristique commune d'une énorme galerie centrale. Dans le cas de l'Arken, cet espace appelé «l'axe de l'art» ne mesure pas moins de 150 m de long. En évoquant des images comme celle de l'Arche, le vaisseau biblique de la survie de l'humanité, l'architecte aurait-il voulu faire allusion à un lien entre l'art et les forces de la nature? Ou l'enjeu est-il simplement architectural? Une autre réponse à ces questions se trouve peut-être dans le monolithe de granit brut de 36 tonnes, installé à l'entrée du musée. Ce geste avait déjà été accompli par Arquitectonica qui avait placé un bloc de granit brut de Normandie à côté de l'entrée principale de sa Banque de Luxembourg (1989–94). L'Arken est consacré à de multiples expressions artistiques, allant du théâtre à la danse et à la musique en passant par la peinture et la sculpture. En évoquant son environnement ou la puissance de la nature, Søren Robert Lund donne à cette œuvre un sentiment de permanence. Ni l'architecture ni beaucoup d'autres formes artistiques ne nous avaient récemment donné cette impression.

Bernard Tschumi, qui a longtemps gravité autour des grandes figures de l'architecture contemporaine, est devenu aujourd'hui un constructeur très actif. Comme Peter Eisenman, qui s'est fait connaître dans le domaine de la théorie architecturale avant de traduire ses idées à échelle appréciable, Tschumi peut déjà

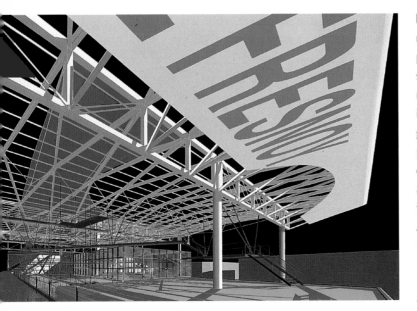

Bernard Tschumi, Le Fresnoy National Studio for
Contemporary Arts, Tourcoing, France, 1991–97.
A computer drawing shows the sweeping roof above
the entrance.

Bernard Tschumi, Medien- und Kulturzentrum
Le Fresnoy, Tourcoing, Frankreich, 1991–97. Die
Computersimulation zeigt das weit ausladende Dach
über dem Eingangsbereich.

Bernard Tschumi, Le Fresnoy, Studio national des Arts
Contemporains, Tourcoing, France, 1991–97. Dessin
par ordinateur montrant le toit en saillie au-dessus de
l'entrée.

had served as a dance hall, an early movie theater, a roller skating
rink, and an indoor pool. Tschumi chose to build an enormous
protective roof over these structures and above all to use the
space created between the old buildings and the new. In his
mind the Fresnoy project is about "How an 'in-between' space
is activated by the motion of bodies in that space; How programmed activities, when strategically located, can charge a non-
programmed space (the in-between); How architecture is about
designing conditions, rather than conditioning designs; How
architecture is about identifying, and ultimately, releasing potentialities hidden in a site, a program, or their social context."[3]
As Bernard Tschumi points out, this is far from being a simple
restoration job. In fact, the poor condition of the existing buildings and the high cost entailed in any thorough reconstruction
led him not only to protect the old roofs with a new one, but also
to put new boxes inside of old spaces in a kind of "Russian doll"
approach. Imagining a cinema perched in the interstitial space,
and students walking to and fro on suspended bridges and stairs,
Tschumi looks toward nothing less than a new rapport between
the past and the present, where users move freely between one
and the other, on occasion making use of the in-between spaces
created by the meeting of one world and another.

Tschumi's Lerner Student Center at Columbia University (New
York, NY, 1994–99) also seeks to bridge a gap in time, although
it is an entirely new structure. This 22,500 square meter student
activity center includes "a combined auditorium/assembly hall
seating 1100–1500, dining facilities, lounges, meeting rooms,
a bookstore, a radio station, student clubs and games rooms,
administrative space, a black box theater, six thousand mailboxes as well as expanded computer facilities for student use."
Making use of building spaces planned but never used in the
original 1890 McKim, Mead and White masterplan for Columbia,
the new structure makes use of the rather steep inclination of
the site to create an internally dynamic layout. As Tschumi says,
"In terms of its exterior, our urban hypothesis is to return to,
even to reinforce the masterplan of McKim, Mead and White,
i.e. the spatial and volumetric logic of the original scheme.

die Art und Weise, wie der Dekonstruktivismus in der Öffentlichkeit wahrgenommen wurde. Mark Wigley lieferte im Katalog eine eher allgemeine Definition: »Bei allen Projekten ist die traditionelle Struktur aus parallelen Ebenen – in einer regelmäßigen Grundform vom Erdgeschoß ausgehend horizontal übereinandergestapelt – verdreht worden. Der Rahmen ist verzerrt. Sogar die Erdgeschoßebene ist verzerrt. Die Infragestellung der reinen Form treibt die Struktur an ihre Grenzen, aber nicht darüber hinaus. Die Struktur wird erschüttert, aber nicht zerstört; sie wird bloß bis zu dem Punkt getrieben, an dem sie verunsichert.«[2] Obwohl auch Frank O. Gehry mit der spektakulären skulpturalen Gestalt von Bauwerken wie dem Guggenheim Museum in Bilbao, Spanien, weiterhin zur Speerspitze derjenigen gehört, welche die Architektur aus ihrer planen Regelmäßigkeit befreien wollen, ist es Bernard Tschumi, vor allem in seiner Funktion als Dekan der Columbia School of Architecture, der die Rolle des führenden Theoretikers einer Bewegung innehat, die trotz der variierenden Ziele ihrer scheinbaren Vertreter nach wie vor als Dekonstruktivismus bezeichnet wird.

Die dekonstruktivistische Ästhetik hat in Europa und in den Vereinigten Staaten weite Verbreitung gefunden. Einer der neueren Bauten mit dieser Formensprache ist das Museum für Moderne Kunst in Kopenhagen, bekannt als Arken, von Søren Robert Lund. Das im Süden der dänischen Hauptstadt gelegene Museum hebt sich kühn gegen die von Dünen und Segelbooten geprägte Landschaft ab, wobei uns seine verwinkelten Formen an die Arbeit einer so entschieden dekonstruktivistischen Architektin wie Zaha Hadid denken lassen. Wie auch ein anderes, im vorliegenden Buch vorgestelltes Museum, das Wissenschaftsmuseum von Renzo Piano in Amsterdam, bedient sich der Entwurf des Arken bestimmter Formelemente aus der Schiffahrt, ein Verweis, der freilich eher aufgrund der landschaftlichen Umgebung als aufgrund der Sammlung gerechtfertigt erscheint. Der Name des Hauses ist das dänische Wort für »Arche«, eine recht ungewöhnliche Metapher für ein Kunstmuseum. Dem Museumscafé mit Blick auf die Bucht von Koge ist auf fast exakte Weise die äußere Gestalt eines Bootes verliehen worden, was an andere

s'enorgueillir d'une réputation substantielle. L'une de ses premières réalisations achevées, depuis le Parc de la Villette, est le Studio national des Arts Contemporains du Fresnoy (Tourcoing, France, 1991–97). Là, sur un espace de 10 000 m² environ, il vient d'aménager un centre international d'art contemporain à partir d'un ensemble en partie préservé de bâtiments des années 20, qui avaient servi de salle de bal, de cinéma, de patinoire ou de piscine. Le Centre comprend une école de cinéma, des espaces d'exposition et de spectacles, deux cinémas, des laboratoires de recherche et de production de son, d'images électroniques, de films et de vidéos, des bureaux administratifs, des logements et un bar-restaurant. Tschumi a décidé de jeter un énorme toit par-dessus ces structures, et surtout d'utiliser l'espace créé entre les anciens et les nouveaux bâtiments. Pour lui, le projet du Fresnoy traite de «la manière dont l'espace ‹intermédiaire› peut être activé par le mouvement des corps dans cet espace; comment des activités programmées, lorsqu'elles se déroulent selon une stratégie, peuvent donner un sens, une charge à un espace non-programmé; comment l'architecture aborde les conditions de la conception plutôt que la conception des conditions; comment elle tient à l'identifi-cation et en dernier lieu au relâchement des potentialités dissimulées dans un site, un programme ou un contexte social.»[3] Ainsi que l'architecte le fait remarquer, ce projet est loin d'être un simple travail de rénovation. En fait, le mauvais état des bâtiments existants et les coûts élevés de reconstruction l'ont non seulement amené à protéger les anciens toits par un nouveau toit, mais encore à disposer des sortes de boîtes à l'intérieur des anciens volumes dans une approche type «poupées gigognes». En perchant un cinéma dans l'espace interstitiel, et en entraînant les étudiants à s'y rendre par des escaliers et des passerelles suspendus, Tschumi crée un nouveau rapport entre le passé et le présent, dans lequel les utilisateurs se déplacent librement de l'un à l'autre, utilisant à l'occasion les espaces de «L'entre-deux» qui se trouvent à la jonction d'un monde ancien et d'un monde nouveau.

Le Lerner Student Center, conçu par Tschumi pour l'Université de Columbia (New York, 1994–99), cherche également à renouer

Some of its original building materials (granite, brick, copper-like material, glass) will also be used. Simultaneously, within this existing framework and its historical constraints, we will strive to provide innovative programmatic spaces – a student 'city' in the 'city' of Columbia in the city of New York. This double strategy could be summarized as a 'quiet building on the outside; a stimulating building on the inside.' By analogy, the Student Center could be described as a dynamic hub that acts as a major social space. The Hub is the main circulatory system of the building. It concentrates lobbies and student lounges, information stands, ramps for 6,000 student mailboxes, exhibitions or student propaganda as well as the overspill of other activities – bar, games and so forth.

Acting as the building's core, the Hub is made possible by the unusual condition of much of the Columbia campus at this location, where the campus side is half a story higher than the neighborhood (Broadway) side. Instead of separating the building's activities into stacked full floors, we connected them into staggered half-floors. Building hallways can act as a continuous link connecting what would normally have been discontinuous and even contradictory activities. It is simultaneously a void (the void of McKim) and a route. During the day, light filters through the suspended glass ramps. At night, as light glows from the inside, figures in movement along this route will appear as in a silent shadow theater."4

Mark Wigley's original definition of the Deconstructivist style evoked the dissolution of the rigid planar organization of architecture. Clearly, the two projects by Bernard Tschumi evoked here do tend toward that goal, although in terms of their external appearance both structures would appear to be less angular and abrupt than for example Søren Robert Lund's Arken. This proves only that Deconstruction survives despite the fact that it is no longer the latest and most fashionable trend. Individual architects will always tend to develop their own ideas in the specific context of the projects they are called upon to create. This pragmatic approach may define contemporary architecture more accurately than any given school.

Beispiele aus der Gegenwartsarchitektur erinnert, etwa den allerdings stilistisch andersartigen Kunstpavillon von Franklin Israel (Beverly Hills, Kalifornien, 1991) mit dem einem Rettungsboot nachempfundenen Balkon. Obgleich nicht angedeutet werden soll, das Arken sei von Gehrys Guggenheim Museum in Bilbao inspiriert, haben beide Gebäude doch eine sehr große zentrale Galerie. Beim Arken ist dieser als »Kunstachse« bezeichnete Raum nicht weniger als 150 m lang. Wollte der Architekt, indem er ein Bild wie das der Arche – jenes archaische Überlebensgefährt – wachruft, auf einen Zusammenhang zwischen Kunst und Naturmächten verweisen? Oder wird hier die Architektur als solche thematisiert? Ein Indiz könnte der 36 Tonnen schwere Monolith aus Granit sein, den man in der Eingangshalle des Museums aufgestellt hat. Auch diese Geste hat ein Vorbild, beispielsweise in der Hauptzentrale der Banque de Luxembourg von Arquitectonica (Luxemburg, 1989–94), wo seitlich des Hauptportals ein 43 Tonnen schwerer Block aus normannischem Granit steht. Das Arken soll einer Vielzahl von Künsten dienen, sowohl Theater-, Ballett- und Musikaufführungen als auch Malerei und Skulptur. Insofern ist es ein Vehikel für kulturellen Ausdruck. Indem er auf das Erscheinungsbild der umgebenden Landschaft oder auf die Naturmächte verwies, ist es Søren Robert Lund gelungen, daß das Arken ein Gefühl von Dauerhaftigkeit vermittelt. Weder die Architektur noch die Kunst sind in jüngerer Zeit mit solchen Leistungen verwöhnt worden.

Bernard Tschumi, der sich lange im Umkreis der Hauptakteure der Gegenwartsarchitektur aufgehalten hat, ist inzwischen ein aktiver Architekt geworden. Wie Peter Eisenman, der sich zunächst auf dem Gebiet der Architekturtheorie einen Namen gemacht hatte, bevor er seine Ideen in nennenswertem Maßstab verwirklichte, muß auch Tschumi seinem guten Ruf gerecht werden. Zu seinen ersten realisierten Entwürfen seit dem Parc de la Villette gehört das Medien- und Kulturzentrum Le Fresnoy (Tourcoing, Frankreich, 1991–97). Innerhalb eines Ensembles von zum Teil restaurierten Gebäuden aus den 20er Jahren, die ehemals als Tanzhalle, frühes Lichtspieltheater, Rollschuhbahn und Hallenbad genutzt worden waren, ist auf rund 10 000 m²

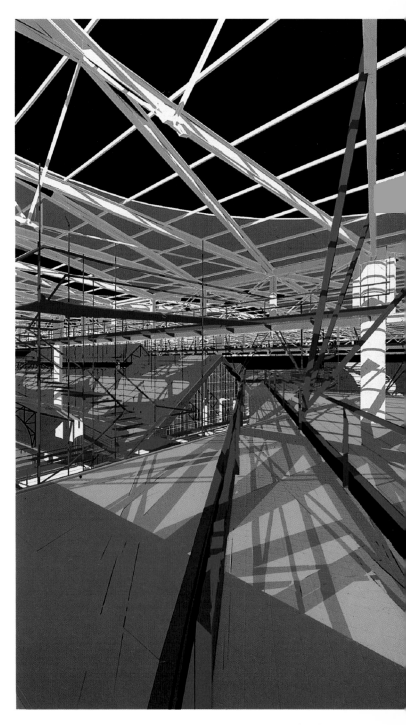

avec les temps anciens, bien que ce soit à travers une construction entièrement nouvelle. Ce centre pour étudiants de 22 500 m²
comprend «une salle de réunion-auditorium de 1100 à 1500
places, une cafétéria, des salles diverses et des salles de réunion,
une librairie, une station de radio, des clubs d'étudiants, des
salles de sport, des espaces administratifs, un petit théâtre,
6 000 boîtes aux lettres, et d'importants équipements informatiques pour les étudiants.» Dans le cadre du schéma directeur
de 1890 dû à McKim, Mead et White, la nouvelle structure met à
profit la pente assez forte du terrain pour créer une dynamique
interne. Tschumi précise: «En ce qui concerne l'extérieur, notre
hypothèse urbaine est de revenir – voire en le renforçant – au
schéma directeur de McKim, Mead et White, c'est-à-dire à la
logique spatiale et volumétrique du plan original. Certains des
matériaux de construction recommandés alors (granit, brique,
métal cuivré, verre) seront également utilisés. Simultanément,
dans ce cadre existant et ses contraintes historiques, nous nous
efforcerons d'offrir des espaces novateurs – une ‹ville› d'étudiants dans la ‹ville› de Columbia dans la ville de New York.
Cette double stratégie pourrait se résumer par la formule
‹un bâtiment calme à l'extérieur, mais stimulant à l'intérieur›.
Par analogie, le Student Center pourrait être décrit comme une
plate-forme dynamique qui agirait tel un espace social majeur.
La plate-forme est le principal système de circulation dans le
bâtiment. Elle concentre les couloirs et les salles d'étudiants,
les stands d'information, les rampes pour les 6 000 boîtes aux
lettres des étudiants, les expositions, les messages des étudiants,
et le surplus des autres activités, bar, sports, etc. Agissant
comme le cœur du bâtiment, cette plate-forme a bénéficié de la
configuration particulière du site du campus à cet endroit,
puisqu'il se trouve d'un demi-niveau plus élevé que son voisinage
immédiat (Broadway). Au lieu de diviser les activités du bâtiment
selon un empilement de niveaux, nous les avons reliées par
des demi-niveaux décalés. Les halls peuvent donc agir comme
un lien de continuité entre ce qui aurait dû normalement rester
des activités discontinues et même contradictoires. C'est en
même temps un vide (le vide McKim) et un cheminement.

Bernard Tschumi, Le Fresnoy National Studio for Contemporary Art, Tourcoing, France, 1991–97. The new roof arches over the existing buildings which were integrated into the complex.

Bernard Tschumi, Medien- und Kulturzentrum Le Fresnoy, Tourcoing, Frankreich, 1991–97. Das neue Dach überragt die bereits existierenden Gebäude, die in den Gesamtkomplex integriert wurden.

Bernard Tschumi, Le Fresnoy, Studio national des Art Contemporains, Tourcoing, France, 1991–97. Le nouveau toit se courbe par-dessus les bâtiments existants qui ont été intégrés au complexe.

Going with the flow

The Dutch architect Erick van Egeraat makes a conscious attempt to break from the conventions that seem to dominate contemporary architecture. As he has said, "In my work, I attempt to get away from the present symmetry and order and instead to introduce asymmetry and disharmony disassociated from its obvious negative connotations. For me, it is the excitement which you can feel whenever encountering something unknown and undefinable to deploy alternative design techniques which enable you to portray the unpresentable and undefinable."[5] His School for Fashion and Graphic Industry, located in Utrecht, The Netherlands, is by any stretch of the imagination an unusual case. In fact, the basic building is not by Erick van Egeraat at all, a fact that curiously highlights the vitality of the architectural scene in Holland. Like any major construction proposal in The Netherlands, the Utrecht Building Department design for a new School for Fashion and Graphic Industry had to be submitted for review by a professional board, which promptly rejected the uninspired three-story concrete structure. Although the board plays only an advisory rule, the Building Department saw fit to call on Erick van Egeraat to see if he could rescue the project, despite tight budgetary constraints. The architect's scheme was to envelope the building with a glass skin, "comparable to a gauze veil," as he says, "an element of fashion that conveys a mysterious lack of definition, yet indicates or proves insights into what is behind. Behind the glass skin is the other, the technical side of the building. Through the glass facade, one sees the hard core of the building: structural members, wood, exposed masonry walls and the yellow insulation pads that cover the building like a woolen blanket." Although it is often said that "beauty is only skin deep," this is an unusually frank exposure of the normally hidden underside of a building. Erick van Egeraat was able to add an auditorium to the original design, an element that confirms his interest in forms that appear to have more to do with the organic world, than with the rigid geometries of neo-minimalism. His frequently published reworking of the Budapest headquarters of the Dutch Nationale Nederlanden Hungary and

ein internationales Zentrum für die zeitgenössischen Künste untergebracht worden, das eine Filmschule, Räumlichkeiten für Ausstellungen und Aufführungen, zwei Kinos, Forschungs- und Produktionsstudios für Ton, elektronisch erzeugte Bilder, Filme und Videos sowie Verwaltungsbüros, Wohnungen und eine Bar bzw. ein Restaurant umfaßt. Tschumi hat sich für ein riesiges schützendes Dach über den Einzelbauten entschieden und, auch dafür, den geschaffenen Raum zwischen den Altbauten und den Neubauten zu nutzen. Das Projekt, so Tschumi, handelt davon, »wie ein ›Zwischenraum‹ durch die Bewegung von Körpern in diesem Raum aktiviert werden kann; Handlungen, die einem definierten Programmablauf folgen, finden an einem strategischen Ort statt, einem Raum, der keinem Programm folgt – dem Zwischenraum; daß Architektur das Entwerfen von Bedingungen zum Gegenstand hat und nicht die Konditionierung von Entwürfen; daß Architektur damit zu tun hat, Möglichkeiten, die in einem Ort, einem Programm oder deren sozialen Kontexten verborgen sind, zu identifizieren und schließlich freizulegen.«[3] Tschumi führt aus, das Projekt sei weitaus mehr gewesen als eine bloße Restaurierung. Der bedauerliche Zustand der bestehenden Bausubstanz und die hohen, mit einer grundlegenden Rekonstruktion verbundenen Kosten hätten ihn dazu veranlaßt, nicht nur die alten Dächer durch eine neue Überstruktur zu schützen, sondern auch in die Altbauten selbst neue Gebäudekerne einzufügen, ähnlich der russischen Puppe in der Puppe. Indem er sich vorstellte, wie ein Kino in einem neu geschaffenen »Zwischenraum« untergebracht werden könnte oder wie die Studenten über aufgehängte Brücken und Treppen hin- und hergehen, machte es sich Tschumi zur Aufgabe, einen neuen Zusammenhang zwischen Vergangenheit und Gegenwart herzustellen, wo sich die Besucher frei zwischen den Zeiten bewegen und gelegentlich jene Zwischenräume nutzen, die durch das Aufeinandertreffen der einen mit der anderen Welt entstanden sind.

Auch bei seinem Lerner Student Center an der Columbia University in New York City (1994–99) versucht Tschumi, eine Brücke zwischen den Zeiten zu schlagen, obwohl es sich um ein gänzlich neues Gebäude handelt. Das 22 500 m² große

Pendant la journée, la lumière filtrera à travers les rampes de verre suspendues. La nuit, lorsque la lumière baignera l'intérieur, les figures en mouvement le long de ce cheminement se détacheront comme dans un théâtre d'ombres silencieux.«[4]

La définition du style déconstructiviste proposée à l'origine par Mark Wigley évoquait la dissolution de l'organisation rigide des plans architecturaux. Les deux projets de Bernard Tschumi présentés ici recherchent cet objectif, bien que du point de vue de leur apparence extérieure, ils paraissent moins anguleux et abrupts que, par exemple, l'Arken de Lund. Ceci prouve seulement que le déconstructivisme survit même s'il n'est plus la dernière des tendances à la mode. Chaque architecte poursuivra toujours ses propres idées dans le contexte spécifique du projet sur lequel il est appelé à intervenir. Cette approche pragmatique est peut-être une définition de l'architecture contemporaine plus précise que celle qui voudrait passer par des écoles données.

Suivre le flux

L'architecte néerlandais Erick van Egeraat veut rompre avec les conventions qui semblent dominer l'architecture contemporaine. Comme il le déclare: «Dans mon travail, j'essaie de m'éloigner de la symétrie et de l'ordre actuels, et d'introduire au contraire une asymétrie et une dysharmonie dissociées de leurs connotations évidentes. Pour moi, c'est l'excitation que l'on ressent en rencontrant quelque chose d'inconnu et d'indéfinissable qui va déployer des techniques de conception alternatives pour représenter ce qui n'est pas représentable et l'indéfinissable.«[5] L'École de mode et de graphique industriel, qu'il a édifié à Utrecht, aux Pays-Bas, en est un exemple étonnant. En fait, à l'origine, le bâtiment n'est pas de Erick van Egeraat, ce qui montre bien une certaine vitalité de la scène architecturale néerlandaise. Comme tout grand projet architectural dans ce pays, la proposition du Service des bâtiments de la ville d'Utrecht fut soumise à un comité de professionnels qui rejeta le projet initial sur trois niveaux, jugé sans inspiration. Bien que le comité ne soit que consultatif, le Service des bâtiments pensa alors à faire appel à Erick van Egeraat pour tenter de sauver le projet,

ING Bank called in a spectacular way on his imagination to produce a kind of bio-mechanical excrescence on the roof of the building that serves as conference space.

Berthold Penkhues is not yet wellknown outside of the area of Kassel, but then again, at the age of forty-three very few architects do have an international reputation. After studies in that city, he worked for Josef Paul Kleihues before attending UCLA. Penkhues was subsequently the project architect for Gehry's Vitra Museum in Weil am Rhein, Germany. Though Kleihues and Gehry have different aesthetic approaches, they are indisputable masters of their profession, and Penkhues, who created his own office in 1989, seems to have profited from his time with them. He won a competition for the History Museum in Korbach, a town of 25,000 persons located near Kassel, against 20 other local architects in 1991. The actual construction work occurred between 1995 and 1997. The competition brief required that the museum, which was originally housed in a medieval stone house and two adjoining buildings, be expanded while a restoration of the existing structures was carried out. A glazed inner courtyard connects a composition of new and old buildings that recalls the town's own narrow alleys. The comment of the jury on this project was: "The special qualities of this design are to be found in the sensitive treatment of the urban space and the related small dimensions. The sculptural forming of the building volumes is notable in their integration of existing buildings and supplementary new structures."

Although the so-called Post-Modern school has long since been out of fashion, the designs of the 1970s did permit architects to once again look back to the past for inspiration. Sadly, the kind of historical pastiches that architects like Michael Graves became famous for had little to do with the actual history of the places the buildings were located in. Although very definitely schooled in current styles of architecture, Berthold Penkhues put the context of this small town, and the specific circumstances of the project, before any attempt to impose a personal or fashionable style. Though the fluidity of the space has been compared to "early Gehry," the Korbach Museum would seem first and fore-

Studentenzentrum umfaßt »eine Aula für 1100–1500 Personen, Speisesäle, Salons, Begegnungsräume, eine Buchhandlung, eine Radiostation, Studentenclubs und Spielzimmer, Verwaltungsbüros, eine Black Box, 6 000 Briefkästen sowie ein umfangreiches Angebot an Computern für die Studenten.« Der Gebäudeentwurf geht zurück auf den ursprünglichen Masterplan für die Columbia-Universität aus dem Jahre 1890 vom Büro McKim, Mead and White, in dem manche Bauplätze zwar verplant wurden, eine tatsächliche Bebauung dann aber unterblieb. Das starke Gefälle des Geländes wird genutzt, um im Inneren eine dynamische Raumaufteilung zu erzeugen. Tschumi bemerkt dazu: »Hinsichtlich der äußeren Gestalt bedeutet unsere städtebauliche Hypothese eine Rückkehr zum Masterplan von McKim, Mead and White, ja sogar dessen Stärkung, nämlich seiner räumlichen und volumetrischen Logik. Auch werden manche der damals vorgeschlagenen Baumaterialien (Granit, Backstein, kupferähnliche Materialien, Glas) verwendet. Innerhalb dieses existierenden Rahmenwerks und seiner historischen Beschränkungen werden wir indes die Schaffung innovativer programmatischer Räume anstreben – eine ›Studentenstadt‹ in der ›Universitätsstadt‹ Columbia in der Stadt New York. Zusammenfassend könnte man diese Doppelstrategie als ›stilles Bauen nach außen, anregendes Bauen im Inneren‹ bezeichnen. Analog dazu könnte das Studentenzentrum beschrieben werden als ein dynamischer Mittelpunkt (›Hub‹), dem wichtige soziale Funktionen zukommen. Dieser Kern repräsentiert im Gebäude das Hauptkreislaufsystem. Er vereint Lobbies und Salons für Studenten, Informationsstände, Rampen mit 6 000 Studentenbriefkästen, Ausstellungen oder studentische Aufrufe sowie andere Aktivitäten – Bars, Spiele und so weiter.

Möglich wird dieser als Gebäudekern fungierende Kern durch die ungewöhnliche topographische Beschaffenheit weiter Teile des Campus an dieser Stelle, denn dieser liegt ein halbes Stockwerk über dem Straßenniveau des Broadways. Anstatt die Gebäudefunktionen auf vollgestopfte ganze Stockwerke zu verteilen, haben wir sie in Gestalt gestaffelter halber Stockwerke miteinander verbunden. Die Korridore eines Gebäudes können als

en dépit des contraintes budgétaires très strictes. L'architecte proposa d'envelopper le bâtiment d'une peau de verre «comparable à un voile de gaze», dit-il, «un élément de mode qui véhicule un manque de définition mystérieux, tout en donnant néanmoins des indications sur ce qu'il masque. À travers la façade de verre, l'on peut voir la structure même: poutres structurelles, bois, murs de maçonnerie brute, et le placage jaune d'isolation qui recouvre le bâtiment comme une couverture de laine.» Si l'on a souvent dit que la beauté n'était qu'apparence, nous sommes confrontés ici à une mise à nu de la face généralement cachée de toute construction, d'une franchise inhabituelle. Erick van Egeraat a ajouté un auditorium au projet d'origine, occasion de confirmer son intérêt pour des formes plus proches de l'univers organique que de la géométrie rigide du néo-minimalisme. Fréquemment publiée, sa rénovation du siège social de la banque néerlandaise NNH et ING à Budapest stimula d'une manière spectaculaire son imagination pour produire une sorte d'excroissance bio-mécanique du toit du bâtiment, aménagé en salle de conférence.

Berthold Penkhues n'est pas encore très connu en-dehors de la région de Cassel, mais il est vrai qu'à l'âge de 43 ans peu d'architectes bénéficient déjà d'une réputation internationale. Après avoir étudié dans sa ville natale, il a travaillé pour Josef Paul Kleihues avant de suivre des cours à l'UCLA. Par la suite, il a été l'architecte du projet de Frank O. Gehry pour le Musée Vitra de Weil am Rhein, en Allemagne. Si Kleihues et Gehry pratiquent des approches esthétiques différentes, ce sont des maîtres incontestés de leur profession, et Penkhues, qui a créé sa propre agence en 1989, semble avoir beaucoup appris de leur fréquentation. Il a ainsi remporté en 1991 le concours pour le Musée historique de Korbach, petite ville de 25 000 habitants proche de Cassel, face à 20 autres architectes locaux. Le cahier de charges voulait que ce musée, installé à l'origine dans une maison médiévale et deux bâtiments voisins, soit agrandi parallèlement à la rénovation des installations existantes. Une cour intérieure vitrée unifie la composition qui regroupe les bâtiments anciens et nouveaux, tout en rappelant les étroites ruelles de

Erick van Egeraat, School for Fashion and Graphic Industry, Utrecht, The Netherlands, 1994–97. A banal building "saved" by the addition of a glass wall, revealing the unadorned structure.

Erick van Egeraat, Fachtechnisches Gymnasium, Utrecht, Niederlande, 1994–97. Ein im Grunde einfacher Bau, »gerettet« durch die Hinzufügung eines Glasmantels, der die bloße Gebäudestruktur enthüllt.

Erick van Egeraat, École de mode et de graphique industrielle, Utrecht, Pays-Bas, 1994–97. Un bâtiment banal, «sauvé» par l'adjonction d'un mur de verre qui met en valeur sa structure brute.

most to be a case of a talented architect acting to solve a specific problem while respecting the village he was working in. Though it does not fit easily into any preconceived trend, this project does provide evidence of the growing maturity of contemporary architects. Budgets are too tight and work too scarce for young architects to make "personal statements." The point is to bring a sense of quality in architecture to a given situation, which implies a pragmatic or perhaps even a modest view of the architect's role.

Renzo Piano is one of a handful of architects who have almost literally built all over the planet. From Kansai Airport in the Bay of Osaka to the Menil Foundation in Houston, he has left a mark that is often associated in the public mind with his first major project, the Centre Georges Pompidou in Paris, which he designed with Richard Rogers. And yet the style of Piano's mature work does not have much to do with the exuberant early 1970s ductwork of Beaubourg. In fact in more recent times, his architecture has tended to a pared-down minimalism. Piano's New Metropolis Science & Technology Center (Amsterdam, The Netherlands) does not, however seem to fit in with the strict lines of works like the Cy Twombly Gallery in Houston or the recent brick veneer addition to the IRCAM next to the Centre Pompidou. Nicknamed the "Titanic" because it does resemble the hull of a great sinking ship, this 32 meter high volume covered with 4,100 square meters of green copper cladding sits in the 17th century maritime heart of Amsterdam, a short walk from the Central Station, and close to the Maritime Museum. Although the architects deny the intentional recourse to a nautical metaphor in this setting, the client's brief did stipulate that the building was to "establish a relation to shipping." Born out of the Dutch Institute for Industry and Technology (NINT), which was founded in 1954, this science museum cost a total of 77.5 million florins to build, of which 42.5 million was for the construction. Within the dark, cavernous interior, there are 4,300 square meters of interactive exhibitions on such areas as Telecommunications, Financial Transactions, The Factory and Synthesis, or Information Technology. A 199-seat cinema and a large museum shop are also included, as is a children's area.

kontinuierliche Verbindungsglieder dienen, die zusammenhalten, was normalerweise nicht zusammenhängende, ja gegensätzliche Funktionen wären. Sie sind gleichzeitig Leerfläche (die Leerfläche von McKim) und Weg. Am Tag strömt Licht in die aufgehängten Glasrampen. Nachts, da das Licht von innen kommt, werden die diesen Weg abschreitenden Menschen wie die Gestalten eines stillen Schattenspiels erscheinen.«[4]

Mark Wigley definierte den dekonstruktivistischen Stil als die Auflösung einer starren, planen Organisation der Architektur. Die beiden vorgestellten Projekte von Bernard Tschumi streben zweifelsohne ein solches Ziel an, obwohl die Bauten rein äußerlich weniger verwinkelt und abrupt erscheinen als beispielsweise Søren Robert Lunds Arken-Museum. Dadurch wird im Prinzip nur belegt, daß der Dekonstruktivismus noch immer lebendig ist, obwohl man ihn nicht länger als neueste und aktuellste Richtung bezeichnen kann. Einzelne Architektenpersönlichkeiten werden immer dazu tendieren, im Rahmen des ihnen durch ein bestimmtes Projekt vorgegebenen Kontextes eigene Ideen zu entwickeln. Dieser Pragmatismus dürfte die Architektur der Gegenwart treffender charakterisieren als irgendeine bestehende Schule.

Alt und Neu

Der holländische Architekt Erick van Egeraat unternimmt ganz bewußt den Versuch, mit den Konventionen zu brechen, die die zeitgenössische Architektur zu dominieren scheinen. »In meiner Arbeit«, so van Egeraat, »versuche ich, von der allgegenwärtigen Symmetrie und Ordnung wegzukommen und dafür Asymmetrie und Disharmonie ins Spiel zu bringen, freilich ohne die negativen Nebenbedeutungen dieser Begriffe. Für mich ist es jene Spannung, die ich immer dann verspüre, wenn ich auf etwas Unbekanntes und Undefinierbares stoße. Sie führt dazu, alternative Entwurfstechniken einzusetzen, wodurch man das Undarstellbare und Undefinierbare zeigen kann.«[5] Sein Fachtechnisches Gymnasium in Utrecht ist nun auch wirklich ein ungewöhnlicher Fall, stammt doch das eigentliche Gebäude gar nicht von Erick van Egeraat, was auf kuriose Weise die Lebendigkeit

Berthold Penkhues, History Museum, Korbach,
Germany, 1995–97. Integrating new buildings into a
dense old village.

Berthold Penkhues, Regionalmuseum, Korbach,
Deutschland, 1995–97. Hier konnten neue Gebäude in
ein dichtes altes Stadtgefüge integriert werden.

Berthold Penkhues, Musée historique, Korbach,
Allemagne, 1995–97. Intégration des bâtiments con-
temporains dans le tissu dense d'un village ancien.

la vieille ville. Le jury du concours a accompagné son choix du commentaire suivant: «Les qualités particulières de ce projet résident dans la sensibilité du traitement de l'espace urbain et ses dimensions raisonnables. La composition formelle des volumes des bâtiments est remarquable dans son intégration des constructions existantes et des extensions nouvelles.»

Si l'école postmoderne est depuis longtemps passée de mode, certains projets des années 70 ont permis de nouveau à des architectes de rechercher leur inspiration dans le passé. Il est néanmoins dommage que les pastiches historiques, du type de ceux qui ont assuré la célébrité d'un architecte comme Michael Graves, n'aient pas grand-chose à voir avec l'histoire réelle des lieux sur lesquels ils ont été édifiés. Bien informé des styles architecturaux actuels, Berthold Penkhues a placé le respect du contexte de la petite cité dans laquelle il intervenait et des circonstances spécifiques du projet avant toute tentative d'imposition d'un style personnel ou à la mode. Même si la fluidité des espaces a été comparée au «jeune Gehry», le musée de Korbach illustre d'abord et avant tout le travail d'un architecte de talent qui s'efforce de résoudre un problème spécifique, tout en respectant la communauté pour laquelle il œuvre. Si elle ne se classe pas facilement dans des tendances préexistantes, cette réalisation met l'accent sur la maturité grandissante des architectes contemporains. Les budgets sont trop resserrés et les chantiers trop rares pour que les jeunes praticiens puissent se permettre des attitudes individualistes. Le problème est d'apporter de la qualité à une architecture correspondant à une situation donnée, ce qui implique une vision pragmatique, voire même modeste, du rôle de l'architecte.

Renzo Piano fait partie de cette poignée d'architectes qui bâtissent pratiquement dans le monde entier. De l'aéroport de Kansai, dans la baie d'Osaka, à la Menil Foundation à Houston, il a laissé sa marque, souvent associée dans l'esprit du public à son premier grand projet, le Centre Pompidou à Paris, conçu avec Richard Rogers. Et pourtant, le style de ces œuvres récentes n'a pas grand-chose à voir avec l'exubérant montage de tuyaux de Beaubourg au début des années 70. En fait, son architecture

Renzo Piano, New Metropolis Science & Technology Center, Amsterdam, The Netherlands, 1995–97. A heavily traveled road leads to a tunnel, whose mouth is just beneath the museum.

Renzo Piano, New Metropolis, Museum für Wissenschaft und Technologie, Amsterdam, Niederlande, 1995–97. Eine stark befahrene Straße führt in einen Tunnel, dessen Eingang sich direkt unterhalb des Museums befindet.

Renzo Piano, New Metropolis, Centre des Sciences et des Technologies, Amsterdam, Pays-Bas, 1995–97. Le musée est situé juste au-dessus de l'entrée d'un tunnel emprunté par une artère très fréquentée.

Open almost from one end of its 208 meter length to the other, the interior space is spectacular, if rather dark. The materials used betray rather tight budgetary constraints, but the gray linoleum floors, perforated galvanized steel balustrades and unpainted concrete surfaces fit in rather well with the factory-like atmosphere. The attention of the visitors is quickly turned toward the exhibits, which is after all the point of the institution.

As intriguing as it is from afar, the New Metropolis Center poses a number of problems. One of them is specifically related to the site. The building is set directly on top of the roof of the iJ tunnel at Oosterdok (East Dock). As the critic Arthur Woortman wrote in a scathing review of the building, "Long before we can enter it, the building beckons from afar. It was argued that building on top of the tunnel would obviate the requirement for foundations, but extra foundation work proved to be necessary. The shape of the building, with its thrusting increase in height, also proved problematic. While the lower part of the building is executed in economical concrete, the upper part has necessarily been executed in steel in order to reduce the weight. Also with an eye to weight, the apparently solid brick plinth – a tribute to the Dutch brick tradition – is in reality a thin brick veneer. New Metropolis stands on top of the tunnel but it has no functional connection with it at all. It may look as if there is a symbiosis between building and infrastructure but anyone who believes their eyes will end up high and dry – in North Amsterdam."[6] Writing in the Dutch magazine Archis, this critic also takes on the surprising form of the structure. "The form dominates," he writes. "The form shouts. Form precedes function. The function of the New Metropolis has nothing to do with the form of the building. Function does not follow form. What was required was a black box. Windows are virtually absent. This green ship, so emphatically present in the city, is totally denied on the inside. We might just as well be in a bunker ten meters underground. At New Metropolis one expects, no demands a spectacle inside, an architectural spectacle to match the spectacular exterior. And this demand is not met. The result is disappointment, no matter how interesting the exhibition material may be."[7]

der holländischen Architekturszene beleuchtet. Wie jedes wichtige Bauvorhaben in den Niederlanden mußte auch der vom Baudezernat der Stadt Utrecht ausgearbeitete Entwurf für diese neue Schule einem Gremium aus Fachleuten zur Prüfung vorgelegt werden, die den uninspirierten dreigeschossigen Betonbau dann auch prompt zurückwiesen. Obwohl das Gremium nur eine beratende Rolle spielt, hielt das Baudezernat es für angebracht, sich an Erick van Egeraat zu wenden, um zu prüfen, ob er das Projekt trotz des engen finanziellen Rahmens würde retten können. Der Entwurf des Architekten sah nun vor, dem ganzen Gebäude eine Hülle aus Glas vorzuhängen, »vergleichbar einem Gazeschleier«, so van Egeraat, »also ein der Mode entlehntes Element, das ein geheimnisvolles Fehlen einer Bestimmung ausdrückt, gleichwohl aber einen Einblick in das, was dahinter ist, zuläßt. Hinter der Glashaut liegt die andere, die technische Seite des Baus. Durch das Glas erblickt man den Kern des Gebäudes: strukturelle Bauglieder, Holz, freiliegendes Mauerwerk und die gelben Isoliermatten, die das Haus wie eine Wolldecke umhüllen.« Obwohl es ja heißt, daß Schönheit nur äußerer Schein sei, handelt es sich hier um eine ungewöhnlich ehrliche Freistellung jener Normalität, die sich unter der Haut eines jeden Gebäudes verbirgt. Erick van Egeraat ist es überdies gelungen, dem ursprünglichen Entwurf noch ein Auditorium hinzuzufügen, ein Element, das sein Interesse an Formen belegt, die sich eher an der organischen Welt denn an der strikten Geometrie des Neo-Minimalismus zu orientieren scheinen. Auch bei dem häufig publizierten Umbau der Hauptzentrale der niederländischen NNH und ING-Bank in Budapest verließ sich Erick van Egeraat auf seine Phantasie, um jenen spektakulären biomechanischen Auswuchs auf dem Dach des Gebäudes schaffen zu können, welcher der Bank als Konferenzsaal dient.

Berthold Penkhues genießt außerhalb Kassels noch keine große Bekanntheit, doch verfügen im Alter von 43 Jahren nur sehr wenige Architekten bereits über einen internationalen Ruf. Nachdem er in der nordhessischen Stadt studiert hatte, arbeitete Penkhues für Josef Paul Kleihues, bevor er an die UCLA (University of California Los Angeles) ging. Anschließend

s'est récemment orientée vers un minimalisme épuré. Par ailleurs, le New Metropolis, Centre des Sciences et des Technologies d'Amsterdam (Pays-Bas), ne semble pas avoir beaucoup de rapports avec des réalisations comme la Cy Twombly Gallery à Houston, ou la récente extension recouverte de plaques de briques de l'IRCAM, à côté du Centre Pompidou. Surnommé le Titanic parce qu'il ressemble à la poupe d'un paquebot en train de couler, le volume du New Metropolis de 32 m de haut recouvert de 4 100 m² de placage de cuivre s'élève au cœur du port d'Amsterdam, non loin de la Gare centrale et du Musée maritime. Même si l'architecte dénie toute intention de métaphore nautique, l'appel d'offre du client stipulait que le bâtiment devait «établir une relation avec le port». Initié par l'Institut néerlandais pour l'industrie et la technologie (NINT), fondé en 1954, ce musée des sciences a coûté 265 millions de F, dont 145 pour sa seule construction. Dans son intérieur caverneux, 4 300 m² sont réservés à des expositions interactives sur des domaines comme les télécommunications, les transactions financières, la production industrielle ou la technologie de l'information. Un cinéma de 199 places, une vaste boutique et un espace pour les enfants complètent l'ensemble. Ouvert pratiquement sur la totalité de ses 208 m de longueur, le volume intérieur est spectaculaire, bien qu'assez sombre. Le choix des matériaux trahit les contraintes budgétaires assez strictes, mais les sols en linoléum gris, les balustrades en acier galvanisé perforé et les surfaces en ciment brut s'accordent bien à cette atmosphère d'usine. L'attention des visiteurs est rapidement orientée vers les pièces exposées, ce qui est après tout l'objectif de ce musée.

Édifice intriguant quand il est vu de loin, le New Metropolis pose un certain nombre de questions. L'une tient spécifiquement au site. Le bâtiment se trouve au-dessus du tunnel iJ de l'Oosterdok (dock est). Le critique Arthur Woortman a écrit à ce sujet un article acerbe paru dans le magazine néerlandais «Archis»: «Bien avant que l'on ne puisse y pénétrer, le bâtiment se signale de loin. On a avancé que sa construction au-dessus du tunnel évitait de nouvelles fondations, mais, en fait, il fallut renforcer celles qui existaient. La forme du bâtiment, avec son envolée ver-

The New Metropolis points to a number of trends and questions relating to contemporary architecture. One trend of recent years all over the world has certainly been toward museums of science and industry. After a glut of art museums throughout the 1970s and 1980s many cities and regions have looked toward science as a new source of municipal pride, but also as a source for tourism. There are some 1,000 of these centers in the world, and no fewer than 25 are currently being developed in Europe. About 250 million people visit science museums every year. As for the form of the New Metropolis, it admittedly has little to do with function, but the client was undoubtedly looking for a spectacular shape in order to attract visitors. The siting on top of the tunnel entrance certainly made the approach to the building more complicated than the architect might have wanted. With its enormous stepped roof, which is open to visitors, the New Metropolis is a large if somewhat incongruous symbol of Dutch openness to the modern world.

Piano's Beyeler Foundation, located in a suburb of the city of Basel called Riehen, is an entirely different kind of building. With its often blank walls made of blocks of porphyry, and its floating metallic roof, this structure recalls Piano's Cy Twombly Gallery in Houston. Within, white walls and light wood floors confirm a certain impression of austerity, which serves to highlight the splendid collection of modern and contemporary art formed by the dealer Ernst Beyeler. A kind of appropriate Swiss modesty permeates the building, which is set near fields close to the German border. A facade dominated by glass faces these fields, while the opposite side of the museum near the entrance faces a busy Wiesental road, which leads from Basel to the Black Forest. On the street side Piano has placed a stone wall, which assures the isolation of the galleries from traffic, but also makes for a rather forbidding presence as visitors approach. Where the New Metropolis places great emphasis on the architectural gesture of the rising green copper hull, here the works of art take center stage, a fact on which the client certainly insisted.

The 1994 Pritzker Prize brought international attention to the work of the French architect Christian de Portzamparc. It is not

fungierte er beim Bau des Vitra-Museums in Weil am Rhein als Projektleiter für Frank O. Gehry. Zwar vertreten Kleihues und Frank O. Gehry verschiedene ästhetische Positionen, doch sind beide Meister ihres Fachs, und Penkhues, der 1989 ein eigenes Büro gründete, konnte anscheinend von der Zeit bei ihnen profitieren. 1991 gewann er gegen 20 andere Architekten den Wettbewerb für das Historische Museum in Korbach, einer Stadt mit 25 000 Einwohnern in der Nähe von Kassel. Errichtet wurde der Bau dann zwischen 1995 und 1997. Die Wettbewerbsausschreibung sah vor, daß das Museum, das zuvor in einem mittelalterlichen Steinhaus und zwei angrenzenden Gebäuden untergebracht war, erweitert und die bestehenden Bauten restauriert werden sollten. Ein verglaster Innenhof verbindet ein Ensemble neuer und alter Gebäude, das an die alten, engen Gassen der Stadt denken läßt. Der Kommentar der Jury zum Entwurf von Penkhues lautete: »Die besonderen Qualitäten des Entwurfs liegen in seiner sensiblen Behandlung des Stadtraums und den damit verbundenen kleinen Abmessungen. Die skulpturale Formung der Baukörper ist bemerkenswert aufgrund der erzielten Integration von bestehender Bausubstanz und hinzugefügten Neubauten.«

Unabhängig davon, daß die sogenannte postmoderne Schule schon längst wieder außer Mode geraten ist, war es den Architekten in den 70er Jahren doch immerhin erlaubt, auf der Suche nach Inspiration einen Blick in die Vergangenheit zu werfen. Zwar hatten jene historischen Pastiches, durch die Architekten wie Michael Graves Berühmtheit erlangten, nur wenig mit der realen Geschichte der Orte zu tun, an denen die Bauten errichtet wurden. Berthold Penkhues hingegen, obwohl ganz unbestreitbar in den modernsten Strömungen der Architektur geschult, gab dem von der Kleinstadt Korbach gestellten Kontext und den spezifischen Bedingungen des Projekts Vorrang vor jeglichen Versuchen, einen persönlichen oder gerade angesagten Stil durchzusetzen. Auch wenn man den erzielten Raumfluß mit dem »frühen Gehry« verglichen hat, scheint das Museum doch zunächst einmal das Werk eines talentierten Architekten zu sein, der sich vorgenommen hat, ein spezifisches Problem zu lösen

Renzo Piano, New Metropolis Science & Technology Center, Amsterdam, The Netherlands, 1995–97. The green copper cladding of the building, as well as its unusual form, make it visible from a considerable distance.

Renzo Piano, New Metropolis, Museum für Wissenschaft und Technologie, Amsterdam, Niederlande, 1995–97. Durch die grüne Kupferverkleidung und seine ungewöhnliche Form ist das Gebäude von weitem sichtbar.

Renzo Piano, New Metropolis, Centre des Sciences et des Technologies, Amsterdam, Pays-Bas, 1995–97. La forme curieuse du bâtiment et son parement de cuivre vert le rendent visible de très loin.

ticale, s'est également révélée problématique. Tandis que la partie basse fut réalisée en béton bon marché, la partie supérieure dut être exécutée en acier pour en diminuer le poids. Toujours dans le même souci, la plinthe qui semble être entièrement édifiée en briques – hommage à la tradition – est en réalité un mince placage. Le New Metropolis se dresse au-dessus du tunnel, mais n'entretient aucune connexion fonctionnelle avec celui-ci. On pourrait penser à une symbiose entre le bâtiment et son infrastructure, mais la perception oculaire est trahie: vous vous retrouvez vite à Amsterdam-Nord.»[6] Le critique s'attaque également à la forme surprenante du Centre: «La forme domine. La forme hurle. La forme précède la fonction. La fonction du New Metropolis n'a rien à voir avec la forme de son bâtiment. La fonction ne suit pas la forme. On avait besoin d'une boîte. Les fenêtres sont pratiquement absentes. Ce vaisseau vert, si présent dans la ville, est totalement nié à l'intérieur. On pourrait tout aussi bien se trouver dans un bunker souterrain. Au New Metropolis, on attend, on réclame un spectacle intérieur, un spectacle architectural qui répond à cet extérieur spectaculaire. Et cette attente n'est pas comblée. Le résultat est une déception, quel que soit l'intérêt du matériel exposé.»[7]

Le New Metropolis met en lumière un certain nombre de tendances et de questions qui agitent l'architecture contemporaine. Un mouvement de ces dernières années – dans le monde entier – a consisté à construire des musées des sciences et de l'industrie. Après une explosion des musées artistiques au cours des années 70 et 80, de nombreuses villes et régions ont constaté que la science pouvait tout aussi bien flatter l'orgueil local et intéresser le tourisme. Il existe quelques 1 000 centres de ce type dans le monde, et pas moins de 25 sont actuellement en cours de construction en Europe. Environ 250 millions de personnes visitent ces musées scientifiques chaque année. Si la forme du New Metropolis n'a pas grand-chose à voir avec sa fonction, le client était certainement à la recherche d'une forme spectaculaire qui attire les visiteurs. Le positionnement au-dessus de l'entrée du tunnel a beaucoup plus compliqué les choses que l'architecte ne l'avait souhaité. Avec son énorme

Renzo Piano, Beyeler Foundation, Riehen, Switzerland, 1993–97. Seen from the fields to the rear of the museum, its long, low design is readily apparent.

Renzo Piano, Fondation Beyeler, Riehen, Schweiz, 1993–97. Blickt man von den umliegenden Feldern auf die Rückseite des Gebäudes, erschließt sich seine langgestreckte, flache Form unmittelbar.

Renzo Piano, Fondation Beyeler, Riehen, Suisse, 1993–97. La forme longue et basse du bâtiment de la Fondation se détache sur un fond de paysage agreste.

obvious that this distinction did much to further his career in any substantive way, but it did focus a certain amount of professional jealousy on him. Winner of a 1997 competition to design the new French embassy in Berlin on the Pariserplatz, next to the Brandenburg Gate, Portzamparc found himself at the center of a controversy. One German newspaper went so far as to say that Portzamparc's choice was "a decision with a political makeup, made in advance." His long-time friend Henri Gaudin, the competition runner-up, went so far as to publicly criticize the outcome, and a vitriolic anonymous text directed at Portzamparc circulated widely in French architectural circles. France, with its long tradition of centralized decision making, may indeed favor certain architects for large, government projects, but Portzamparc hardly has the profile of an "official" architect. Nor did any alleged friendship between the architect and the former Minister of Foreign Affairs Hervé de Charette actually have any impact on the outcome.

It should be noted that any construction on the Pariserplatz is subject to great scrutiny. Given its name in 1814 after the return from France of the Brandenburg Gate's quadriga, the square was devastated during World War II, a situation that was perpetuated by the proximity of the Berlin Wall. When the Wall came down, the Senate insisted that any reconstruction be aesthetically "in the spirit of the time" of the square, despite the fact that precious little aside from the Brandenburg Gate itself remained. The faithful reconstruction of the Hotel Adlon (Patzschke, Klotz & Partner) gives the tone for what is to come, even if Günter Behnisch of Stuttgart has been allowed to conceive a glass facade for his Art Academy directly next door. Even Frank O. Gehry has been persuaded to moderate his facade for the Deutsche Genossenschaftsbank, which will be next to the new U.S. Embassy (Moore, Ruble, Yudell). Everything possible was done to impress upon the architects and their clients that the Pariserplatz was a very special location, which could not admit architectural "fantasy."[8]

As prestigious as the commission to build a new French embassy in Berlin may be, the site, an L-shaped lot measuring

und dabei das Umfeld seines Schaffens zu respektieren. In einen Trend läßt sich das Projekt zwar nicht so leicht einordnen, doch legt es Zeugnis ab von der zunehmenden Reife der Gegenwartsarchitekten. Die Budgets sind zu knapp und die Arbeitsgelegenheiten zu selten für junge Architekten, um leichtfertig »persönliche Aussagen« zu treffen. Die Aufgabe muß vielmehr darin bestehen, einer architektonischen Lösung angesichts einer gegebenen Situation Qualität zu verleihen, was eine pragmatische und vielleicht sogar bescheidene Sichtweise des Architekten nahelegt.

Renzo Piano gehört zu jener Handvoll Architekten, die fast überall gebaut haben. Vom Kansai-Flughafen in der Bucht von Osaka bis zur Menil Collection in Houston – überall hat Piano seine Spuren hinterlassen, obgleich er in der Öffentlichkeit häufig noch immer mit seinem ersten Großprojekt, dem Centre Georges Pompidou in Paris, identifiziert wird, das er zusammen mit Richard Rogers entworfen hatte. Freilich haben die späteren Bauten Pianos stilistisch nur noch wenig mit jenem aus den 70er Jahren stammenden, überschwenglichen Röhrenwerk auf dem Place Beaubourg zu tun. In jüngerer Zeit tendiert seine Architektur vielmehr zu einem auf das Wesentliche reduzierten Minimalismus. Indes scheint sich New Metropolis, das Zentrum für Wissenschaft und Technologie in Amsterdam, nicht in die strikte Linienführung von Projekten wie der Cy Twombly Gallery in Houston oder dem neuen, backsteinverblendeten Anbau des IRCAM-Instituts neben dem Centre Pompidou in Paris einzufügen. Das wegen seiner Ähnlichkeit mit dem Rumpf eines großen, sinkenden Schiffs mit dem Spitznamen »Titanic« bedachte Zentrum in Amsterdam erreicht eine Höhe von 32 m und ist mit insgesamt 4 100 m² grüner Kupferplatten verkleidet; es steht in dem aus dem 17. Jahrhundert stammenden, maritimen Herzen Amsterdams, in der Nähe des Schiffahrtsmuseums und nicht weit vom Hauptbahnhof entfernt. Obwohl die Architekten den bewußten Rückgriff auf nautische Metaphern bestreiten, verlangte doch bereits die Ausschreibung des Projekts, der Entwurf solle einen »Zusammenhang mit der Schiffahrt herstellen«. Das Zentrum, ein Projekt des 1954 gegründeten Niederländischen Instituts für Industrie und Technologie, kostete insgesamt 77,5

toit en décrochements – ouvert aux visiteurs – le New Metropolis est un imposant symbole, mais légèrement incongru, de l'ouverture des Pays-Bas au monde moderne.

Toujours de Piano, la Fondation Beyeler à Riehen, dans la banlieue de Bâle, est un bâtiment d'esprit totalement différent. Avec ses murs souvent aveugles en blocs de porphyre et son toit métallique flottant, elle rappelle la Cy Twombly Gallery édifiée par Piano à Houston. À l'intérieur, des murs blancs et des sols en parquet clair confirment une certaine impression d'austérité, qui met en valeur la splendide collection d'art moderne et contemporain constituée par le marchand Ernst Beyeler. Une sorte de réserve suisse, qui convient parfaitement, émane de ce bâtiment situé en bordure de champs qui marquent la frontière allemande. Une façade essentiellement en verre ouvre sur la nature, tandis que la face opposée, prés de l'entrée, donne sur une route fréquentée qui va de Bâle à la Forêt Noire. Côté route, Piano a disposé un mur de pierre qui isole la galerie de la circulation, mais ne semble guère inviter à entrer. Alors que le New Metropolis met fortement l'accent sur le geste architectural de cette énorme coque de cuivre vert, ici, ce sont les œuvres d'art qui sont mises en évidence, ce qui était certainement le souhait du client.

Le Prix Pritzker 1994 a attiré l'attention internationale sur les travaux de l'architecte français Christian de Portzamparc. Il n'est pas certain que cette distinction ait beaucoup fait pour sa carrière, mais elle a assurément concentré sur sa personne un certain nombre de jalousies professionnelles. Après avoir remporté en 1997 le concours pour la nouvelle ambassade de France à Berlin, Pariser Platz, près de la porte de Brandebourg, Portzamparc s'est retrouvé au centre d'une controverse. Un journal allemand est allé jusqu'à écrire que le choix de Portzamparc était «une décision politique, prise d'avance». Son ami de longue date, Henri Gaudin, l'un de ses adversaires pour ce concours, en a publiquement critiqué les résultats, et un texte anonyme au vitriol dirigé contre Portzamparc a été largement diffusé parmi les cercles français d'architecture. La France, où règne encore une longue tradition de centralisation,

4,600 square meters offers no obvious solutions. "I entered the competition with a great deal of perplexity and uncertainty," says Christian de Portzamparc. "I found the site to be very difficult, because it is enclosed by the long high walls of neighboring buildings. I have always objected to what I call 'closed islands' in the construction of housing projects, and here it seemed impossible to create what I found to be a necessary openness. Bit by bit, I found a solution which permitted me to open the interior space to the sky, creating courtyards and gardens. My own claustrophobic reaction permitted me to find the key to open up the space, to avoid what seemed like the inevitable enclosure of the embassy 'island.'"[9] By building around the interior perimeter of the site Portzamparc was able to create a raised garden, and a walkway against the very large wall that faces the rear of the lot. His project is also in conformity, though just barely, with the rather austere facade requirements intended by city authorities to give a harmony to the square. He was in fact obliged to change the surface of some windows so that they would not exceed the maximum permitted of 40 square meters. The design also takes into account the strict environmental requirements of Berlin.

Elegant, if a bit complex, Portzamparc's embassy is further evidence of the willingness of well-known contemporary architects to take on projects that oblige them to make stylistic concessions. Whether because of the demands of clients or local authorities, or through the insistence of the architects themselves, contemporary buildings, especially in Europe, are increasingly aware of their surroundings, in terms both of their appearance and of their ecological impact on the environment. Gone, except for the odd exception, is the architectural work built on the tabula rasa that Modernism claimed as its territory.

An awareness of history, but also of the interaction of any building with its neighborhood, has tempered European contemporary architecture, indeed has made it mature. With some luck and perspicacity on the part of clients this new awareness can be brought to types of structures that generally do not take into account the basics of architectural quality, whether they be sports facilities, fair ground halls or embassies.

Millionen Gulden, von denen 42,5 Millionen Gulden für den eigentlichen Bau aufgewendet wurden. In seinem dunklen, höhlenähnlichen Inneren finden sich auf 4 300 m² interaktive Ausstellungen über Gebiete wie Telekommunikation, Finanztransaktionen, industrielle Fabrikation oder Informationstechnologie. Außerdem gibt es ein Kino mit 199 Sitzen, einen großen Museumsshop sowie einen Bereich für Kinder. Der fast über die gesamte Länge von 208 m offene Innenraum ist sehr eindrucksvoll, wenn auch ziemlich dunkel. Die verwendeten Materialien deuten einen recht engen finanziellen Rahmen an, doch passen die grauen Linoleumböden, die Balustraden aus gelochtem, galvanisertem Stahl und die unbehandelten Betonoberflächen gut zu der fabrikähnlichen Atmosphäre. Die Aufmerksamkeit der Besucher richtet sich vorrangig auf die Exponate, und das ist ja schließlich auch der Sinn der Einrichtung.

Mag das Wissenschaftszentrum aus der Ferne auch einen faszinierenden Anblick bieten, so zeigen sich bei näherer Betrachtung dennoch einige problematische Aspekte. Diese haben zunächst einmal mit seiner Lage zu tun. Der Bau befindet sich direkt über dem iJ-Tunnel des Oosterdoks (Östlichen Docks). Der Kritiker Arthur Woortman schrieb in einer vernichtenden Besprechung des Entwurfs: »Lange bevor wir den Bau betreten können, winkt er uns von fern zu. Man hatte behauptet, die Errichtung auf dem Tunnel würde ein Fundament überflüssig machen, aber dann stellten sich entsprechende Arbeiten doch als notwendig heraus. Auch die Grundgestalt des Gebäudes mit dem jähen Höhenanstieg erwies sich als problematisch. Während der untere Teil in kostengünstigem Beton ausgeführt ist, mußte der obere Teil aus Stahl konstruiert werden, um das Gewicht zu reduzieren. Gleichfalls aus Gewichtsgründen ist der scheinbar solide Backsteinsockel – eine Referenz an die holländische Backsteintradition – in Wirklichkeit nur eine dünne Verkleidung aus diesem Material. New Metropolis steht zwar auf dem Tunnel, hat aber nicht die geringste funktionale Verbindung zu ihm. Es mag so aussehen, als bestünde eine Symbiose zwischen Gebäude und Infrastruktur, doch bleibt jeder, der seinen Augen traut, auf dem Trockenen sitzen – in Nord-Amsterdam.«[6]

*Christian de Portzamparc, French Embassy, Berlin,
Germany, 1997–2000. In this model view, the main
facade of the Embassy is visible above the Brandenburg
Gate.*

*Christian de Portzamparc, Französische Botschaft,
Berlin, Deutschland, 1997–2000. Bei diesem Modell
blickt man über das Brandenburger Tor auf die Hauptfassade der Botschaft.*

*Christian de Portzamparc, Ambassade de France,
Berlin, Allemagne, 1997–2000. Dans cette maquette,
on aperçoit la façade principale de l'ambassade juste
au-dessus de la porte de Brandebourg.*

favorise probablement certains architectes à l'occasion de grands
projets gouvernementaux, mais Portzamparc ne correspond
guère au portrait d'un architecte «officiel». Et l'on ne peut dire
si son amitié supposée avec l'ancien ministre des Affaires
étrangères, Hervé de Charette, a réellement joué un rôle dans
cette affaire.

Il reste néanmoins que toute construction sur la Pariser Platz
est sujette à des examens minutieux. Baptisée Place de Paris
après le retour de France du quadrige de la porte de Brandebourg,
la place fut dévastée au cours de la Seconde Guerre mondiale,
situation gelée par la construction toute proche du mur de
Berlin. Lorsque le mur fut abattu, le Sénat insista pour que toute
reconstruction soit traitée «dans l'esprit de l'époque» de la
place, bien que rien de réellement précieux n'ait subsisté dans
le voisinage en dehors de la porte elle-même. La reconstitution
fidèle de l'Hôtel Adlon (Platzschke, Klotz & Partner) a donné
le ton de ce qui allait suivre, même si Gunter Behnisch, de
Stuttgart, a eu l'autorisation de donner une façade en verre à
son Académie des arts, la porte à côté. Même Frank O. Gehry
a été persuadé de modérer sa façade pour la Deutsche
Genossenschaftsbank, à côté de la nouvelle ambassade des
États-Unis (Moore, Ruble, Yudell). Tout ce qui était possible a
été entrepris pour faire comprendre aux architectes et à leurs
clients que la Pariser Platz était un lieu très particulier, ne
pouvant admettre aucune «fantaisie» architecturale.[8]

Si la commande d'une nouvelle ambassade de France à Berlin
est prestigieuse, le site, un terrain en forme de L de 4 600 m²
n'offrait guère de possibilités évidentes. «J'ai participé au concours avec beaucoup de perplexité et d'incertitude», commente
Christian de Portzamparc. «Je me suis engagé dans l'étude du
projet pour Berlin avec beaucoup de perplexité et d'incertitude
après avoir vu le site, tant je le trouvais difficile, par sa situation
terriblement encaissée entre des mitoyens hauts, longs, resserrés. Vu ma réticence aux îlots fermés, c'était pour moi mission
impossible... Et peu à peu les idées et les dispositifs me sont
venus pour dilater et ouvrir au ciel et aux arbres des espaces
de cours et de jardins intérieurs. Cette sorte de claustrophobie

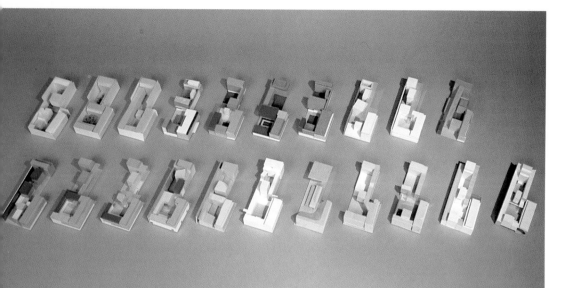

Christian de Portzamparc, French Embassy, Berlin, Germany, 1997–2000. A series of models shows the architect's different ideas for this rather difficult site.

Christian de Portzamparc, Französische Botschaft, Berlin, Deutschland, 1997–2000. Diese Modelle zeigen verschiedene Entwurfsideen des Architekten für das schwierige Grundstück.

Christian de Portzamparc, Ambassade de France, Berlin, Allemagne, 1997–2000. Différentes maquettes montrant les multiples approches inspirées à l'architecte par cet emplacement difficile.

1 Riley, Terence: *Light Construction*. The Museum of Modern Art, New York, 1995.
2 Johnson, Philip and Mark Wigley: *Deconstructivist Architecture*. The Museum of Modern Art, New York, 1988.
3 Tschumi, Bernard: *Architecture In/Of Motion*. NAI Publishers, Rotterdam, 1997.
4 ibid.
5 Sudjic, Deyan: *Erick van Egeraat, Six Ideas About Architecture*. Birkhäuser, Basel, 1997.
6 Woortman, Arthur: "Form, Function, Location – Renzo Piano, New Metropolis in Amsterdam," *Archis*, 1997.
7 ibid.
8 Ambassade de France à Berlin, Ministère des Affaires Etrangères, Paris, 1997.
9 Letter from Christian de Portzamparc, August 29, 1997. "Je me suis engagé dans l'étude du projet pour Berlin avec beaucoup de perplexité et d'incertitude après avoir vu le site, tant je le trouvais difficile, par sa situation terriblement encaissée entre des mitoyens hauts, longs, resserrés. Vu ma réticence aux îlots fermés, c'était pour moi mission impossible... Et peu à peu les idées et les dispositifs me sont venus pour dilater et ouvrir au ciel et aux arbres des espaces de cours et de jardins intérieurs. Cette sorte de claustrophobie m'a obligé à trouver des clés pour ouvrir les lieux, pour déjouer l'enfermement de l'îlot."

Der für die holländische Zeitschrift »Archis« schreibende Kritiker befaßt sich auch mit der überraschenden Form des Baus. »Die Form dominiert. Die Form schreit. Die Form geht der Funktion voran. Die Funktion von New Metropolis hat nichts mit seiner äußeren Gestalt zu tun. Die Funktion folgt nicht der Form. Benötigt wurde eine schwarze Kiste. Fenster fehlen fast vollständig. Das grüne Schiff, das so nachdrücklich in der Stadt präsent ist, findet im Inneren überhaupt keine Entsprechung. Wir könnten uns genausogut in einem Bunker 10 m unter der Erde befinden. In New Metropolis würde man auch im Inneren ein Schauspiel, ein architektonisches Spektakel, erwarten, nein verlangen, welches der spektakulären Außenform gerecht wird. Und dieses Verlangen wird nicht erfüllt. Das Resultat ist zwangsläufig enttäuschend, ganz gleich, wie interessant das Ausstellungsmaterial auch sein mag.«[7]

Das New Metropolis-Zentrum weist auf eine Reihe von Tendenzen und Fragestellungen der Gegenwartsarchitektur hin. Ein weltweiter Trend der vergangenen Jahre war die Errichtung von Wissenschafts- und Industriemuseen. Im Anschluß an die Schwemme von Kunstmuseen in den 70er und 80er Jahren haben viele Städte und Regionen ihren Blick nun auf die Wissenschaft als neue Quelle des lokalen Stolzes, aber auch als Quelle für den Tourismus gerichtet. Momentan gibt es rund 1 000 solcher Zentren auf der Welt, nicht weniger als 25 werden zur Zeit allein in Europa geplant und gebaut. Rund 250 Millionen Menschen besuchen jedes Jahr diese Wissenschaftsmuseen. Sicherlich war dies einer der Gründe dafür, daß der Auftraggeber nach einer solch spektakulären Gestaltung verlangte, um so Touristenströme anzuziehen, leider jedoch mit dem Ergebnis, daß das Äußere des New Metropolis wenig mit seiner Funktion zu tun hat. Die Lage oberhalb der Tunneleinfahrt macht die Erschließung des Gebäudes gewiß schwieriger, als der Architekt sich das gewünscht hätte. Mit seinem riesigen gestuften Dach, das übrigens besucht werden kann, ist New Metropolis ein kraftvolles, wenn auch etwas unglücklich plaziertes Symbol für die Offenheit der Niederlande gegenüber der modernen Welt.

m'a obligé à trouver des clés pour ouvrir les lieux, pour déjouer l'enfermement de l'îlot.«[9] En construisant sur le périmètre du site, l'architecte a créé un jardin suspendu et une passerelle le long du grand mur qui bloque l'arrière du terrain. Son projet est également en conformité (mais tout juste) avec les contraintes assez sévères imposées aux façades par les autorités municipales pour harmoniser la place. Il a été en fait obligé de modifier la surface de certaines baies pour qu'elles ne dépassent pas la hauteur maximum autorisée de 40 m². Le projet prend également en compte la stricte réglementation berlinoise sur l'environnement. Élégante, quoiqu'un peu complexe, l'ambassade de France Portzamparc est une preuve supplémentaire de la volonté d'architectes connus de prendre en charge des projets qui les forcent à des concessions stylistiques. Que ce soit à cause des demandes des clients ou des autorités locales, ou à travers l'insistance des architectes eux-mêmes, les constructions contemporaines, en particulier en Europe, sont de plus en plus conscientes de leur environnement, tant en ce qui concerne l'aspect que l'impact écologique. L'œuvre architecturale faisant table rase du passé, si chère aux modernistes, n'est plus de mise, à quelques exceptions près. Une conscience de l'histoire, mais également de l'interaction de toute construction avec son voisinage a tempéré l'architecture contemporaine européenne, en lui permettant d'accéder à une maturité nouvelle. Avec un peu de chance et une attention renouvelée de la part des clients, cette nouvelle prise de conscience peut s'appliquer à des types de structures qui généralement ne prennent pas en compte les bases de la qualité architecturale, que ce soit des salles de sport, des halls de foire ou des ambassades.

Pianos Entwurf für die Fondation Beyeler in Riehen, einem Vorort von Basel, brachte einen völlig anderen Gebäudetyp hervor. Die häufig unverputzten Wände aus Porphyrstein und das schwebende, metallische Dach rufen dem Betrachter Pianos Twombly Gallery in Houston in Erinnerung. Auch im Inneren bekräftigen die weißen Wände und die hellen Holzböden den Eindruck einer strengen Einfachheit, die der großartigen Sammlung moderner und zeitgenössischer Kunst, die der Kunsthändler Ernst Beyeler zusammengetragen hat, Vorrang vor der Architektur geben soll. Der in einer Felderlandschaft an der Grenze zu Deutschland errichtete Bau ist von schweizerischer Zurückhaltung gekennzeichnet. Eine von Glasflächen dominierte Fassade öffnet sich zur Landschaft, während die gegenüberliegende Seite mit dem Eingangsbereich zur stark befahrenen Wiesentalstraße weist, die von Basel zum Schwarzwald führt. Auf dieser Straßenseite hat Piano eine Steinmauer vorangestellt, die die Ausstellungsräume vom Verkehr abschirmt und auch für ein recht düsteres Erscheinungsbild sorgt, nähert sich der Besucher dem Museum von dort. Wurde beim New Metropolis-Zentrum großer Wert auf die architektonische Geste des in die Höhe ragenden grünen Kupferrumpfes gelegt, spielen in Riehen die Kunstwerke die Hauptrolle, worauf der Auftraggeber zweifellos bestanden hat.

Durch die Verleihung des Pritzker-Preises 1994 wurde man auf den französischen Architekten Christian de Portzamparc international aufmerksam. Auch wenn diese Auszeichnung seine Laufbahn als Architekt nicht wesentlich gefördert hat, so trug sie ihm mit Gewißheit ein nicht geringes Maß an Neid aus den Reihen seiner Kollegen ein. Portzamparc, der Gewinner eines 1997 ausgetragenen Wettbewerbs für den Neubau der französischen Botschaft am Pariser Platz in Berlin, fand sich plötzlich im Zentrum einer Kontroverse wieder. Eine deutsche Tageszeitung behauptete sogar, die Wahl Portzamparcs sei »aus politischen Gründen vorab entschieden worden«. Sein langjähriger Freund Henri Gaudin, zweiter Preisträger des Wettbewerbs, kritisierte das Ergebnis öffentlich, und in französischen Architektenkreisen kursierte ein an Portzamparc gerichteter, haßerfüllter Text. Es mag wohl zutreffen, daß Frankreich mit seiner langen Tradition zentralisierter Entscheidungsprozesse bestimmte Architekten für große Regierungsprojekte bevorzugt, doch hat gerade Portzamparc wohl kaum das Profil eines »offiziellen« Architekten. Ebensowenig hat die angebliche Freundschaft zwischen dem Architekten und dem früheren Außenminister Hervé de Charette irgendeinen Einfluß auf das Ergebnis genommen.

Nicht unerwähnt bleiben sollte, daß jedes Bauvorhaben auf dem Pariser Platz Gegenstand einer eingehenden Prüfung ist. Der Platz, der seinen Namen im Anschluß an die 1814 erfolgte Rückkehr der Quadriga des Brandenburger Tores aus Frankreich erhielt, wurde im Zweiten Weltkrieg weitgehend zerstört, ein Zustand, der dann durch die unmittelbare Nähe der Berliner Mauer über Jahrzehnte bestehen blieb. Als die Mauer fiel, bestand der Senat darauf, daß jede Rekonstruktion ästhetisch »im Geist der Zeit« der Entstehung des Platzes erfolgen müsse, ungeachtet der Tatsache, daß außer dem Brandenburger Tor so gut wie nichts erhalten geblieben war. Der dem zerstörten Original nachempfundene Wiederaufbau des Hotels Adlon (Patzschke, Klotz & Partner) lieferte den Grundton für alles weitere, auch wenn Günter Behnisch aus Stuttgart die Genehmigung erhalten hat, die unmittelbar benachbarte Kunstakademie mit einer Glasfassade zu versehen. Selbst Frank O. Gehry konnte davon überzeugt werden, die Fassade der Deutschen Genossenschaftsbank moderat zu gestalten, die direkt neben der neuen Botschaft der USA (Moore, Ruble, Yudell) zu sehen sein wird. Alles Denkbare ist getan worden, um auf die Architekten und ihre Auftraggeber Einfluß auszuüben, daß der Pariser Platz ein ganz besonderer Ort sei, an dem architektonische »Phantasie« nichts zu suchen habe.[8]

So prestigeträchtig der Auftrag zum Bau der neuen französischen Botschaft in Berlin auch sein mag – das L-förmige Grundstück von rund 4 600 m² Größe legt keine offensichtlichen Lösungen nahe. »Als ich die Arbeit am Wettbewerbsentwurf begann, war ich perplex und sehr verunsichert«, sagt Portzamparc. »Ich fand das vorgesehene Grundstück außerordentlich schwierig, denn es ist von den langen, hohen Mauern benachbarter Häuser eingeschlossen. Ich habe mich bei meinen Ent-

würfen für Wohnbauten immer dagegen gewehrt zu bauen, was ich ›geschlossene Inseln‹ nenne, und hier nun schien es unmöglich, das zu schaffen, was ich für eine notwendige Offenheit hielt. Schritt für Schritt näherte ich mich dann einer Lösung, die es mir erlaubte, die innen gelegenen Räume zum Himmel hin zu öffnen sowie Innenhöfe und Gärten zu planen. Meine eigene klaustrophobische Reaktion machte es mir möglich, den Schlüssel zu finden, um den zur Verfügung stehenden Raum zu öffnen und so zu vermeiden, was zunächst wie eine unumgängliche Botschafts-›Insel‹ ausgesehen hatte.«[9] Portzamparc baute entlang der inneren Begrenzungslinien des Grundstücks einen höher gelegenen Garten und schuf einen Weg gegen eine sehr große Mauer, welche die Rückseite des Geländes markiert. Sein Entwurf genügt, wenn auch knapp, den recht strengen Auflagen für Hausfassaden, mithilfe derer die städtischen Behörden ein harmonisches Zusammenspiel des Bauensembles am Pariser Platz sicherstellen wollen. Portzamparc mußte sogar die Größe einiger Fenster verringern, um die maximal erlaubten 40 m² nicht zu überschreiten. Schließlich hält der Entwurf auch die strengen Umweltbestimmungen der Stadt Berlin ein.

Das elegante, recht komplexe Botschaftsgebäude von Portzamparc ist ein weiteres Anzeichen für die Bereitschaft bekannter Gegenwartsarchitekten, sich auch solchen Projekten zu widmen, die sie zu stilistischen Konzessionen verpflichten. In zunehmendem Maße wird mit zeitgenössischen Bauten, vor allem in Europa, auf deren jeweilige Umgebung Rücksicht genommen – sei es aufgrund der Vorgaben der Auftraggeber oder der lokalen Behörden oder auch aus Überzeugung der Architekten –, sowohl in Hinblick auf das äußere Erscheinungsbild als auch im Zusammenhang mit den ökologischen Auswirkungen. Abgesehen von gelegentlichen Ausnahmen sind die Zeiten einer Architektur, die auf Grundlage der »tabula rasa« entstand, was die Moderne einst als ihr ureigenes Vorrecht begriff, vorüber. Das Bewußtsein für den historischen Kontext, aber auch für die Interaktion jedes Bauwerks mit seiner Nachbarschaft, hat die europäische Architektur der Gegenwart zur Mäßigung veranlaßt,

Christian de Portzamparc, French Embassy, Berlin, Germany, 1997–2000. A drawing by the architect shows the inner garden of the Embassy.

Christian de Portzamparc, Französische Botschaft, Berlin, Deutschland, 1997–2000. Eine Zeichnung des Architekten zeigt den Garten im Innenhof der Botschaft.

Christian de Portzamparc, Ambassade de France, Berlin, Allemagne, 1997–2000. Dessin de l'architecte pour le jardin intérieur de l'ambassade.

ja hat ihr zur Reife verholfen. Mit etwas Glück und Weitsicht auf Seiten der Auftraggeber kann sich dieses neue Bewußtsein auch auf solche Gebäudetypen auswirken, bei denen die Grundregeln der architektonischen Qualität nicht unbedingt berücksichtigt werden, seien es Sporteinrichtungen, Messehallen oder Botschaftsgebäude.

Page 51: *Thomas Herzog + Partner, Hall 26, Deutsche Messe, Hanover, Germany, 1994–96. A peak of one of the wave-like forms of this exhibition hall.*
Pages 52–53: *Renzo Piano, New Metropolis Science & Technology Center, Amsterdam, The Netherlands, 1995–97. The building seen from the footbridge which leads to its port side facade.*

Seite 51: *Thomas Herzog + Partner, Halle 26, Deutsche Messe Hannover, Deutschland, 1994–96. Die Spitze einer der Wellenformen der Messehalle.*
Seite 52–53: *Renzo Piano, New Metropolis, Museum für Wissenschaft und Technologie, Amsterdam, Niederlande, 1995–97. Blick auf das Gebäude von der Fußgängerbrücke, die zu der dem Hafen zugewandten Seitenfassade führt.*

Page 51: *Thomas Herzog + Partner, Hall 26, Foire d'Allemagne, Hanovre, Allemagne, 1994–96. Faîte de l'une des «vagues» qui constituent ce hall d'exposition.*
Pages 52–53: *Renzo Piano, New Metropolis, Centre des Sciences et des Technologies, Amsterdam, Pays-Bas, 1995–97. Le bâtiment vu de la passerelle qui conduit à sa façade côté port.*

Mario Botta

Born in Mendrisio, Switzerland (1943), Mario Botta left school at fifteen to become an apprentice in a Lugano architectural office. He designed his first house the following year. After studies in Milan and Venice, Botta worked briefly in the entourage of Le Corbusier and Louis Kahn and worked often with Luigi Snozzi. He built private houses in Cadenazzo (1970–71), Riva San Vitale (1971–73), and Ligornetto (1975–76), all in Switzerland. The Médiathèque in Villeurbanne, France (1984–88) and Cultural Center in Chambéry, France (1982–87) followed. More recent projects include the Évry Cathedral, France (1988–95), the San Francisco Museum of Modern Art, California (1989/92–95), the Tamaro Chapel, Switzerland (Monte Tamaro, 1990–96), the Jean Tinguely Museum in Basel, Switzerland (1993–96), a little church in Mogno, Switzerland (1986–98), and a design for the renovation of the Presbytery of the Cathedral of Santa Maria del Fiore in Florence, Italy (1997), as well as the Synagogue and Cultural Center in Tel Aviv, Israel (1996–98). Working with geometric forms, such as truncated cylinders, Mario Botta often uses brick cladding. His mastery of shapes at the juncture between the contemporary and the profoundly traditional is perhaps most evident in his chapels and churches.

Mario Botta, geboren 1943 im schweizerischen Mendrisio, verließ die Schule bereits im Alter von 15 Jahren und durchlief eine Lehre in einem Architekturbüro in Lugano. Schon im darauffolgenden Jahr entwarf er sein erstes Haus. Nach Studien in Mailand und Venedig wirkte Botta kurzzeitig im Mitarbeiterstab von Le Corbusier und Louis Kahn und arbeitete oft mit Luigi Snozzi zusammen. Er entwarf Einfamilienhäuser wie in Cadenazzo (1970–71), Riva San Vitale (1971–73) oder Ligornetto (1975–76), alle in der Schweiz. Es folgten eine Médiathèque in Villeurbanne, Frankreich (1984–88) und ein Kulturzentrum in Chambéry, Frankreich (1982–87). Zu Bottas jüngeren Projekten gehören die Kathedrale von Évry, Frankreich (1988–95), das Museum of Modern Art in San Francisco, Kalifornien (1989/92–95), die Kapelle auf dem Monte Tamaro, Schweiz (1990–96), das Jean Tinguely Museum in Basel, Schweiz (1993–96), eine kleine Kirche in Mogno, Schweiz (1986–98), ein Entwurf für die Neugestaltung des Presbyteriums der Kirche Santa Maria del Fiore in Florenz, Italien (1997) sowie eine Synagoge mit jüdischem Kulturzentrum in Tel Aviv, Israel (1996–98). Bei seiner Entwurfsarbeit, die sich meist geometrischer Grundformen wie etwa dem Zylinderstumpf bedient, setzt Botta häufig Klinkerverblendungen ein. Seine meisterhafte Formbeherrschung am Schnittpunkt zwischen dem Zeitgenössischen und dem Traditionellen kommt vielleicht am deutlichsten in seinen Kapellen und Kirchen zum Ausdruck.

Né en 1943 à Mendrisio (Suisse), Mario Botta quitte l'école à 15 ans pour commencer son apprentissage dans une agence d'architecture de Lugano. Il dessine sa première maison l'année suivante. Après des études à Milan et Venise, il travaille brièvement dans l'entourage de Le Corbusier et de Louis Kahn et collabore souvent avec Luigi Snozzi. Il construit des maisons individuelles comme à Cadenazzo (1970–71), Riva San Vitale (1971–73) ou Ligornetto (1975–76), toutes situées en Suisse, puis la Maison de la culture de Chambéry, France (1982–87), et la Médiathèque de Villeurbanne, France (1984–88). Parmi ses réalisations récentes: la cathédrale d'Évry, France (1988–95), le Musée d'art moderne de San Francisco, Californie (1989/92–95), la Chapelle sur le Mont Tamaro, Suisse (1990–96), le Musée Jean Tinguely à Bâle, Suisse (1993–96), une petite église à Mogno, Suisse (1986–98), le projet de rénovation du presbytère de la cathédrale de Santa Maria del Fiore à Florence, Italie (1997), ainsi que la synagogue et le centre culturel juif à Tel Aviv, Israël (1996–98). Travaillant à partir de formes géométriques comme le cylindre tronqué, Botta recouvre souvent ses réalisations d'un parement de briques. Sa maîtrise des formes, à la jonction du langage contemporain et de la haute tradition, est particulièrement évidente dans ses chapelles et ses églises.

Mario Botta, Private House, Montagnola, Ticino, Switzerland, 1989/91–94.

Mario Botta, Privathaus, Montagnola, Tessin, Schweiz, 1989/91–94.

Mario Botta, résidence privée, Montagnola, Tessin, Suisse, 1989/91–94.

Private House

Montagnola, Ticino,
Switzerland, 1989/91–1994

Built on a 3,666 square meter site located not far from Lugano, this house has a net floor area of 670 square meters. It is a reinforced concrete structure with brick facing. The entrance and a part of the "night" area of the house are located on the intermediate level, where there are two bedrooms. The rest of the night area, including three more bedrooms, is on the lower floor, which also contains a studio and bar, a pool, sauna and large garage intended for an automobile collection. These facilities are situated in the long, low volume, which extends from the main, semicircular form. The part of the house that is set aside for the day is on the upper floor of the semicircle, marked from the outside by a line of portholes and a recessed loggia near the living room. This large house does bring to mind much of Botta's previous residential work, usually situated in the Canton of Ticino. Set on a sloping piece of land, this structure is immediately identifiable as a Mario Botta building, both because of its circular forms and because of its brick facing.

Das in der Nähe von Lugano auf einem 3 666 m² großen Grundstück errichtete Haus bietet eine Fläche von 670 m². Es handelt sich um einen Stahlbetonbau mit Backstein- verblendung. Die Eingangszone und ein Teil des »Nachtbereichs« mit zwei Schlafzimmern befinden sich auf einer Zwischenetage. Weitere drei Schlafzimmer liegen im Unterge- schoß neben einem Atelierraum, einer Bar, einem Swimmingpool, einer Sauna und einer großen Garage für eine Automobilsammlung. All diese Räumlichkeiten sind in einem langen, flach gehaltenen Baukörper untergebracht, der aus der halbkreisförmigen Hauptform hervorragt. Im Obergeschoß des Rundbaus liegen die Bereiche, die dem Aufenthalt bei Tag vorbehalten sind, äußerlich gekennzeichnet durch eine Reihe Bullaugen und eine zurückspringende Loggia neben dem Wohnzimmer. Das weitläufige Haus ruft viele der früheren Wohnbauten Bottas ins Gedächtnis, die er größtenteils im Kanton Tessin errichtet hat. Auf abfallendem Gelände stehend, ist das Gebäude sofort als ein Botta- Entwurf identifizierbar, sei es wegen seiner Rundformen oder auch aufgrund der Backsteinverblendung.

Édifiée sur un terrain de 3 666 m² non loin de Lugano, cette maison en béton armé paré de briques occupe une surface au sol nette de 670 m². L'entrée et une partie de la zone «nocturne» sont implantées au niveau inter- médiaire, où deux chambres à coucher ont été prévues. Le reste de cette même zone, dont trois chambres supplémentaires, se situe au niveau inférieur, qui contient également un studio avec bar, une piscine, un sauna et un grand garage prévu pour une collection de voitures. Le tout se trouve dans le long volume bas qui se déploie à partir du bâtiment princi- pal de forme semi-circulaire. La partie de la maison réservée à la zone de jour occupe le niveau supérieur du demi-cercle, caractérisée à l'extérieur par une rangée d'œils-de-bœuf et une loggia en retrait, desservant la salle-de- séjour. Cette grande maison fait beaucoup penser aux premières résidences construites par l'architecte, la plupart dans le Tessin. Implantée sur un terrain en pente, cette struc- ture circulaire parée de briques porte indéni- ablement la signature de Mario Botta.

Pages 56–59: The two main facades of the house, one straight and the other semicircular, are part of a geo- metric composition, which includes a long, elevated walkway over the garage and part of the ground floor area.

Seite 56–59: Die zwei Hauptfassaden des Hauses – eine gerade und eine halbkreisförmige – bilden eine geometrische Komposition, die auch einen langen Zufahrtsweg über der Garage und einen Teil der Wohnfläche im Erdgeschoß einschließt.

Pages 56–59: Les deux principales façades de la mai- son, l'une rectiligne, l'autre semi-circulaire, font partie de la composition géométrique générale qui comprend un long passage surélevé au-dessus du garage et d'une partie du rez-de-chaussée.

Pages 60–61: *Within, large glazed surfaces admit ample natural light and permit the house to be in direct visual contact with its surroundings.*
Page 60 bottom: *Drawings of the first and second floors emphasize the semicircular shape of the main house and the projecting volume of the pool, sauna and garage to the right.*

Seite 60–61: *Im Inneren bewirken große Glasflächen die großzügige Versorgung mit Tageslicht und einen direkten Sichtkontakt mit der unmittelbaren Umgebung.*
Seite 60 unten: *Grundrisse des ersten und zweiten Stockwerkes zeigen die halbrunde Form des Haupt-gebäudeteils und rechts das auskragende Bauvolumen, das das Schwimmbad, die Sauna und die Garage beherbergt.*

Pages 60–61: *À l'intérieur, de grandes baies vitrées laissent entrer une abondante lumière naturelle et maintiennent un contact visuel direct entre la maison et son environnement.*
Page 60 en bas: *Dessins du premier et second niveaux mettant en valeur la forme semi-circulaire de la maison principale et les volumes en projection de la piscine, du sauna et du garage, à droite.*

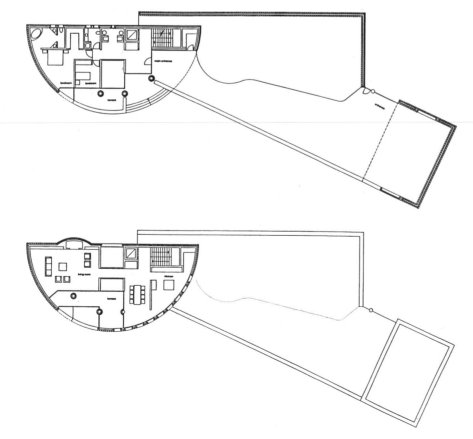

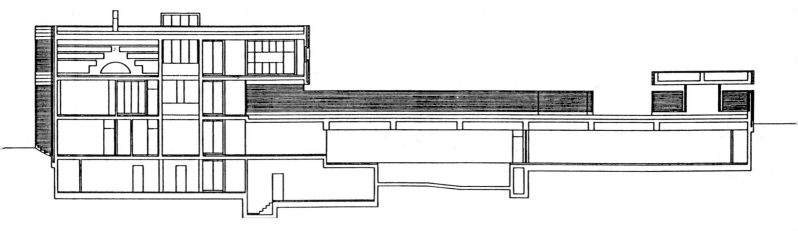

Chaix & Morel

J.-P. Morel   Ph. Chaix

Philippe Chaix and Jean-Paul Morel were both born in 1949. Chaix attended the École des Beaux-Arts in Paris, where he received his diploma in 1972 (UP6, DPLG), while Morel graduated from the École UP1 in Nancy in 1976 (DPLG). They have been associates since 1983. It was the following year that they built the 6,000 seat Zénith, a concert hall located in the Parc de la Villette in Paris. This experience led them to work on similar structures in Montpellier (1986) and Orléans (1996) – both in France. They have participated extensively in competitions, and their entries have frequently been among those most appreciated by the juries, as was the case for the Bibliothèque Nationale de France in Paris. As well as the Archeological Museum of Saint-Romain-en-Gal and the Avancée of the Renault Technocenter published here, they recently completed the new École des Ponts et Chaussées in Marne-la-Vallée. Current work includes a soccer stadium in Amiens, France (1995–98), and the European Center of Federal Express at Roissy near Paris (1998–99). Their work can be considered part of a wave of technologically oriented new French architecture, which includes such other firms as Valode & Pistre or Architecture Studio.

Philippe Chaix und Jean-Paul Morel wurden beide 1949 geboren. Chaix besuchte die École des Beaux-Arts in Paris, wo er 1972 sein Diplom erhielt (UP6, DPLG), während Morel 1976 an der École UP1 in Nancy graduierte (DPLG). Seit 1983 unterhalten sie eine Bürogemeinschaft. Im darauffolgenden Jahr bauten sie die mit 6 000 Sitzen ausgestattete Konzerthalle Zénith im Parc de la Villette in Paris. Die dort gemachten Erfahrungen führten sie zu ähnlichen Bauten in Montpellier (1986) und Orléans (1996) – beide in Frankreich. Chaix & Morel haben sich ausgiebig an Wettbewerben beteiligt, und ihre Entwürfe zählen häufig zu den von den Gutachtern meistgeschätzten, wie etwa im Fall der Bibliothèque Nationale de France in Paris. Neben dem Archäologischen Museum in Saint-Romain-en-Gal und dem Avancée des Renault-Technologiezentrums, beide hier vorgestellt, stellten Chaix & Morel auch die neue École des Ponts et Chaussées in Marne-la-Vallée fertig. Zu ihren laufenden Projekten gehören ein Fußballstadion in Amiens, Frankreich (1995–98), und die Europazentrale von Federal Express in Roissy nahe Paris (1998–99). Chaix & Morel repräsentieren jene Bewegung einer technologisch ausgerichteten, neuen französischen Architektur, der auch Büros wie Valode & Pistre oder Architecture Studio angehören.

Associés depuis 1983, Philippe Chaix et Jean-Paul Morel sont tous deux nés en 1949. Chaix étudie à l'École des Beaux-Arts de Paris (UP6), dont il sort diplômé (DPLG) en 1972, tandis que Morel est diplômé (DPLG) de l'École UP1 de Nancy. En 1984, ils construisent un premier «Zénith», salle de concert de 6 000 places en bordure du Parc de la Villette à Paris. Ils travaillent sur des structures similaires à Montpellier (1986) et Orléans (1996). Participant à de nombreux concours, leurs projets sont souvent très appréciés par les jurys, dont celui de la Bibliothèque Nationale de France à Paris. En dehors du Musée archéologique de Saint-Romain-en-Gal et de l'Avancée du Technocentre Renault reproduits ici, ils ont récemment achevé la nouvelle École des Ponts et Chaussées à Marne-la-Vallée. Ils travaillent actuellement sur un stade de football à Amiens (1995–98), et le Centre européen de Federal Express, à l'aéroport de Roissy (1998–99). Leur œuvre appartient à cette vague de la nouvelle architecture française à orientation technologique, à laquelle se rattachent des agences comme Valode & Pistre ou Architecture Studio.

Chaix & Morel, Archeological Museum, Saint-Romain-en-Gal, France, 1994–96.

Chaix & Morel, Archäologisches Museum, Saint-Romain-en-Gal, Frankreich, 1994–96.

Chaix & Morel, Musée archéologique de Saint-Romain-en-Gal, France, 1994–96.

Archeological Museum

Saint-Romain-en-Gal, France, 1994–1996

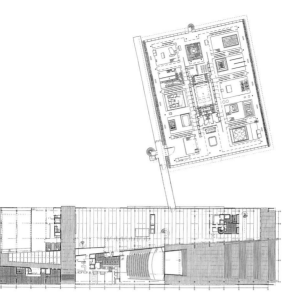

Located opposite the city of Vienne on the Rhone, the former Roman Colonia Iulia Viennensium is an important archeological site, having yielded no fewer than 250 mosaics to date. It is in the midst of this site that it was decided in 1988 to build a museum of Roman civilization. The 12,000 square meter structure is divided into two sections. A more traditional concrete building contains the entrance area, a bookshop, cafeteria, amphitheater, offices, storage areas, and a 2,300 square meter restoration laboratory. More unexpected, the permanent exhibition building, made of steel and glass, is suspended from four rows of six pillars over the location of an actual archeological dig. Its large windows offer views out onto the site, and an inclined ramp offers direct access to the ground level. Set in a 7 hectare lot, which is classified by the French government as an historic monument, the museum cost 181.5 million francs to build, a budget that was divided between the region and the central government.

Bei der gegenüber der Stadt Vienne auf der anderen Seite der Rhône gelegenen ehemaligen römischen Siedlung Colonia Iulia Viennensium handelt es sich um eine wichtige archäologische Grabungsstätte, bei der bislang nicht weniger als 250 Mosaike zutage gebracht wurden. Im Jahre 1988 entschied man, inmitten dieser Anlage ein Museum für römische Kultur zu errichten. Die insgesamt 12 000 m² Nutzfläche des neuen Museums verteilen sich auf zwei Baukörper. Ein eher konventioneller Betonbau nimmt die Eingangszone, eine Buchhandlung, eine Cafeteria, ein Amphitheater, Büros, Magazine sowie eine 2 300 m² große Restaurierungswerkstatt auf. Im Gegensatz dazu wird der zweite, aus Stahl und Glas erstellte Baukörper, in der die Dauerausstellung gezeigt wird, von vier Reihen aus jeweils sechs Pfeilern getragen. Dieses Gebäude befindet sich unmittelbar über einer Grabungsstätte. Große Fensterflächen bieten dem Besucher einen guten Überblick über die Gesamtanlage, und eine Fußgängerrampe ermöglicht den direkten Zugang zum Bodenniveau. Die Baukosten des Museums, dessen 7 Hektar umfassendes Gelände von der französischen Regierung zum »Historischen Monument« erklärt worden ist, betrugen 181,5 Millionen Francs, für die Region und Zentralregierung gemeinsam aufkamen.

Situé face à la ville de Vienne, sur l'autre rive du Rhône, l'ancienne Colonia Iulia Viennensium est un site archéologique important qui a déjà révélé pas moins de 250 mosaïques. C'est au milieu de ce champ de fouilles qu'il a été décidé, en 1988, de construire un musée de la civilisation romaine. La structure de 12 000 m² est divisée en deux sections. Un bâtiment en béton, d'aspect plus traditionnel, contient la zone d'accueil du public, une librairie, une cafétéria, un amphithéâtre, des bureaux, des réserves et un laboratoire de restauration de 2 300 m². Le bâtiment de l'exposition permanente est plus inhabituel: en verre et acier, il est surélevé sur quatre rangées de six piliers au-dessus d'un champ de fouilles archéologiques. Ses vastes baies s'ouvrent sur le site, tandis qu'une rampe inclinée permet un accès direct au rez-de-chaussée. Construit sur un terrain de 7 hectares classé Monument historique, ce musée à coûté 181,5 millions de F, répartis entre la région et l'État.

Pages 64–67: The museum is divided into two buildings, one, more massive and set on the earth, the other, with its large glass facades, literally set up above the site of an archeological dig.

Seite 64–67: Das Museum verteilt sich auf zwei Gebäude: einen massiven, auf dem Erdboden ruhenden Bau und einen auf Pfeiler gelagerten, gläsernen Bau, der sich unmittelbar über einer archäologischen Grabungsstätte befindet.

Pages 64–67: Le musée est divisé en deux bâtiments. L'un, plus massif, repose sur le sol, tandis que l'autre, aux vastes façades de verre, est littéralement en surélévation au-dessus du site des fouilles archéologiques.

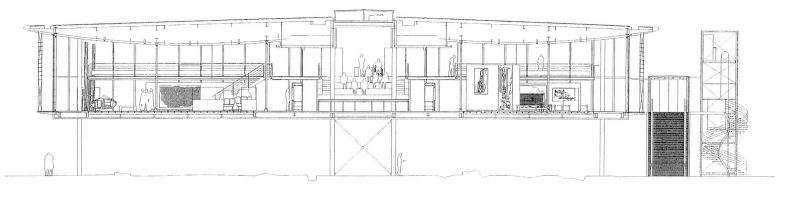

Pages 68–70: Since the museum is in the midst of the site where many of the objects displayed were discovered, the architects chose to give the main display areas a view to the outside. Since mosaics are involved, the museum does not have the same low-light requirements that some other institutions might.

Seite 68–70: Da sich das Gebäude unmittelbar auf dem Gelände befindet, wo viele der gezeigten Objekte gefunden wurden, haben die Architekten im Hauptausstellungsbereich die Möglichkeit geschaffen, nach draußen zu schauen. Weil es sich hier größtenteils um Mosaike handelt, ist in diesem Fall gedämpftes Licht weniger erforderlich als bei anderen Einrichtungen.

Pages 68–70: Comme le musée est implanté au milieu du site sur lequel de nombreux objets exposés ont été découverts, les architectes ont choisi d'ouvrir les principales zones d'exposition sur l'extérieur. Les collections étant en grande partie composées de mosaïques, le musée n'est pas soumis à des exigences de contrôle d'éclairage particulières.

Page 71: The stairs leading to heavier concrete structure housing the bookshop, cafeteria (page 70 top), offices and storage areas.

Seite 71: Der Treppenaufgang führt zu einem massiveren Baukörper aus Beton, in dem ein Buchladen, eine Cafeteria (Seite 70 oben), Büros und Lagerräume untergebracht sind.

Page 71: L'escalier menant à la structure en béton, plus massive, qui abrite la librairie, la caféteria (page 70 en haut), les bureaux et des espaces de stockage.

L'Avancée, Renault Technocenter

Guyancourt, France, 1995–1997

Located to the west of Paris, Renault's Technocenter was for some time the largest industrial construction project in Europe. The 350 hectare site is to include a total of 350,000 square meters of buildings for a staff of 6,500 persons, set out on a masterplan designed by the architects Valode & Pistre. The Avancée with its distinctive wedge-like shape is symbolically and in reality the entrance to this complex. Including an entrance lobby, a 380-seat conference center, three restaurants, and areas for the presentation of vehicles, the 74,000 square meter building is intended to house the research and design facilities of the French auto maker. In order to carefully control costs, prefabricated construction materials such as the aluminum chassis were used. Seen by the architects as a "fifth facade" of the building, the long, inclined roof is made largely of poured-in-place concrete. The 295 meter long forward edge of the structure is set on an artificial lake, making for a spectacular image of modernity, which symbolizes the ambitions of Renault.

Das westlich von Paris gelegene Technologie-zentrum von Renault war eine Zeitlang das größte industrielle Bauvorhaben in Europa. Auf dem 350 Hektar umfassenden Gelände, für welches die Architekten Valode & Pistre einen Gesamtplan erstellt haben, werden rund 350 000 m² Gebäudenutzfläche für 6 500 Beschäftigte geschaffen. Das durch eine auffällige Keilform ausgezeichnete Avancée bildet dabei sowohl symbolisch als auch real den Eingang des Zentrums. Auf 74 000 m² sind neben der eigentlichen Eingangshalle ein Konferenzsaal mit 380 Plätzen, drei Restaurants sowie Präsentationsflächen für Automobile untergebracht, vor allem aber dient das Gebäude den Forschungs- und Entwicklungs-labors des französischen Autoherstellers. Um die Kosten niedrig zu halten, wurde verstärkt auf vorgefertigte Konstruktionsteile wie etwa eine Aluminiumfassade zurückgegriffen. Das von den Architekten als »fünfte Fassade« bezeichnete schräge Dach des Gebäudes besteht zum größten Teil aus vor Ort gegos-senem Beton. Die 295 m lange, keilförmige Vorderseite des Gebäudes liegt inmitten eines künstlichen Sees – ein spektakuläres Symbol für Modernität, das die Ambitionen von Renault zum Ausdruck bringen soll.

Situé à l'ouest de Paris, le Technocentre Renault a été pendant quelque temps le plus important projet industriel d'Europe. Ce terrain de 350 hectares devrait recevoir à terme 350 000 m² de bâtiments dans lesquels tra-vailleront 6 500 personnes. Le plan directeur a été conçu par les architectes Valode & Pistre. L'Avancée – en forme de coin originale – con-stitue aussi bien l'entrée que le symbole de ce complexe. Comprenant un hall d'entrée, un centre de conférences de 380 places, trois restaurants et des espaces pour la présenta-tion des véhicules, ce bâtiment de 74 000 m² abritera les services de recherche et de design du constructeur automobile français. Pour limiter les coûts, des matériaux de construction préfabriqués, dont des châssis d'aluminium, ont été utilisés. Présenté par les architectes comme une «cinquième façade», le long toit incliné est essentiellement construit en béton, coulé sur place. Ce coin plongeant, qui mesure 295 m dans sa plus grande longueur, domine un bassin artificiel. Il donne une spectaculaire image de modernité, symbole des ambitions de Renault.

Chaix & Morel, L'Avancée, Renault Technocenter, Guyancourt, France, 1995–97.

Chaix & Morel, L'Avancée, Technologiezentrum von Renault, Guyancourt, Frankreich, 1995–97.

Chaix & Morel, L'Avancée, Technocentre Renault, Guyancourt, France, 1995–97.

The long, wedge-like shape of the building starts in the large artificial basin, which also reflects the structure, especially at night.

Die lange Keilform des Gebäudes steigt aus dem großen künstlichen Wasserbecken empor, das den Bau, besonders nachts, reflektiert.

La forme en coin étiré du bâtiment surplombe en partie le grand bassin artificiel dans lequel il se reflète, particulièrement pendant la nuit.

Pages 76–79: Serving as the entrance building to the Renault Technocenter, L'Avancée is laid out along the lines of the grid established by project lead architects Valode & Pistre.

Seite 76–79: Das Avancée, das im Technologiezentrum von Renault als Eingangsgebäude dient, folgt dem Raster, das die projektleitenden Architekten Valode & Pistre entwickelt haben.

Pages 76–79: L'Avancée, l'entrée du Technocentre Renault, est calée sur la trame mise au point par les architectes en chef du projet, Valode & Pistre.

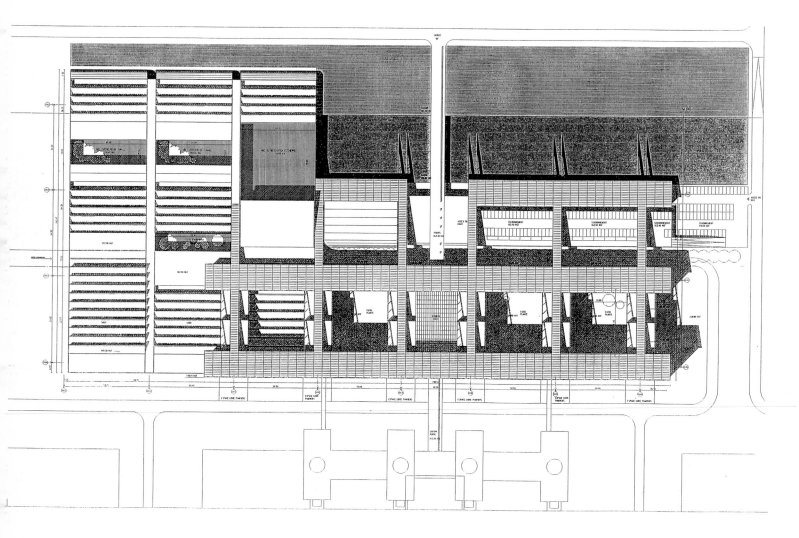

Although it does take on an original form, L'Avancée was built as much as possible with prefabricated materials in order to control costs.

Obwohl das Avancée aus Kostengründen soweit als möglich mit vorgefertigten Teilen realisiert wurde, hat das Gebäude eine originelle Form.

Même si sa forme est originale, L'Avancée a fait appel autant que possible à des matériaux préfabriqués pour réduire les coûts de construction.

David Chipperfield

Born in London in 1953, David Chipperfield obtained his Diploma in Architecture from the Architectural Association in London in 1977. He worked in the offices of Norman Foster and Richard Rogers before establishing David Chipperfield Architects in 1984. He has designed shops for Issey Miyake, Joseph and Equipment in London, Paris, Tokyo and New York. He completed a Design Store for Toyota Automobiles in Kyoto in 1989 for which he won the 1993 Andrea Palladio Prize. He finished the Matsumoto Headquarters Building in Okayama, Japan in 1990, the Plant Gallery and Central Hall of the Natural History Museum in London in 1993, and the Wagamama Restaurant in London in 1996, as well as the River & Rowing Museum at Henley-on-Thames published here. His current work includes the Landeszentralbank in Gera, Germany, the Grassimuseum in Leipzig, Germany, three hotels in the US, a private house in Spain, and a house in Martha's Vineyard, US. In December 1997 he won the contract to rebuild Berlin's Neues Museum, which will exhibit part of the Egyptian collection of Berlin's museums. This $150 million project is to be completed six to eight years after construction begins in the year 2000.

Der 1953 in London geborene David Chipperfield erhielt 1977 sein Diplom an der Architectural Association in London. Nachdem er in den Büros von Sir Norman Foster und Richard Rogers gearbeitet hatte, gründete er 1984 das Büro David Chipperfield Architects. Er hat Läden für Issey Miyake, Joseph und Equipment in London, Paris, Tokio und New York entworfen. Für den 1989 fertiggestellten Design Store des Automobilunternehmers Toyota in Kyoto erhielt Chipperfield den Andrea Palladio Preis des Jahres 1993. Im gleichen Jahr konnte er auch die Hauptzentrale von Matsumoto im japanischen Okayama vollenden; 1993 folgten die Pflanzengalerie und die zentrale Haupthalle des Natural History Museum in London, 1996 dann das Restaurant Wagamama in London und das hier vorgestellte River & Rowing Museum in Henley-on-Thames. Zu seinen laufenden Projekten zählen die Landeszentralbank in Gera, Deutschland, drei Hotels in den USA, ein Privathaus in Spanien und ein weiteres Haus in Martha's Vineyard. Im Dezember 1997 schloß Chipperfield den Vertrag zum Umbau des Neuen Museums in Berlin, in dem Teile der Ägypten-Sammlung der Berliner Museen präsentiert werden sollen. Das 150 Millionen $ teure Projekt wird nach Beginn der Bauarbeiten im Jahre 2000 innerhalb von sechs bis acht Jahren abgeschlossen.

Né à Londres en 1953, David Chipperfield est diplômé de l'Architectural Association de cette même ville, en 1977. Il travaille dans les agences de Norman Foster et de Richard Rogers, avant de fonder David Chipperfield Architects en 1984. Il conçoit des boutiques pour Issey Miyake, Joseph et Équipement à Londres, Paris, Tokyo et New York. Sa boutique de design pour Toyota Automobiles (Kyoto, 1989) remporte le Prix Andrea Palladio 1993. Il termine le siège social de Matsumoto à Okayama, au Japon, la même année, ainsi que la galerie des plantes et le hall central du Natural History Museum de Londres. En 1996, il réalise le Wagamama Restaurant à Londres, et le River & Rowing Museum à Henley-on-Thames, publié dans ce livre. Parmi ses réalisations récentes: le siège social de la Landeszentralbank de Gera, en Allemagne, le Grassimuseum de Leipzig, Allemagne, trois hôtels aux États-Unis, une résidence privée en Espagne, et une autre maison sur Martha's Vineyard, aux États-Unis. En décembre 1997, il remporte le contrat pour la reconstruction du Neues Museum de Berlin, où une partie de la collection égyptienne des musées de Berlin sera exposée. Ce projet de 150 millions de $ devrait être achevé six ou huit ans après le début des travaux en l'an 2000.

David Chipperfield, River & Rowing Museum, Henley-on-Thames, Great Britain, 1989/96–97.

David Chipperfield, Fluß- und Rudermuseum, Henley-on-Thames, Großbritannien, 1989/96–97.

David Chipperfield, River & Rowing Museum, Henley-on-Thames, Grande-Bretagne, 1989/96–97.

River & Rowing Museum

Henley-on-Thames, Great Britain, 1989/96–1997

Despite an international reputation forged with fashion boutiques for Joseph, Equipment and Issey Miyake, or with buildings in Japan, this is David Chipperfield's first major building in England. Built in meadowland near the Thames, the structure is set up on concrete piles, and sits on a slab made of the same material. The form of its stainless steel roofs recalls local agricultural architecture, but also that of tents set up each year nearby for the Henley Regatta. Reversing the typical logic of materials, Chipperfield uses a transparent glass skin on the lower part of the buildings, and finely detailed English green oak boards above. This pattern recalls upturned rowing shells drying in their dock. The simplicity and power of the design brings to mind some of the work of the Japanese architect Tadao Ando, even if concrete is not the primary material of the buildings themselves. Louis Kahn's work has also been cited as a reference in this instance, but through his materials and detailing Chipperfield confirms that his is in fact a personal approach, which is very much in tune with the times.

Trotz Chipperfields internationalen Rufes, der vor allem auf den Entwürfen für Boutiquen von Joseph, Equipment und Issey Miyake oder auch auf seinen Bauten in Japan gründet, handelt es sich hierbei um sein erstes größeres realisiertes Projekt in England. Der inmitten von Weideland am Ufer der Themse errichtete Bau ruht auf einer von Betonpfeilern getragenen Betonplatte. Die Form der aus Edelstahl gefertigten Dächer nimmt die ländliche Architektur der Umgebung auf, verweist aber auch auf jene Zelte, die jedes Jahr anläßlich der dort ausgetragenen Henley-Ruderregatta aufgestellt werden. In Umkehrung der normalerweise üblichen Materialabfolge verwendet Chipperfield für den unteren Teil des Gebäudes eine transparente Glashaut und darüber schön gearbeitete Verkleidungen aus grüner englischer Eiche. Diese Anordnung läßt an auf den Kopf gestellte Ruderboote denken, die in den Docks trocknen. Die Einfachheit und Kraft des Entwurfs erinnert an Arbeiten des japanischen Architekten Tadao Ando, selbst wenn Chipperfield als Hauptmaterial nicht Beton verwendet. Auch das Werk Louis Kahns ist in diesem Zusammenhang genannt worden. Chipperfield vermag jedoch durch seine Materialwahl und Detaillösungen klarzustellen, daß es sich bei ihm um einen ganz individuellen Ansatz handelt, der sehr in seiner Zeit verwurzelt ist.

S'il jouit déjà d'une solide réputation due à plusieurs boutiques de mode sophistiquées (Joseph et Équipement, Issey Miyake), et quelques réalisations au Japon, ce musée est la première œuvre importante signée par Chipperfield dans son pays. Édifiés au milieu des champs au bord de la Tamise, les bâtiments sont surelevés sur une dalle de béton qui repose sur des pilotis du même matériau. La forme des toits en acier inoxydable rappelle l'architecture rurale locale, ou les tentes dressées chaque années à l'occasion des régates de Henley. Inversant la logique habituelle des matériaux, l'architecte a recouvert la partie basse d'une «peau» de verre transparente, et la partie haute d'un revêtement en bardeaux de chêne anglais teinté en vert. Ce traitement évoque des coques de bateaux sèchant au soleil. La simplicité et la puissance du dessin rappellent également certaines œuvres de l'architecte japonais Tadao Ando, même si le béton n'est pas, ici, le matériau principal. L'œuvre de Louis Kahn a pu également être citée. À travers son choix des matériaux et la qualité de l'exécution, Chipperfield confirme la personnalité d'une approche en harmonie avec l'esprit du temps.

The closed forms and elevated design of the River & Rowing Museum, together with the extensive use of wood, bring to mind certain Japanese temples, such as the Shosoin storehouse at Todaiji (Nara, 8th century).

Die geschlossenen Formen, die Pfeilerkonstruktion sowie der Gebrauch von Holz lassen beim River & Rowing Museum an japanische Tempelbauten denken, wie etwa das Tempelschatzhaus Shosoin im Todaiji-Tempel (Nara, 8. Jahrhundert).

Les formes hautes et fermées de ce musée et la forte présence du bois rappellent certains bâtiments de temples japonais, comme le Shosoin de Todaiji (Nara, VIIIe siècle).

While making multiple references to the avowed theme of river and rowing, Chipperfield also engages a dialog with local agricultural architecture, in a palette of materials and forms that identifies him with current minimalist trends.

Neben zahlreichen Verweisen auf das gegebene Thema – den Fluß und das Rudern – geht Chipperfield auch einen Dialog mit der lokalen landwirtschaftlichen Architektur ein, bedient sich dabei aber einer Material- und Formenpalette, die ihn als Vertreter der gegenwärtigen minimalistischen Strömung ausweist.

Tout en multipliant les références au thème avoué du fleuve et de l'aviron, Chipperfield a également noué un dialogue avec l'architecture agricole locale à travers une palette de matériaux et de formes qui le relie aux tendances minimalistes actuelles.

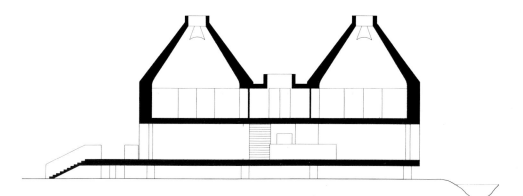

In every carefully designed detail, the River & Rowing Museum maintains a rigorous purity and simplicity.

In allen sorgfältig ausgearbeiteten Details beweist das Fluß- und Rudermuseum eine strenge Einfachheit und Klarheit.

Dans chacun des ses détails soigneusement pensés, le River & Rowing Museum maintient une pureté et une simplicité rigoureuses.

Jo Coenen

Born in 1949 in Heerlen, The Nederlands, Jo Coenen graduated from the Eindhoven University of Technology in 1975. Between 1976 and 1979 he lectured both in Eindhoven and in Maastricht, and worked with Luigi Snozzi, James Stirling, and Aldo van Eyck. He opened his own office in 1979, and built his first important project, a library and exhibition gallery in Heerlen (1983–86). His Chamber of Commerce in Maastricht (1988–91), situated next to the River Maas combines a modernist simplicity and the use of pilotis with large brick surfaces leading to the old city and nearby factory complex. Water is again an element in the composition of his structures for the Haans Company in Tilburg (1989–91), a complex that shows numerous stylistic similarities with the Netherlands Architecture Institute in Rotterdam (1993). Though inevitably contested by other architects because of its highly symbolic presence for the profession, the NAI confirmed Jo Coenen as an competent and inventive designer. More recent work includes a police station in Sittard (1997), and an apartment building in the Rijswijkseplein area of The Hague (1997).

Der 1949 in Heerlen, Niederlande, geborene Jo Coenen erhielt 1975 sein Diplom an der Technischen Universität in Eindhoven. Zwischen 1976 und 1979 lehrte er in Eindhoven und in Maastricht und arbeitete in den Büros von Luigi Snozzi, James Stirling und Aldo van Eyck. Nachdem er 1979 ein eigenes Büro gegründet hatte, realisierte er als sein erstes wichtiges Projekt eine Bibliothek samt Ausstellungsfläche in Heerlen (1983–86). Der Bau für die Handelskammer in Maastricht (1988–91) am Ufer der Maas vereint Einfachheit in der Tradition der Moderne und den Gebrauch von Pfahlbau mit großflächigen Backsteinfassaden, die auf die Altstadt und eine nahegelegene Fabrik verweisen. Das Element Wasser spielt eine große Rolle bei der Auslegung der Baukörper für die Firma Haans in Tilburg (1989–91), das zahlreiche stilistische Ähnlichkeiten mit Coenens Gebäude für das Niederländische Architektur-Institut in Rotterdam (1993) widerspiegelt. Obwohl er wegen des damit verbundenen hohen Symbolwerts für den Berufsstand unweigerlich unter starken Wettbewerbsdruck durch andere Architekten geriet, bestätigte das NAI Coenen als einen kompetenten und erfindungsreichen Baumeister. Zu seinen jüngeren Arbeiten zählen eine Polizeiwache in Sittard (1997) und ein Apartmenthaus im Stadtteil Rijswijkseplein von Den Haag (1997).

Né en 1949 à Heerlen (Pays-Bas), Jo Coenen sort diplômé de l'Université de Technologie d'Eindhoven en 1975. De 1976 à 1979, il enseigne à Eindhoven et Maastricht, et travaille pour Luigi Snozzi, James Stirling et Aldo van Eyck. Il ouvre son agence en 1979, et réalise son premier projet, une bibliothèque et une galerie d'exposition pour Heerlen (1983–86). Sa Chambre de Commerce de Maastricht, au bord de la Meuse (1988–91), combine simplicité moderniste, pilotis et larges surfaces de briques, qui rappellent la vieille cité et le complexe industriel tout proche. L'eau joue également un rôle dans la composition de son ensemble pour la société Haans, à Tilburg (1989–91), qui présente de nombreuses similarités stylistiques avec l'Institut néerlandais d'architecture (NAI), à Rotterdam (1993). Bien qu'inévitablement contesté par d'autres architectes du fait de son importance pour la profession, le NAI a confirmé le talent et l'inventivité de Jo Coenen. Parmi ses réalisations plus récentes figurent un poste de police à Sittard (1997), et un immeuble d'appartements dans le quartier du Rijswijkseplein à la Haye (1997).

Jo Coenen, Kunstcluster, Tilburg, The Netherlands, 1992–96.

Jo Coenen, Kunstcluster, Tilburg, Niederlande, 1992–96.

Jo Coenen, Kunstcluster, Tilburg, Pays-Bas, 1992–96.

Kunstcluster
Tilburg, The Netherlands, 1992–1996

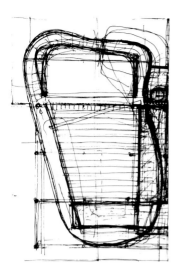

Tilburg is located in the southern Netherlands. It is an industrial center linked to the Rhine and Maas rivers by the Wilhelmina Canal. As a result of the collapse of its textile industry in the 1960s, large areas of the city center were left unused. After giving a priority to housing, the city is now concentrating on culture. Jo Coenen's Kunstcluster is a combined 840-seat concert hall, conservatory, and ballet academy, situated just opposite the town hall on the site of a former monastery garden. Using wood as a primary cladding material and by spreading the rather large volume of the complex over an elongated site, Coenen has succeeded in giving the Kunstcluster a friendly feeling – an impression that is heightened by the ease of pedestrian access and the way in which the park to the rear of the concert hall fits into a series of convivial spaces in this area of Tilburg, for which the architect has been responsible since 1989. Physically connected to existing municipal theater, the Kunstcluster brings a measure of dignity and spatial calm to an otherwise largely undistinguished city center.

Tilburg liegt in den südlichen Niederlanden und ist ein Industriezentrum, das der Wilhelmina-kanal mit Rhein und Maas verbindet. Als Folge des Niedergangs der örtlichen Textilindustrie in den 60er Jahren lagen weite Bereiche der Innenstadt brach. Nachdem sich die Stadt zunächst auf den Wohnungsbau konzentriert hat, richtet sie ihr Augenmerk nun auf die Kultur. Auf dem Gelände eines ehemaligen Klostergartens direkt gegenüber dem Rathaus vereint der Kunstcluster von Jo Coenen unter einem Dach eine Konzerthalle mit 840 Sitzen, ein Konservatorium und eine Ballettschule. Indem er das Gebäude vornehmlich mit Holz verkleidete und den recht großvolumigen Baukörper über einem langgezogenen Grund-riß errichtete, gelang es Coenen, dem Kunst-cluster ein einladendes Erscheinungsbild zu geben. Dieser Eindruck wird noch dadurch verstärkt, daß das Gebäude für Fußgänger leicht zu erschließen ist und durch die Art, wie sich der Park hinter der Konzerthalle in die Abfolge heiterer öffentlicher Räume in diesen Teil von Tilburg einfügt, für dessen Gestaltung der Architekt seit 1989 verantwortlich war. Der baulich mit dem schon zuvor existierenden Stadttheater verbundene Kunstcluster verleiht dem architektonisch sonst eher gesichtslosen Stadtzentrum eine gewisse Würde und räumliche Ausgewogenheit.

Centre industriel du Sud des Pays-Bas, relié au Rhin et à la Meuse, Tilburg s'étend en bordure du canal Wilhelmina. À la suite de l'effondre-ment de l'industrie textile dans les années 60, de vastes zones du centre ville ont été désaf-fectées. Après avoir donné priorité à la con-struction de logements, la ville se consacre maintenant à des projets culturels. Le Kunst-cluster de Jo Coenen associe une salle de con-cert de 840 places, un conservatoire et une académie de danse. Il se dresse juste en face de l'hôtel de ville sur le jardin d'un ancien cou-vent. En étalant les volumes assez importants requis par ce programme sur le terrain allongé, et en privilégiant le bois pour le parement des bâtiments, l'architecte a réussi à donner à l'ensemble une atmosphère conviviale que renforce la facilité des accès piétonniers et la création d'espaces agréables donnant sur le parc à l'arrière de l'auditorium. Coenen est d'ailleurs responsable de l'urbanisme de cette partie de Tilburg depuis 1989. Le Kunstcluster, relié au théâtre municipal existant, apporte une sorte de dignité et de sérénité spatiale à un centre ville sinon sans grand intérêt.

The Kunstcluster is located on a wide central square in Tilburg, just opposite the city hall. Despite its large volume, it does not by any means dominate the square.

Der Kunstcluster befindet sich auf einem großen zentralen Platz in Tilburg, genau gegenüber dem Rathaus. Trotz seiner Größe dominiert der Bau den Platz keineswegs.

Le Kunstcluster se situe sur la grande place centrale de Tilburg, face à l'hôtel de ville. Malgré son important volume, il ne domine en aucune façon le site.

Page 94: The long, narrow building of the ballet academy extends to the rear of the concert hall and conservatory, in the ground of a former monastery park.

Seite 94: Auf der Rückseite der Konzerthalle und des Konservatoriums erstreckt sich der lange, schmale Bau der Ballettakademie auf dem Gelände eines ehemaligen Klostergartens.

Page 94: Le long et étroit bâtiment de l'académie de danse s'étend derrière la salle de concert et le conservatoire, sur le jardin d'un ancien couvent.

Pages 95–97: *The inner courtyard of the concert hall is accessible to pedestrians even when the rest of the complex is closed, creating a convivial space in the heart of the city. Below, a view of the interior of the concert hall.*

Seite 95–97: *Der Innenhof der Konzerthalle ist auch dann für Passanten zugänglich, wenn der übrige Gebäudekomplex geschlossen ist, wodurch ein heiterer, geselliger Ort im Herzen der Stadt geschaffen wurde. Unten: Innenansicht der Konzerthalle.*

Pages 95–97: *La cour intérieure de la salle de concert reste accessible aux piétons, même lorsque le reste du complexe est fermé, créant ainsi un espace convivial au cœur de la ville. Ci-dessous, vue de l'intérieur de la salle de concert.*

Erick van Egeraat

One of the most promising Dutch architects of his generation, Erick van Egeraat was born in 1956 in Amsterdam. He created Mecanoo architects with Henk Döll, Chris de Weijer, and Francine Houben in Delft in 1983. Their work included large housing projects such as the Herdenkingsplein in Maastricht, The Netherlands (1990–92), and smaller-scale projects such as their 1990 Boompjes Pavilion, a cantilevered structure overlooking the harbor of Rotterdam, close to the new Erasmus Bridge, and a private house in Rotterdam, The Netherlands (1989–91). Signature features of these projects include unexpected use of materials, as in the Rotterdam house where bamboo and steel are placed in juxtaposition with concrete, for example, or an apparent disequilibrium, as in the Boompjes Pavilion. In his headquarters for NNH and ING in Budapest Erick van Egeraat, who left Mecanoo in 1995, confronted organic and mechanical forms, and presented an innovative solution to the reuse of a 19th century building. An extension to this building was completed in 1997. Current work includes a design for the Royal Netherlands Embassy and Embassy housing for the Embassy in New Delhi, the Photographer's Gallery in London, Crawford Municipal Art Gallery in Cork, Ireland (1996–98) and theatres for the Royal Shakespeare Company in Stratford-upon-Avon, Great Britain (1998–2004).

Der 1956 in Amsterdam geborene Erick van Egeraat gehört zu den vielversprechendsten Talenten der niederländischen Architekten seiner Generation. 1983 gründete er zusammen mit Henk Döll, Chris de Weijer und Francine Houben in Delft das Büro Mecanoo. Zu dessen realisierten Entwürfen zählen große Wohnanlagen wie das Herdenkingsplein in Maastricht, Niederlande (1990–92), und kleinere Projekte wie etwa der Boompjes Pavillon von 1990, ein Auslegerbau mit Blick über den Hafen von Rotterdam in der Nähe der neuen Erasmus-Brücke, sowie ein Privathaus in Rotterdam, Niederlande (1989–91). Markenzeichen dieser Projekte sind unter anderem unerwartete Materialkombinationen – so treffen etwa in dem Rotterdamer Haus Bambus und Stahl auf Beton – sowie das scheinbare Ungleichgewicht der Konstruktion, beispielsweise beim Boompjes Pavillon. In seinem Entwurf für die Budapester Zentrale der Nationale Nederlanden Hungary und ING-Bank konfrontierte Erick van Egeraat, der 1995 das Büro Mecanoo verließ, organische mit mechanischen Formen, wodurch ihm eine innovative Umgestaltung eines Gebäudes aus dem 19. Jahrhundert gelang. 1997 konnte auch eine Erweiterung dieses Baus fertiggestellt werden. Zu van Egeraats laufenden Projekten zählen Entwürfe für die niederländische Botschaft in Neu-Delhi und dazugehörige Wohnungen, die Photographer's Gallery in London, die Crawford Municipial Art Gallery im irischen Cork (1996–98) und Theater für die Royal Shakespeare Company in Stratford-upon-Avon, Großbritannien (1998–2004).

L'un des architectes néerlandais les plus prometteurs de sa génération, Erick van Egeraat, naît en 1956 à Amsterdam. Il crée Mecanoo Architects à Delft en 1983, en association avec Henk Döll, Chris de Weijer et Francine Houben. Ils interviennent sur d'importants programmes de logements, comme le Herdenkingsplein à Maastricht, Pays-Bas (1990–92), ou d'autres projets de taille plus réduite, comme le Boompjes Pavilion, structure en porte-à-faux dominant le port de Rotterdam près du pont Erasmus, ou une résidence privée à Rotterdam, Pays-Bas (1989–91). Ses projets se reconnaissent au recours à des matériaux inattendus, comme dans cette maison de Rotterdam, où le bambou et l'acier voisinent avec le béton, et au déséquilibre apparent, comme dans le Boompjes Pavilion. Dans le siège social de NNH et ING à Budapest, Erick van Egeraat, qui quitte Mecanoo en 1995, contraste des formes organiques et mécaniques, et propose une solution novatrice à la réutilisation d'un immeuble du XIXe siècle. Une extension de ce bâtiment lui est demandée en 1997. Il travaille actuellement sur les plans de l'ambassade royale des Pays-Bas et ses appartements de fonction à New Delhi (Inde), la Photographer's Gallery à Londres, la Crawford Municipal Art Gallery à Cork, Irlande (1996–98), et théâtres pour la Royal Shakespeare Company à Stratford-upon-Avon, Grande-Bretagne (1998–2004).

Erick van Egeraat, School for Fashion and Graphic Industry, Utrecht, The Netherlands, 1994–97.

Erick van Egeraat, Fachtechnisches Gymnasium, Utrecht, Niederlande, 1994–97.

Erick van Egeraat, École de mode et de graphique industrielle, Utrecht, Pays-Bas, 1994–97.

School for Fashion and Graphic Industry

Utrecht, The Netherlands, 1994–1997

Called on to "rescue" a project originally designed by the building department of the city of Utrecht, Erick van Egeraat chose to enclose the structure in a "glass envelope, comparable to a gauze veil – an element of fashion that conveys a mysterious lack of definition, yet indicates or proves insights into what is behind," according to the architect. Unexpectedly, as Erick van Egeraat says, "Behind the glass skin is the other, the technical side of the building. Through the glass facade, one sees the hard core of the building: structural members, wood, exposed masonry walls and the yellow insulation pads that cover the building like a woolen blanket." This 15,000 square meter building obviously retains the basic forms laid out before the intervention of Erick van Egeraat, but in his hands, for a limited budget and in a short period of time, it has become not only a commentary on fashion, but also, perhaps more durably, on the act of building and designing architecture. The fact that a committee of design professionals called on Erick van Egeraat for this job is also a testimony to the vitality of contemporary architecture in The Netherlands.

Der zur »Rettung« eines ursprünglich vom Baudezernat der Stadt Utrecht entworfenen Gebäudes herbeigerufene Erick van Egeraat versah den Bau mit einer »Hülle aus Glas, vergleichbar einem Gazeschleier – ein der Mode entlehntes Mittel, das zwar auf mysteriöse Weise jede genaue Bestimmung verwischt, gleichwohl aber einen Einblick in das, was dahinter ist, zuläßt«, so der Architekt. »Hinter der Glashaut liegt die andere, die technische Seite des Baus. Durch das Glas erblickt man den Kern des Gebäudes: strukturelle Bauglieder, Holz, freiliegendes Mauerwerk und die gelben Isoliermatten, die das Haus wie eine Wolldecke umhüllen.« Das 15 000 m² Nutzfläche bietende Gebäude behält offensichtlich die vor dem Eingreifen Erick van Egeraats festgeschriebene Grundform bei, wird aber unter seinen Händen – mit einem sehr begrenzten Budget- und Zeitrahmen – nicht nur zu einem Kommentar über Mode, sondern auch – und das vielleicht dauerhafter – zu einem Kommentar über die Handlung des Bauens und das Gestalten von Architektur. Daß Erick van Egeraat von einem aus professionellen »Gestaltern« bestehenden Komitee berufen wurde, ist ein Beweis, wie lebendig die gegenwärtige Architekturszene in den Niederlanden ist.

Appelé pour «sauver» un programme conçu à l'origine par le Service des travaux publics de la ville d'Utrecht, Erick van Egeraat a choisi d'enfermer la structure «dans une enveloppe de verre, comparable à un voile de gaze, élément de mode qui provoque un subtil brouillage de définition, tout en donnant une indication sur ce qui se cache derrière ces murs», précise l'architecte. «Derrière la peau de verre, se perçoit la structure du bâtiment: poutres structurelles, bois, murs en maçonnerie brute et épais matériau jaune d'isolation qui recouvre le tout comme une couverture dense.» Cette construction de 15 000 m² ne peut dissimuler totalement les formes basiques décidées avant l'intervention d'Erick van Egeraat, mais grâce à lui, pour un budget limité et dans des délais resserrés, elle s'est transformée en un commentaire sur la mode, mais aussi – et peut-être de façon plus durable – sur l'acte de concevoir et de construire l'architecture. Qu'un comité de professionnels ait fait appel à cet architecte pour ce travail témoigne d'ailleurs de la vitalité de l'architecture néerlandaise contemporaine.

Pages 101–103: The otherwise uninteresting facades of the building are brought to life through the use of a glass curtain wall, which reveals the unfinished surfaces below.

Seite 101–103: Durch einen Glasvorhang, der die darunterliegenden, nicht fertiggestellten Wände zeigt, werden die Gebäudefassaden, die ansonsten eher uninteressant wären, belebt.

Pages 101–103: Les façades sans intérêt du bâtiment sont animées par un mur-rideau en verre, qui met en valeur leurs surfaces brutes.

The elevated auditorium, which shows the architect's
predilection for organic forms, was the only element he
was permitted to add to the original design.

*Das erhöhte Auditorium – das einzige Element, das
van Egeraat hinzufügen konnte – belegt sein Interesse
an Formen von fast organischer Komplexität.*

*L'auditorium surélevé montre le goût de l'architecte
pour des formes d'une complexité quasi organique.*

Sir Norman Foster

Sir Norman Foster is undoubtedly one of the most active and best-known contemporary architects in the world. His current work includes such significant projects as the massive new Airport at Chek Lap Kok in Hongkong (inaugurated in July 1998), the renovation of the Reichstag, for the new German Parliament in Berlin, Germany (1995–99); or the redevelopment of the British Museum in London (1997–2000). Born in Manchester in 1935, Norman Foster studied architecture and city planning at Manchester University. After graduating in 1961 he was awarded a Henry Fellowship to Yale University, where he received an M. Arch. degree, and met Richard Rogers with whom he created Team 4. Although his architecture has always had a technological element, perhaps best symbolized by the Hongkong and Shanghai Banking Corporation Headquarters in Hong Kong (1981–86), the method of his office has consisted in adapting their approach to each individual situation. With work such as the Commerzbank Headquarters published here, Norman Foster has demonstrated his capacity to bring innovative solutions to a building type that most frequently is subjected to severe economic constraints.

Sir Norman Foster ist zweifellos einer der aktivsten und bekanntesten Architekten der heutigen Zeit. Zu seinen Projekten zählen solch bedeutende Bauten wie der neue Chek Lap Kok-Flughafen in Hongkong (eröffnet im Juli 1998), die Umbauten des Reichstaggebäudes für den Deutschen Bundestag in Berlin (1995–99) sowie die des British Museum in London (1997–2000). Geboren 1935 in Manchester, studierte Norman Foster Architektur und Städteplanung an der University of Manchester. Nach seiner Abschlußprüfung (1961) erhielt er ein Stipendium (Henry Fellowship) für die Yale University, wo er 1963 seinen Master's Degree in Architektur erlangte und Richard Rogers kennenlernte, mit dem er das Team 4 gründete. Auch wenn Fosters Architektur immer durch einen technischen Aspekt gekennzeichnet ist – was vielleicht bei dem Gebäude der Hongkong und Shanghai Bank am besten deutlich wird (Hongkong, 1981–86) – berücksichtigt er stets die jeweilige Bausituation. Die in diesem Buch vorgestellte Hauptverwaltung der Commerzbank in Frankfurt zeigt seine Fähigkeit für innovative Lösungen in Hinblick auf einen Gebäudetypus, der meist drastischen wirtschaftlichen Bedingungen unterworfen ist.

Sir Norman Foster est sans aucun doute l'un des architectes les plus actifs et les plus célèbres au monde. Il travaille sur des projets aussi importants que le gigantesque aéroport de Chek Lap Kok à Hongkong (inauguré en juillet 1998), la rénovation du Reichstag pour le parlement allemand à Berlin, Allemagne (1995–99), ou le redéploiement du British Museum à Londres (1997–2000). Né à Manchester en 1935, il étudie l'architecture et l'urbanisme à l'Université de Manchester (1961). Il bénéficie d'un Henry Fellowship pour l'Université de Yale, où il passe son M. Arch. et rencontre Richard Rogers avec lequel il fonde Team 4. Bien que ses créations soient toujours marquées par une forte présence technologique, dont le siège social de la Hongkong and Shanghai Banking Corporation à Hong Kong (1981–86) en est un bon exemple, la méthode de travail de son agence passe par une adaptation systématique à chaque problème posé. À travers des réalisations comme le siège social de la Commerzbank, présenté ici, Foster fait preuve de sa capacité à apporter des solutions novatrices à un type de construction fréquemment soumis à des contraintes économiques drastiques.

Norman Foster, Commerzbank Headquarters, Frankfurt am Main, Germany, 1994–97.

Norman Foster, Hauptverwaltung der Commerzbank, Frankfurt am Main, Deutschland, 1994–97.

Norman Foster, siège social de la Commerzbank, Francfort-sur-le-Main, Allemagne, 1994–97.

Commerzbank Headquarters
Frankfurt am Main, Germany, 1994–1997

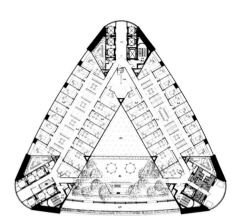

The Commerzbank is one of Germany's most important private sector banks, with a staff of 30,000 people and 1,000 branches in Germany. These figures may explain why the bank recently completed the tallest office building in Europe (298.74 meters with its aerial) for a staff of 2,400. Norman Foster describes this as the "world's first ecological high-rise tower – energy efficient and user friendly." Four-story gardens spiral around the gently curved triangular plan with its service cores placed in the corners. The central atrium serves as a "natural ventilation chimney." Windows of the tower both inward and outward facing can be opened in each office for reasons of energy efficiency. An automatic system closes the windows under extreme climatic conditions, just as it can open them to allow cooling at night. As is often the case in Foster's buildings, the offices are column-free. Another frequent feature of his designs, a careful attention to the immediate environment of the building is here respected. Neighboring buildings have been restored, maintaining the height of the surrounding structures, and a winter garden with restaurants and exhibition space is open to the public.

Mit 30 000 Beschäftigten und 1 000 inländischen Geschäftsstellen gehört die Commerzbank zu den großen Privatbanken in Deutschland. Diese Zahlen mögen erklären, weshalb die Bank vor kurzem das höchste Bürogebäude Europas (298,74 m mit Antenne) für 2 400 Angestellte einweihte. Der Architekt, Sir Norman Foster, nennt es »den ersten ökologischen Wolkenkratzer der Welt – energiesparend und benutzerfreundlich«. Gärten winden sich über vier Geschosse spiralförmig um den sanft abgerundeten, dreieckigen Grundriß, dessen Versorgungskerne in die Ecken verlegt worden sind. Ein zentrales Atrium dient als »natürlicher Luftkanal«. Aus Gründen der Energieeinsparung können die Fenster aller Büros – sowohl der zum Atrium hin als auch der außen gelegenen – geöffnet werden. Eine Automatik schließt die Fenster bei extremen Klimabedingungen und öffnet sie, um bei Nacht für Abkühlung zu sorgen. Wie häufig bei den Bauten Fosters sind die Büros stützenfrei. Und noch ein weiteres Merkmal vieler seiner Projekte, die sorgfältige Berücksichtigung der unmittelbar benachbarten Bebauungssituation, läßt sich hier feststellen. Die umliegenden Gebäude wurden restauriert, wobei man die Traufhöhe beibehalten hat. Ein Wintergarten mit Restaurants und Ausstellungsflächen ist öffentlich zugänglich.

Avec plus de 30 000 employés et 1 000 agences, la Commerzbank est l'une des grandes banques allemandes privées. Ces chiffres expliquent que l'entreprise vienne de faire élever cette tour, le plus haut immeuble de bureaux d'Europe (298,74 m, antennes comprises), prévu pour 2 400 collaborateurs. Norman Foster la décrit comme «la première tour de grande hauteur au monde qui soit écologique, conviviale et offre un bon rendement énergétique». Quatre niveaux de jardins s'imbriquent autour d'un plan triangulaire à angles arrondis, ceux-ci recevant les installations techniques. L'atrium central sert de «cheminée de ventilation naturelle». Pour des raisons d'économie d'énergie, les fenêtres, qui s'ouvrent à la fois vers l'intérieur et l'extérieur, se commandent de chaque bureau. Un système automatique les ferme lors de conditions climatiques extrêmes, ou les ouvre la nuit pour faciliter la ventilation. Comme souvent chez Foster, les bureaux sont sans piliers, et une attention particulière a été portée à l'environnement immédiat de l'immeuble. Les bâtiments voisins ont été restaurés pour maintenir les hauteurs et leurs proportions, tandis qu'un jardin d'hiver, des restaurants et un espace d'exposition ont été ouverts au public.

The unusual triangular plan of the Commerzbank tower is echoed in the skylights, which bring ample natural light into the heart of the building.

Der ungewöhnliche dreieckige Grundriß des Commerzbank-Hochhauses findet sein Echo im Atrium, durch das reichlich Tageslicht in den Gebäudekern gelangt.

Le plan inhabituel en triangle de la tour de la Commerzbank se retrouve dans les verrières qui diffusent une abondante lumière naturelle jusqu'au cœur du bâtiment.

The Commerzbank stands out against the Frankfurt skyline. A drawing, below, shows how natural air ventilation is encouraged through the center of the building.

Die Commerzbank ragt aus der Frankfurter Skyline heraus. Unten: Die Zeichnung zeigt, wie eine natürliche Belüftung durch das Gebäude geführt wird.

La Commerzbank se détache sur le panorama de la ville. Ci-dessous, un dessin montre la façon dont la ventilation naturelle pénètre jusqu'au centre du bâtiment.

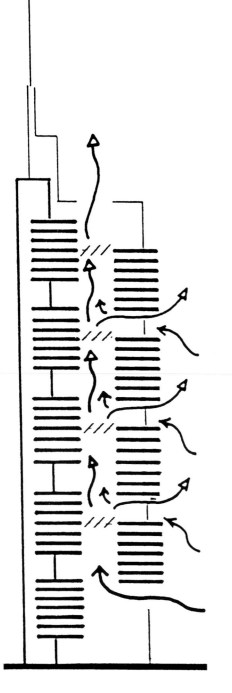

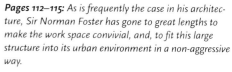

Pages 112–115: *As is frequently the case in his architecture, Sir Norman Foster has gone to great lengths to make the work space convivial, and, to fit this large structure into its urban environment in a non-aggressive way.*

Seite 112–115: *Wie so häufig in seinen Entwürfen hat Sir Norman Foster alles daran gesetzt, ein angenehmes Arbeitsumfeld zu schaffen und den Großbau in das urbane Umfeld einzufügen.*

Pages 112–115: *Comme souvent dans ses réalisations, Sir Norman Foster s'est réellement efforcé de rendre les espaces de travail conviviaux et d'intégrer cette énorme construction dans son environnement urbain d'une manière non-agressive.*

Thomas Herzog + Partner

Thomas Herzog was born in 1941 in Munich. He was granted his diploma by the Technical University in Munich in 1965. After obtaining a Doctorate from the University of Rome "La Sapienza" with a dissertation on "Pneumatic Constructions" (1972), he opened his own office the same year. He created a partnership with Hanns Jörg Schrade in 1994. He has taught at universities in Kassel, Darmstadt, Lausanne and Munich. His buildings include the Burghardt House in Regensburg, Germany (1978–79), the Richter housing complex in Munich, Germany (1981–83), a Solar House Module in Sulmona, Italy (1983–85), a Conference and Exhibition Hall in Linz, Austria (1988–93), Production Halls and Central Energy Plant for Wilkhahn in Eimbeckhausen, Germany (1989–92), and Hall 26 at the Deutsche Messe, Hanover (1994–96), published here. He has worked on experimental energy-saving structures since the mid-1970s. Thomas Herzog won the Gold Medal of the Bund Deutscher Architekten (BDA) in 1993, in 1996 the August-Perret-Prize of the UIA, and in 1998 La grande medaille d'or of the French Academy of Architects.

Thomas Herzog wurde 1941 in München geboren und erhielt 1965 sein Diplom an der dortigen Technischen Universität. Nachdem er über das Thema »Pneumatische Konstruktionen« an der Universität »La Sapienza« in Rom promoviert hatte, gründete er 1972 ein eigenes Architekturbüro. 1994 ging er eine Büropartnerschaft mit Hanns Jörg Schrade ein. Herzog hat an Universitäten in Kassel, Darmstadt und München gelehrt. Zu seinen wichtigsten Bauten zählen das Wohnhaus Burghardt in Regensburg (1978–79), die Wohnanlage Richter in München (1981–83), ein durch Solarenergie gespeistes Hausmodul im italienischen Sulmona (1983–85), eine Kongreß- und Ausstellungshalle in Linz, Österreich (1988–93), Fertigungshallen und eine Energieversorgungszentrale für die Firma Wilkhahn in Eimbeckhausen, Deutschland (1989–92), und schließlich die hier vorgestellte Halle 26 der Deutschen Messe in Hannover (1994–96). Seit Mitte der 70er Jahre arbeitet Herzog an experimentellen Entwürfen für die Nutzung von Solarenergie. 1993 erhielt er die Goldmedaille des Bundes Deutscher Architekten (BDA), 1996 den Auguste-Perret-Preis des Weltverbandes der Architekten UIA und 1998 La grande medaille d'or der französischen Akademie für Architektur.

Thomas Herzog naît en 1941 à Munich, et sort diplômé de l'Université technique de Munich en 1965. Docteur de l'Université de Rome, La Sapienza, avec une thèse sur les constructions pneumatiques (1972), il ouvre son agence la même année. Il s'associe à Hanns Jörg Schrade en 1994. Il enseigne aux Universités Cassel, Darmstadt, Lausanne et Munich. Parmi ses réalisations: la maison Burghardt à Ratisbonne, Allemagne (1978–79), la résidence Richter à Munich, Allemagne (1981–83), un module de maison solaire à Sulmona, Italie (1983–85), un hall de conférence et d'exposition à Linz, Autriche (1988–93), des halls de production et une centrale d'énergie pour Wilkhahn à Eimbeckhausen, Allemagne (1989–92), le hall 26 de la Deutsche Messe à Hanovre (1994–96), publié dans ce livre. Il travaille sur des structures expérimentales pour utiliser l'énergie solaire depuis le milieu des années 70. Il reçut en 1993 la médaille d'or du Bund Deutscher Architekten (BDA), en 1996 le Prix Auguste Perret de la fédération internationale des architectes UIA, et en 1998 la grande médaille d'or de l'académie d'architecture française.

Thomas Herzog + Partner, Hall 26, Deutsche Messe, Hanover, Germany, 1994–96.

Thomas Herzog + Partner, Messehalle 26, Deutsche Messe Hannover, Deutschland, 1994–96.

Thomas Herzog + Partner, Hall 26, Foire d'Allemagne, Hanovre, Allemagne, 1994–96.

Hall 26, Deutsche Messe

Hanover, Germany, 1994–1996

This 220 by 115 meter structure rises to a height of 25 meters on the grounds of the Deutsche Messe complex. A light tensile steel suspension roof was chosen to provide large unencumbered spans for fairs. High points were created to facilitate natural ventilation, and the skylights were arranged in such a way that ample natural lighting could be provided without unduly increasing solar gain. Timber composite panels with thermal insulation were used on the roof, and timber louvers for some exterior cladding such as that of the six cubic service structures along the sides of the building. For energy efficiency reasons fresh air is fed into the building at a height of 4.7 meters, a system that permitted a 50% savings for the cost of the mechanical ventilation. Although these technical elements are essential to the success of the building, it is its light-filled, generous space and spectacular wave-like profile that make it attractive to users and visitors.

Der 220 x 115 m große Bau erhebt sich 25 m über das Messegelände in Hannover. Um weite, nicht durch Stützen unterbrochene Flächen für die Messen zu gewährleisten, entschied der Architekt sich für eine leichte Hängedachkonstruktion aus Stahl. Die Hochpunkte des Daches wurden so ausgebildet, daß eine natürliche Belüftung der Halle ermöglicht wird. Die Oberlichter sind so angeordnet, daß die Halle zwar großzügig mit Tageslicht versorgt wird, aber gleichzeitig vor zu starker Sonneneinstrahlung geschützt ist. Für die Dachkonstruktion verwendete man zusammengesetzte und wärmeisolierte Holzelemente, dagegen waren es bei der Außenverkleidung – wie bei den sechs kubischen Servicewürfeln entlang der Hallenseiten – Lamellen aus Holz. Aus Gründen der Energieeinsparung strömt Frischluft in einer Höhe von 4,7 m in das Gebäude, ein Verfahren, das die Kosten gegenüber einer mechanischen Ventilation um 50% senkt. Obgleich solche technischen Merkmale wesentlich zum Erfolg des Baus beigetragen haben, sind es doch der lichtdurchflutete und großzügige Innenraum sowie das spektakuläre wellenförmige Profil der Halle, das sie für Aussteller und Besucher besonders attraktiv macht.

Cette structure de 220 x 115 m s'élève à une hauteur de 25 m à l'intérieur du complexe de la Deutsche Messe. La formule du toit léger suspendu en acier a été choisie pour offrir de vastes espaces d'exposition dégagés. Les points hauts facilitent la ventilation naturelle, et les verrières laissent pénétrer une lumière généreuse sans trop laisser passer la chaleur solaire. Des panneaux d'isolation thermique en bois composite ont été utilisés pour le toit, ainsi que des volets de bois pour certains revêtements extérieurs, comme par exemple pour les six structures techniques cubiques qui flanquent les bâtiments. Pour des raisons de rendement énergétique, l'air frais est insufflé à 4,7 m de haut, système qui permet de réduire de moitié le coût de la ventilation mécanique. Bien que l'aspect technique joue un rôle essentiel dans le succès de ce bâtiment, ce sont surtout ses espaces généreux inondés de lumière et son profil en forme de vagues qui séduisent surtout les visiteurs et les exposants.

Pages 118–121: The wave-like structure of the roof makes for an aesthetically pleasing design, but its origin is just as much related to the factors of natural lighting and ventilation, which the architect is very interested in.

Seite 118–121: Die wellenförmige Dachstruktur ergibt ein ästhetisch gelungenes Erscheinungsbild, sie ist jedoch auch auf funktionale Faktoren wie die Versorgung mit Tageslicht oder eine natürliche Ventilation zurückzuführen, an denen der Architekt sehr interessiert ist.

Pages 118–121: La structure du toit en forme de vagues est réussie du point de vue esthétique, mais elle s'explique tout autant par une recherche sur l'éclairage et la ventilation naturels auxquels l'architecte s'intéresse beaucoup.

The spectacular interior spaces of Hall 26 have brought
to mind comparisons with early industrial-age halls
such as Paxton's Crystal Palace.

Der spektakuläre Innenraum der Messehalle 26 hat zu
Vergleichen mit Hallen aus der Frühzeit des Industrie-
zeitalters angeregt, so etwa mit Paxtons Kristallpalast.

Les spectaculaires espaces intérieurs du Hall 26 incitent
à la comparaison avec les vastes constructions métalli-
ques des débuts de l'ère industrielle, comme le Crystal
Palace de Paxton.

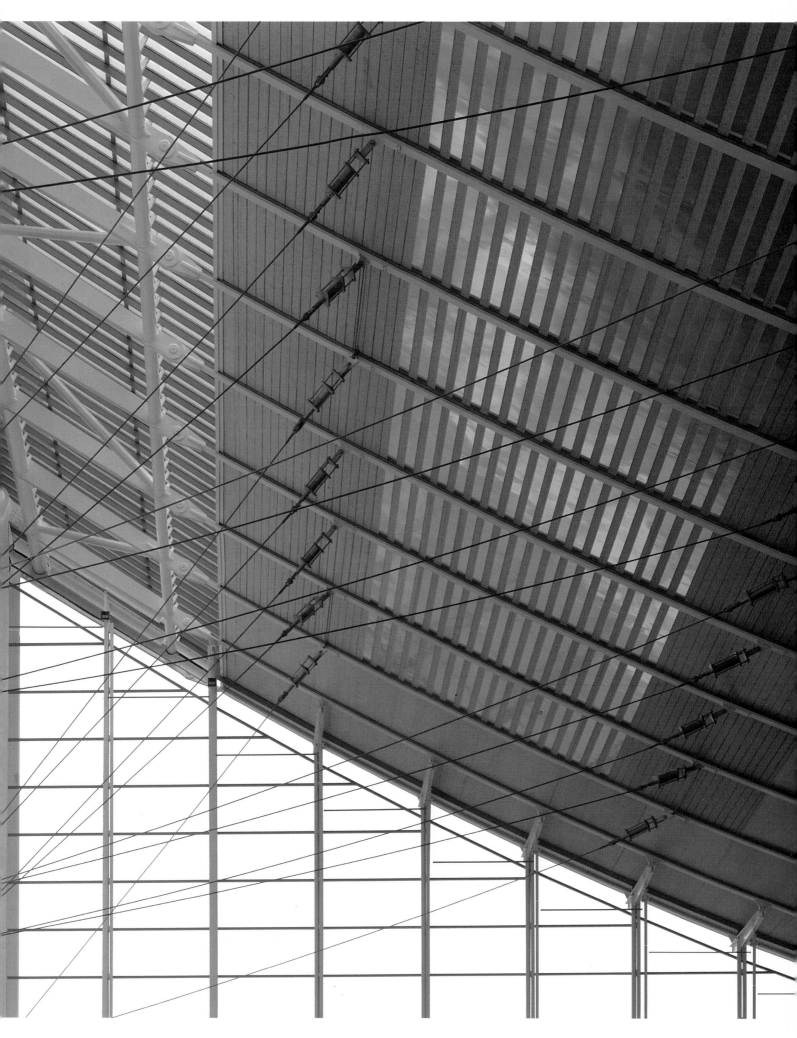

Thomas Herzog + Partner: Hall 26, Deutsche Messe, 1994–96

Søren Robert Lund

Born in Copenhagen in 1962, Søren Robert Lund attended the Royal Academy of Fine Arts in that city from 1982 to 1989. He established his own architectural office in 1991. Aside from the Arken Museum, his largest completed project to date, Lund has designed the main lobby of a mall in Lyngby, Denmark (with Busk Design, 1991), the entrance area of the Skagen Museum with the same partner (1991), and a brick one-family house in Allerød, Denmark (1996–97). Current work includes a new printing factory in Slagelse, Denmark (phase one to be completed in 1999), and a global shop concept for a shoemaker. He also participated in the 1989 competition for the library in Alexandria, Egypt (Special Merit Award), and the Aga Khan's 1991 ideas competition for the center of Samarkand, Uzbekistan. An exhibition on his work, organized by the Deutsche Werkbund, took place in Ennigerich, Germany (1998).

Der 1962 in Kopenhagen geborene Søren Robert Lund besuchte von 1982–89 die dortige Königliche Akademie der Schönen Künste. 1991 gründete er ein eigenes Architekturbüro. Neben dem Arken-Museum, seinem bislang größten realisierten Projekt, hat Lund die Lobby eines Einkaufszentrums in Lyngby entworfen (gemeinsam mit Busk Design, Dänemark, 1991), die Eingangszone des Skagen-Museums (ebenfalls mit Busk-Design, 1991) und ein Einfamilienhaus aus Backstein in Allerød, Dänemark (1996–97). Zur Zeit arbeitet er an einem Druckereigebäude in Slagelse (Bauphase 1 wird 1999 fertiggestellt) sowie an einem Konzept für die weltweiten Geschäftsfilialen eines Schuhherstellers. Außerdem nahm Lund 1989 an einem Wettbewerb für die Bibliothek im ägyptischen Alexandria teil (Spezialpreis) sowie an dem 1991 von Aga Khan ausgeschriebenen Ideenwettbewerb für das Stadtzentrum von Samarkand (Usbekistan). Eine vom Deutschen Werkbund organisierte Ausstellung seines Werks war 1998 im deutschen Ennigerich zu sehen.

Né à Copenhague en 1962, Søren Robert Lund suit les cours de l'Académie royale des Beaux-Arts de cette ville de 1982 à 1989, et fonde son agence en 1991. En dehors du musée de l'Arken – son plus important projet achevé jusqu'à ce jour – il a dessiné en 1991 le hall principal d'un centre commercial à Lyngby (Danemark) en collaboration avec Busk Design; la zone d'entrée du Musée de Skagen (1991), toujours en collaboration avec Busk Design, et une maison en briques à Allerød, Danemark (1996–97). Actuellement, il travaille sur le projet d'une imprimerie à Slagelse (Danemark), dont la première phase sera achevée en 1999, ainsi que sur le concept de boutiques globales pour un fabricant de chaussures. Il a également remporté le Prix spécial du mérite au concours pour la bibliothèque d'Alexandrie, Égypte (1989), et le concours d'idées organisé par l'Aga Khan (1991) pour le centre de Samarkand (Ouzbékistan). Une exposition sur son œuvre, organisée par le Deutsche Werkbund, s'est tenue à Ennigerich, Allemagne (1998).

Søren Robert Lund, Arken Museum of Modern Art, Copenhagen, Denmark, 1988–96.

Søren Robert Lund, Arken-Museum für Moderne Kunst, Kopenhagen, Dänemark, 1988–96.

Søren Robert Lund, Musée d'art moderne de l'Arken, Copenhague, Danemark, 1988–96.

Arken Museum of Modern Art
Copenhagen, Denmark, 1988–1996

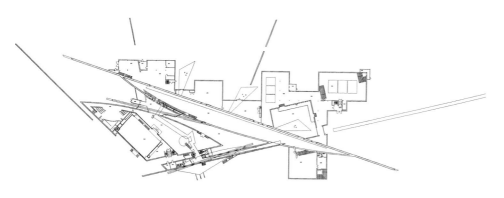

Set on Koge Bay to the south of Copenhagen, this museum's shape was inspired by its maritime surroundings. As the architect says, "The metaphor of the shipwreck has been very significant in the design of the building. By using this metaphor, the design is inscribed into the history of the landscape." Definitely conceived in the spirit of "deconstructivist" architecture, the museum is located on a 72,000 square meter site, and has a total area of 9,200 square meters, of which 3,500 square meters is intended for the exhibitions. Built for the County of Copenhagen following a 1988 national competition with a $27 million budget, the Arken Museum is centered around a 150 meter long gallery called the "Art Axis." At its largest, this space is 10 meters wide and 12 meters high. A passage called the "Red Axis," colored ruby red with tilted walls and a black floor-bisects the building "stretching from the Main Foyer to the boat-bridge at the harbor." Intended for visual arts, the museum also gives space to film, ballet, theater, and music.

Die äußere Gestalt des Museums an der Koge-Bucht im Süden von Kopenhagen wurde von seiner maritimen Umgebung inspiriert. »Die Metapher des Schiffswracks«, so der Architekt, »war beim Entwurf des Gebäudes sehr wichtig. Indem wir uns auf diese Metapher stützten, konnte der Entwurf in die Geschichte der Landschaft eingeschrieben werden.« Das Museum, dessen Architektur entschieden den Geist des Dekonstruktivismus verkörpert, befindet sich auf einem 72 000 m² großen Gelände und hat eine Gesamtfläche von 9 200 m², von denen 3 500 m² für Ausstellungen vorgesehen sind. Der Entwurf ging aus einem 1988 ausgetragenen nationalen Wettbewerb hervor und wurde mit einem Budget von 27 Millionen $ verwirklicht. Im Zentrum des Baus steht eine 150 m lange Galerie, die sogenannte »Kunstachse«, die maximal 10 m breit und 12 m hoch ist. Eine »Rote Achse« genannte Passage, rubinrot mit geneigten Wänden und schwarzem Fußboden, schneidet das Gebäude entzwei und erstreckt sich vom Hauptfoyer bis zur Schiffsbrücke am Hafen. Das für alle visuellen Kunstarten konzipierte Museum bietet auch dem Film, dem Ballett, dem Theater und der Musik Raum.

Situé au bord de la baie de Koge, au sud de Copenhague, les formes de ce musée se sont inspirées de son environnement maritime. Pour l'architecte: «La métaphore de l'épave a joué un rôle significatif dans le dessin du bâtiment. À travers elle, il s'inscrit dans l'histoire du paysage». Conçu dans un esprit résolument déconstructiviste, il se situe sur un terrain de 72 000 m² pour une surface totale de 9 200 m², dont 3 500 réservés aux expositions. Édifié pour le comté de Copenhague à l'issue d'un concours national organisé en 1988 et pour un budget de 27 millions de $, le musée de l'Arken s'organise autour d'une galerie de 150 m de long appelée «l'axe de l'art». Dans sa partie la plus importante, cet espace mesure 10 m de large sur 12 de haut. Un passage appelé «l'axe rouge», de couleur rubis avec des murs carrelés et un sol noir, coupe le bâtiment en deux «se déployant du hall principal jusqu'à la jetée du port.» Conçu pour les arts plastiques, le musée accueillera également films, ballets, pièces de théâtre et concerts.

Pages 126–129: Both its plan (page 126) and views from the sea or from the surrounding dunes make it clear that this is a "deconstructivist" design, but it seems nonetheless to blend into its environment in an appropriate manner.

Seite 126–129: Sowohl der Grundriß (Seite 126) als auch verschiedene Ansichten des Gebäudes zeigen, daß es sich um einen dekonstruktivistischen Entwurf handelt, der sich dennoch auf angemessene Weise in seine natürliche Umgebung einfügt.

Pages 126–129: Les vues prises de la mer ou des dunes, tout comme le plan (page 126), montrent clairement la nature déconstructiviste du projet, qui ne s'en s'intègre pas moins bien pour autant à son environnement.

Søren Robert Lund: Arken Museum of Modern Art, 1988–96 **127**

The lifeboat-like café confirms the frequent use of nautical metaphors, which are also apparent in interior volumes. The very name of the museum – Arken – intentionally evokes the image of the ark.

Das an ein Rettungsboot erinnernde Café bestätigt einmal mehr den Rückgriff auf nautische Metaphern, die auch in den Innenräumen augenscheinlich sind. Der Name des Museums, Arken, verweist bewußt auf das Bild der Arche.

Le café en forme de canot de sauvetage s'inscrit dans une multiplicité de métaphores nautiques, également présentes dans les volumes intérieurs. Le nom même du musée – Arken – est une allusion à l'Arche biblique.

The main gallery, called the "Art Axis", is no less than 150 meters long. A passageway colored bright red also runs through the building, bringing the only touch of strong color to the interior.

Der Hauptausstellungsraum, »Kunstachse« genannt, ist beeindruckende 150 m lang. Eine leuchtend rot gehaltene Passage kreuzt den Bau und verleiht dem Inneren den einzigen starken Farbakzent.

La galerie principale, appelée «l'axe de l'art», ne mesure pas moins de 150 m de long. Un passage peint en rouge vif court à travers le bâtiment, seule touche de couleur forte à l'intérieur.

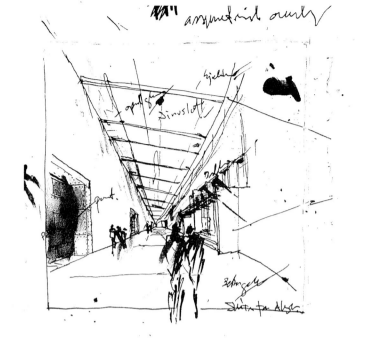

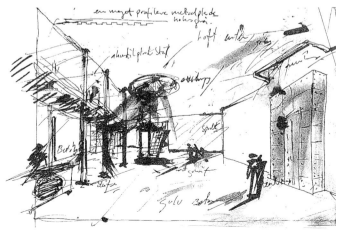

Berthold Penkhues

Born in Schloss Holte, Westphalia, in 1955, Berthold Penkhues studied architecture and urban planning at the University of Kassel from 1976 to 1984. In 1980 he worked for the firm of Josef Kleihues, but four years later he obtained a scholarship which permitted him to study at the UCLA Graduate School of Architecture and Urban Planning, under Charles Moore and Ricardo Legoretta (1984–86), where he obtained a Master of Architecture degree. During the same period he was a visiting critic at the Southern California Institute of Architecture in Santa Monica. From 1986 to 1989 he worked in the office of Frank O. Gehry in Santa Monica, before returning to found his own firm in Kassel in 1989. Aside from the museum in Korbach published here, he has participated in numerous competitions in Germany, and built a villa in Kassel (1993–98). Current work includes a design for town houses on Sternstrasse in Kassel, scheduled for 1998 completion.

Der 1955 im westfälischen Schloß Holte geborene Berthold Penkhues studierte von 1976 bis 1984 Architektur und Stadtplanung an der Universität Kassel. 1980 arbeitete er im Büro von Josef Kleihues, erhielt vier Jahre später aber ein Stipendium, das es ihm ermöglichte, an der UCLA Graduate School of Architecture and Urban Planning unter Charles Moore und Ricardo Legoretta zu studieren (1984–86), wo er als Abschluß den Master of Architecture erlangte. Während dieser Zeit war er auch als Gastkritiker am Southern California Institute of Architecture in Santa Monica tätig. Von 1986 bis 1989 arbeitete er im Büro von Frank O. Gehry in Santa Monica, bevor er nach Deutschland zurückkehrte, um in Kassel sein eigenes Büro zu gründen. Neben dem hier vorgestellten Museum in Korbach hat Penkhues sich an zahlreichen Wettbewerben in Deutschland beteiligt und in Kassel eine Villa gebaut (1993–98). Zur Zeit arbeitet er an der Planung für Stadtvillen in der Kasseler Sternstraße, die 1998 fertiggestellt sein sollen.

Né à Schloss Holte en Westphalie en 1955, Berthold Penkhues étudie l'architecture et l'urbanisme à l'Université de Cassel, de 1976 à 1984. En 1980, il travaille pour l'agence de Josef Kleihues, et quatre ans plus tard, il obtient une bourse qui lui permet de poursuivre ses études à l'UCLA Graduate School of Architecture and Urban Planning sous la direction de Charles Moore et de Ricardo Legoretta (1984–86), où il passe son Master en architecture. Au cours de la même période, il est critique invité au Southern California Institute of Architecture, à Santa Monica. De 1986 à 1989, il travaille pour Frank O. Gehry à Santa Monica avant de revenir à Cassel pour créer son agence en 1989. En dehors du Musée historique de Korbach publié ici, il a participé à de nombreux concours en Allemagne, et construit une villa à Cassel (1993–98). Il a récemment conçu les plans pour des résidences urbaines sur la Sternstrasse à Cassel, qui devraient être achevées en 1998.

Berthold Penkhues, History Museum, Korbach, Germany, 1995–97.

Berthold Penkhues, Regionalmuseum, Korbach, Deutschland, 1995–97.

Berthold Penkhues, Musée historique, Korbach, Allemagne, 1995–97.

History Museum
Korbach, Germany, 1995–1997

Berthold Penkhues won a competition restricted to architects from the Kassel region in 1991 to restore and expand a local history museum. Museum construction was divided into two stages. The first began in March 1995, and was completed in January 1997. The museum as a whole was inaugurated in June 1997. A glazed inner courtyard is used by the architect to connect the older, stone or half-timber houses with new spaces in the form of two-story cubes. Particular attention was paid to creating contemporary structures that fit into the existing street and architectural pattern of Korbach, a town of 25,000 inhabitants, located near Kassel. As the competition jury said, "The special qualities of this design are to be found in the sensitive treatment of the urban space and the related small dimensions. The sculptural forming of the building volumes is notable in their integration of existing buildings and supplementary new structures." Although this project was built with a low budget (about $5 million), it is indicative of both a respect for historical tradition and an ability to fit contemporary architecture into a traditional context.

Im Jahre 1991 gewann Berthold Penkhues einen den Architekten der Region Kassel vorbehaltenen Wettbewerb, der die Restaurierung und Erweiterung eines Museums für lokale Geschichte zum Gegenstand hatte. Die Arbeiten wurden in zwei Abschnitte unterteilt. Die erste Bauphase begann im März 1995 und wurde im Januar 1997 abgeschlossen. Im Juni 1997 konnte das Museum dann als Ganzes eingeweiht werden. Der Architekt schuf einen glasüberdachten Innenhof, um die alten, aus Stein oder halb aus Holz errichteten Gebäude mit den Neubauten in Gestalt zweigeschossiger Kuben zu verbinden. Besondere Aufmerksamkeit wurde darauf gelegt, eine zeitgenössische Formensprache zu entwickeln, die sich in die bestehende Bausituation von Korbach, einer Stadt mit 25 000 Einwohnern in der Nähe von Kassel, einfügt. »Die besonderen Qualitäten des Entwurfs«, so das Urteil der Jury, »liegen in der sensiblen Behandlung des Stadtraums und den damit zusammenhängenden, klein dimensionierten Abmessungen. Die skulpturale Formung der Baukörper ist bemerkenswert aufgrund der Integration von bereits existierenden Gebäuden und hinzugefügten Neubauten.« Auch wenn das Projekt mit einem kleinen Budget (rund 5 Millionen $) verwirklicht werden mußte, zeigt sich in ihm sowohl Respekt für eine historisch gewachsene Situation, wie auch die Fähigkeit, zeitgenössische Architektur in einen traditionellen Kontext einzupassen.

Berthold Penkhues a remporté en 1991 le concours, réservé aux architectes de la région de Cassel, pour la restauration et l'extension du musée d'histoire locale. La construction s'est déroulée en deux phases. La première, qui a débuté en mars 1995, s'est achevée en janvier 1997. Le musée a été inauguré dans sa totalité en juin 1997. Une cour intérieure vitrée relie les parties anciennes, en pierre ou à colombage, aux nouveaux espaces répartis entre deux cubes de deux niveaux. Une attention particulière a été portée à la création de ces structures contemporaines qui s'intègrent dans le schéma architectural et de voirie de Korbach, petite ville de 25 000 habitants, proche de Cassel. Le jury avait accompagné sa décision du commentaire suivant: «Les qualités particulières de ce projet tiennent au traitement plein de sensibilité de l'espace urbain et à ses dimensions modestes et adéquates. Les formes sculpturales des volumes sont remarquables pour leur intégration des bâtiments existants et des constructions nouvelles.» Bien que réalisé pour un budget minimal (30 millions de F), ce projet traduit à la fois un respect pour la tradition historique et une capacité à intégrer l'architecture contemporaine dans un contexte ancien.

Pages 137–139: The new forms added by Berthold Penkhues are intended to fit in with the scale and volumes of the existing village, while maintaining their modern identity.

Seite 137–139: Die von Berthold Penkhues neu hinzugefügten Gebäude sollen sich in das Stadtgefüge in Hinblick auf Größe und Volumina eingliedern, dabei aber ihre Modernität keineswegs verleugnen.

Pages 137–139: Les nouveaux volumes créés par Berthold Penkhues s'adaptent aux volumes et à l'échelle de la petite ville, tout en maintenant leur identité contemporaine.

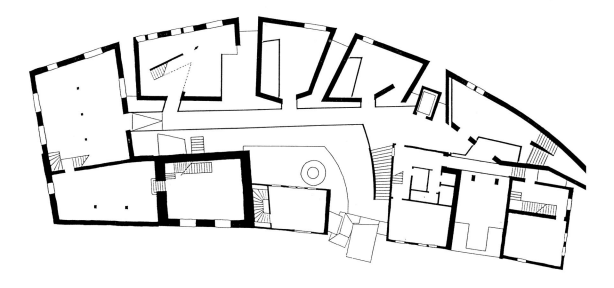

Covered walkways link the old and new components of the museum, while keeping to the rhythm of the narrow streets of the town.

Überdachte Wege verbinden die alten und neuen Teile des Museums und behalten dabei den Rhythmus der engen Straßen des Ortes bei.

Des passages couverts relient les bâtiments anciens et nouveaux, tout en reprenant le rythme des étroites ruelles de la ville.

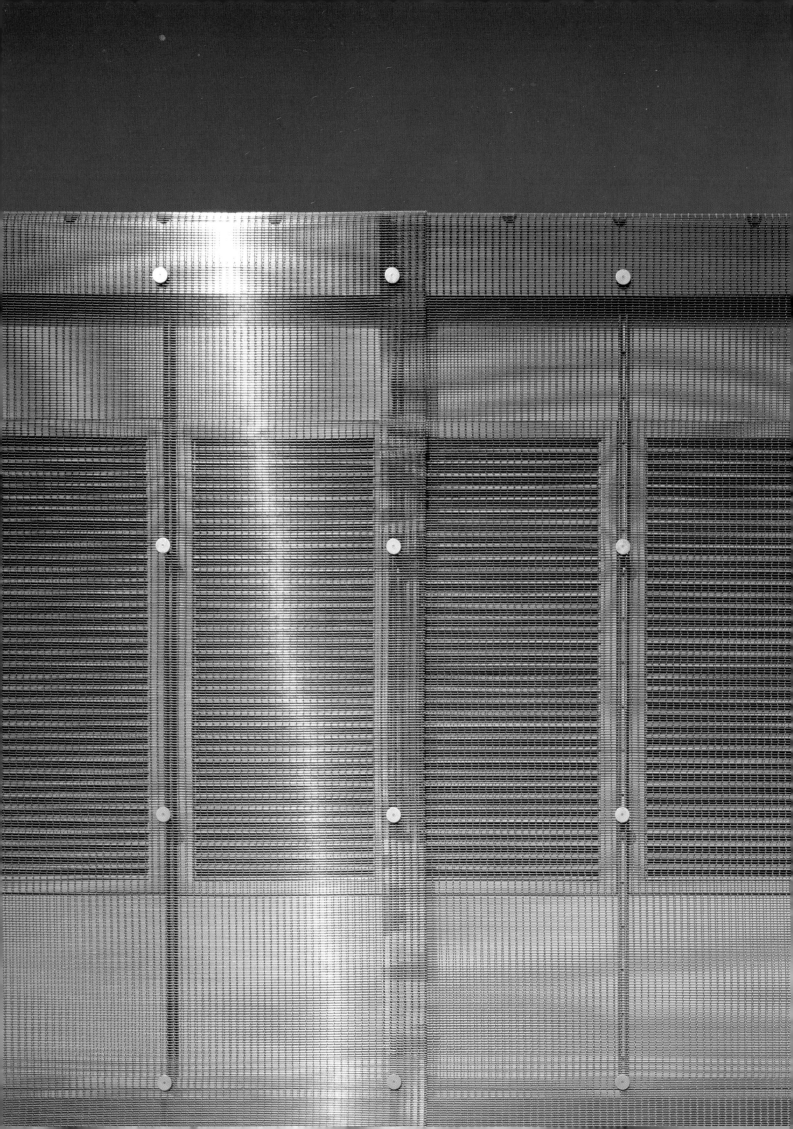

Dominique Perrault

Born in 1953, Dominique Perrault was not the most obvious candidate to win the 1989 competition to build a new French national library, to replace the aging facilities located on the rue de Richelieu in Paris. Having defeated the likes of Meier, Koolhaas, Nouvel, and Stirling in the competition, Perrault faced a storm of often politically motivated protest against his project, which provided for library stacks placed in four, symmetrical 100 meter high towers, arranged around a large interior garden with 250 mature trees. Although the towers were reduced to a height of 80 meters and more books were placed in the base of the structure, the basic plan of Perrault survived this criticism, and he also designed most of the interiors. This in itself is a substantial accomplishment for a young architect. His Velodrome and Swimming Pool for Berlin have in common with the library a use of metals and a digging into the earth, as well as a continued admiration for the kind of simple forms seen in the work of Minimalist artists, or perhaps in this case more specifically, a reference to Land Art.

Daß der 1953 geborene Dominique Perrault den Wettbewerb für den Neubau der Französischen Nationalbibliothek, der die veralteten Räumlichkeiten an der Rue de Richelieu in Paris ersetzen sollte, im Jahre 1989 für sich entscheiden würde, war nicht unbedingt zu erwarten gewesen. Nachdem er Architektenpersönlichkeiten wie Meier, Koolhaas, Nouvel und Stirling ausgestochen hatte, sah sich Perrault einem oftmals politisch motivierten Proteststurm gegen seinen Entwurf ausgesetzt. Dieser sah Bücherstellflächen in vier symmetrischen, jeweils 100 m hohen Türmen vor, die um einen großen eingefaßten Garten mit 250 ausgewachsenen Bäumen gruppiert sein sollten. Obgleich die Höhe der Türme schließlich auf 80 m reduziert und ein größerer Teil der Bücher in der Gebäudebasis untergebracht wurde, überstand die Grundidee Perraults alle geäußerte Kritik; außerdem entwarf Perrault einen Großteil der Innenausstattung. Das allein ist schon eine beachtliche Leistung für einen jungen Architekten. Sein Velodrom und die Schwimmhalle für Berlin haben mit der Nationalbibliothek sowohl den Gebrauch von Metall als Baumaterial wie auch ein weites Eingraben ins Erdreich gemeinsam. Die anhaltende Bewunderung für einfache Formen, derer sich auch die Künstler des Minimalismus bedienen, oder – in diesem Fall noch genauer – die Vertreter der Land-Art, wird bei Perrault in seinen bisherigen Bauwerken deutlich.

Né en 1953, Dominique Perrault n'était pas le candidat le plus évident pour remporter le concours de la nouvelle Bibliothèque nationale de France, organisé en 1989 pour remplacer les installations usagées de la rue de Richelieu à Paris. Après avoir battu des concurrents tels que Meier, Koolhaas, Nouvel et Stirling, Perrault doit faire face à une tempête de protestations, souvent à motivations politiques. Son projet prévoyait de conserver les livres dans quatre tours symétriques de 100 m de haut, disposées autour d'un vaste jardin intérieur planté de 250 arbres de haute fûtaie. Bien que la hauteur des tours aient été réduite à 80 m et que l'on ait décidé d'entreposer davantage de livres dans le socle du bâtiment, la proposition initiale a survécu à toutes les critiques, et l'architecte a également conçu la plus grande partie des aménagements intérieurs. Tout ceci est, en soi, une réussite remarquable pour un jeune architecte. Son vélodrome et ses piscines pour Berlin partagent avec cette bibliothèque le recours au métal et l'enfouissement dans le sol, ainsi qu'une admiration renouvelée pour les formes simples des artistes minimalistes, ou peut-être même, dans ce cas spécifique, une référence au Land Art.

Dominique Perrault, Velodrome and Olympic Swimming Pool, Berlin, Germany, 1993–98.

Dominique Perrault, Rad- und Schwimmsporthallen, Berlin, Deutschland, 1993–98.

Dominique Perrault, vélodrome et piscine olympique, Berlin, Allemagne, 1993–98.

Velodrome and Olympic Swimming Pool

Berlin, Germany, 1993–1998

Launched in 1992 when Berlin was a candidate for the Olympic Games of the year 2000 (Sydney was chosen over Berlin), this sports complex is highly unusual in that its structures emerge no more than 1 meter above the earth. The Velodrome, completed before the Swimming Pool, appears above the surface as a shiny disk, 140 meters in diameter. Intentionally eschewing the heavy symbolism typical of Olympic architecture, Perrault meant his design to be a willful counterpoint to the structures of the 1936 Berlin Olympics. By burying the complex as much as 17 meters below ground, the architect also obtained a particularly energy-efficient design (60% less energy use). The most outstanding technical feature of the Velodrome is the 3,500 ton roof, which has a clear span of 115 meters and is supported by 16 concrete columns. Forty-eight trussed girders laid out in radial form transmit the load to the columns. Though it bears obvious comparison to a spoked bicycle wheel this roof has also been compared to the underside of a flying saucer. With a capacity of 5,800 persons, which can be increased to 9,500, and a ceiling height of 13 meters, the structure can be used for all indoor sports.

Die 1992 entworfene Sportanlage entstand im Zusammenhang damit, daß Berlin sich um die Austragung der Olympischen Spiele des Jahres 2000 bewarb – wobei dann allerdings die Wahl auf Sydney fiel. Als Projekt ist die Anlage insofern höchst ungewöhnlich, als sie nur 1 m über Bodenniveau hinausragt. Das zuerst fertiggestellte Velodrom erscheint über der Geländeoberfläche als eine glänzende Scheibe mit einem Durchmesser von 140 m. In der Absicht, jenen schweren Symbolismus zu vermeiden, der olympischen Bauten häufig anhaftet, sieht Perrault seinen Entwurf auch als bewußten Kontrapunkt zu den architektonischen Manifestationen der Berliner Olympiade von 1936. Indem er 17 m tief ins Erdreich vordrang, gelang dem Architekten zudem ein außerordentlich energiesparender Bau, der Einsparungen von 60% vorweisen kann. Herausragendes technisches Merkmal des Velodromes ist das 3 500 Tonnen schwere Dach, das stützenfrei 115 m überspannt und von 16 Betonpfeilern getragen wird. Insgesamt 48 radial angeordnete, versteifte Träger verteilen das Gewicht auf die Pfeiler. Die Gestalt des Dachs legt den Vergleich mit dem gespeichten Rad eines Fahrrads nahe, ist aber auch mit der Unterseite einer »fliegenden Untertasse« verglichen worden. Mit seiner Deckenhöhe von 13 m und einer Besucherkapazität, die von 5 800 bis 9 500 Personen reicht, kann das Bauwerk für alle Hallensportarten genutzt werden.

Conçu en 1992, alors que Berlin était candidate aux Jeux Olympiques de l'an 2000 (Sydney fut préférée), ce complexe sportif étonnant ne dépasse pas de plus d'un mètre le niveau du sol. Le vélodrome, achevé avant la piscine, ressemble à un disque étincelant de 140 m de diamètre qui serait posé sur le sol. Échappant volontairement au lourd symbolisme fréquent dans l'architecture olympique, Perrault a voulu que ce projet vienne en contrepoint des constructions entreprises pour les Jeux de Berlin de 1936. En creusant jusqu'à 17 m en dessous du niveau du sol, il a également pu bénéficier d'économies d'énergie importantes (60%). L'élément technique le plus remarquable du vélodrome est son toit de 3 500 tonnes et 115 m de diamètre, soutenu par 16 colonnes en béton. 48 poutres radiales en treillis transmettent la charge sue les colonnes. S'il évoque une roue de bicyclette, ce toit fait aussi penser à un ovni. Pour une capacité de 5 800 à 9 500 places, et une hauteur de plafond de 13 m, cette structure peut servir à tous les sports d'intérieur.

Pages 145–147: Inside the Velodrome, the most visible feature of the structure is the spoked 115 meter clear-span roof.

Seite 145–147: Das auffälligste konstruktive Merkmal im Inneren des Velodroms ist das 115 m Raum überspannende, gespeichte Dach.

Pages 145–147: L'élément le plus caractéristique de l'intérieur du vélodrome est son toit rayonnant de 115 m de portée sans piliers.

Page 148: Plans show the juxtaposition of the round (Velodrome) and rectangular (Swimming Pool) volumes, the whole surrounded by an orchard of apple trees.
Page 149: The chain-mail-type cladding of the Velodrome.

Seite 148: Die Pläne zeigen die Gegenüberstellung eines runden (Velodrom) und eines rechteckigen (Schwimmstadion) Baukörpers. Umgeben werden die Gebäude von einem Park mit Apfelbäumen.
Seite 149: Die an ein Kettenhemd erinnernde Außenverkleidung des Velodroms.

Page 148: Les plans montrent la juxtaposition de volumes rond (vélodrome) et carré (piscine), entourés d'un verger de pommiers.
Page 149: Le revêtement en «cottes de mailles» du vélodrome.

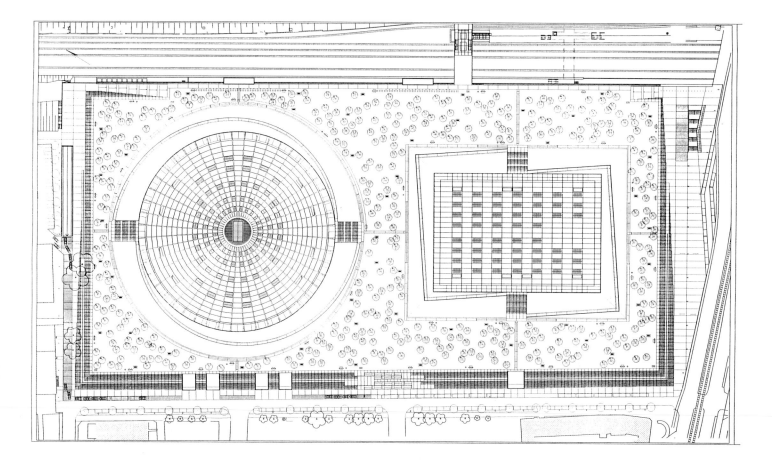

By sinking the structures into the earth, the architect makes them visually and symbolically unobtrusive, while obtaining important gains in energy efficiency.

Indem der Architekt die beiden Bauwerke in die Erde versenkt, sind sie nicht nur optisch und symbolisch unauffällig, sondern es kann auch sehr viel Energie gespart werden.

En enterrant ses structures, l'architecte leur assure une discrétion visuelle et symbolique, tout en obtenant d'importantes économies d'énergie.

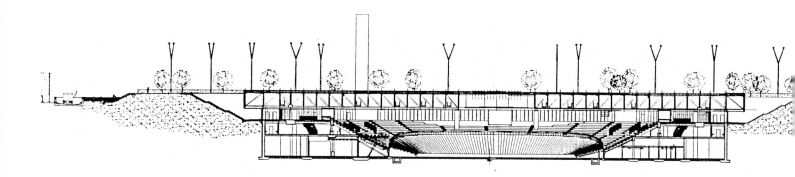

Dominique Perrault: Velodrome and Olympic Swimming Pool, 1993–98 **151**

Renzo Piano

Born in 1937 in Genoa, Renzo Piano associated with Richard Rogers completed the Georges Pompidou Center in Paris in 1977, which brought him almost instantly to international attention. Since that time, he has become one of the most active "stars" of the world of architecture, completing the Menil Collection Museum, Houston, Texas (1981–86), or the San Nicola stadium in Bari, Italy (1987–90). Although he has no regrets about the aggressive design of the Pompidou Center, he does say, "We were young and we wanted the building to be noticed," opting in his more recent work for a more sophisticated and subtle kind of technologically oriented architecture. He is capable of a wide variety of stylistic expressions, as evidenced by his Jean-Marie Tjibaou Cultural Center in New Caledonia (1994–98), his 1989 extension for the IRCAM, a calm brick structure, just opposite the multi-colored tubes and pipes of the Pompidou Center, or, in a different context, the renovation of the Lingotto complex in Turin, Italy (1989). Recent work in includes the Mercedes-Benz Center, Stuttgart, Germany (1992–96), as well as the massive Kansai International Airport Terminal, Osaka, Japan (1988–94), and work on the Potsdamer Platz, Berlin.

Der 1937 in Genua geborene Renzo Piano stellte 1977 in Zusammenarbeit mit Richard Rogers das Centre Georges Pompidou in Paris fertig, was ihm fast unmittelbar zu internationaler Bekanntheit verhalf. Seit dieser Zeit wurde Piano zu einem der aktivsten »Stars« der Architektenwelt, beispielsweise mit Projekten wie der Menil Collection in Houston, Texas (1981–86), oder dem San Nicola-Stadion in Bari, Italien (1987–90). Obwohl er die provokative Gestaltung des Centre Pompidou keineswegs bedauert, meint er doch: »Wir waren jung und wollten, daß das Gebäude beachtet wurde«. Mit seinen neueren Entwürfen vertritt Piano indes eher eine ausgefeilte und subtile Richtung der High-Tech-Architektur. Er verfügt über eine enorme Bandbreite an stilistischen Ausdrucksformen, was angesichts des Kulturzentrums Jean-Marie Tjibaou in Neukaledonien (1994–98), der Erweiterung des IRCAM-Instituts in Paris (1989) – einem ruhigen Backsteinbau direkt gegenüber dem vielfarbigen Röhrenwerk des Centre Pompidou – oder der von ihm umgebauten, ehemaligen Lingotto-Fabrik in Turin, Italien (1989), deutlich wird. Zu Pianos jüngsten Projekten zählen das Mercedes Benz-Center in Stuttgart, Deutschland (1992–96), das riesige Terminalgebäude des Flughafens Kansai in Osaka, Japan (1988–94) und Bauwerke für den Potsdamer Platz in Berlin.

Né en 1937 à Gênes, Renzo Piano, associé à Richard Rogers, achève le Centre Georges Pompidou à Paris en 1977, qui lui vaut une reconnaissance internationale immédiate. Depuis cette époque, il est devenu l'une des vedettes internationales de l'architecture, réalisant, par exemple, le Menil Collection Museum à Houston, Texas (1981–86), ou le Stade San Nicola à Bari, Italie (1987–90). Bien que sans regret pour le design agressif du Centre Pompidou, il précise cependant: «Nous étions jeunes et nous voulions que ce bâtiment soit remarqué». Dans ses œuvres plus récentes, il opte pour un type d'architecture d'esprit technologique plus sophistiqué et plus subtil. Il est capable d'expressions stylistiques très variées, comme pour le Centre culturel Jean-Marie Tjibaou en Nouvelle-Calédonie (1994–98), l'extension de l'IRCAM à Paris (1989), discrète petite structure de briques face au Centre Pompidou avec ses tubes et tuyaux colorés, ou, dans un contexte différent, la rénovation de l'usine du Lingotto à Turin, Italie (1989). Parmi ses travaux récents: le Centre Mercedes-Benz à Stuttgart, Allemagne (1992–96), l'énorme aéroport international de Kansai à Osaka, Japon (1988–94), et des interventions autour de la Postdamer Platz, à Berlin.

Renzo Piano, New Metropolis Science & Technology Center, Amsterdam, The Netherlands, 1995–97.

Renzo Piano, New Metropolis, Museum für Wissenschaft und Technologie, Amsterdam, Niederlande, 1995–97.

Renzo Piano, New Metropolis, Centre des Sciences et des Technologies, Amsterdam, Pays-Bas, 1995–97.

New Metropolis
Science & Technology Center

Amsterdam, The Netherlands, 1995–1997

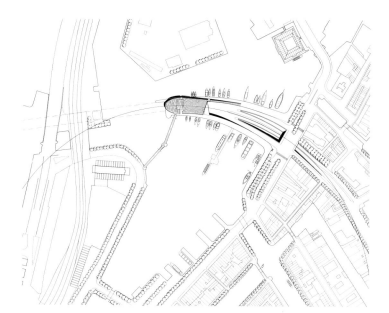

The very unexpected green shape of the New Metropolis Center appears from a distance to rise up from the old 17th century port of Amsterdam, near the Central railroad station. Built on the roof of the 1968 iJ tunnel at Oosterdok (East Dock), this 208 meter long, 32 meter high structure with a total net surface 10,258 square meters is bright green, due to its 4,100 square meters of copper facing. Inside, 4,300 square meters of interactive exhibitions and a 199-seat cinema greet a large number of visitors. Built for a total cost of 77.5 million florins (including exhibitions), the building itself cost 42.5 million florins. The vast, almost undivided interior space is finished in a summary, but interesting manner, with concrete columns and ceilings, perforated steel barriers, unpainted wood handrails and gray linoleum floors. Criticized because its exterior seems to have little to do with the inside, the New Metropolis Center nonetheless makes a convincing landmark in the skyline of old Amsterdam, a testimony to the continued interest of the Dutch in contemporary architecture.

Aus der Distanz gesehen scheint die unerwartete, grüne Gestalt des neuen New Metropolis-Museums mitten aus dem alten, im 17. Jahrhundert entstandenen Hafen von Amsterdam – nahe dem Hauptbahnhof – emporzuwachsen. Errichtet über dem iJ-Tunnel von 1968 am Oosterdock, dem östlichen Dock, erstrahlt das 208 m lange und 32 m hohe Gebäude mit einer Nutzfläche von 10 258 m² in einem leuchtenden Grün, was auf die Kupferverkleidung zurückzuführen ist, die insgesamt 4 100 m² Außenfläche bedeckt. Im Inneren laden 4 300 m² interaktive Ausstellungsfläche und ein Kino mit 199 Plätzen eine große Zahl von Besuchern ein. Von den Gesamtkosten in Höhe von 77,5 Millionen Gulden entfielen 42,5 Millionen Gulden auf den eigentlichen Bau. Der riesige, fast nicht unterteilte Innenraum bietet sich mit seinen Betonpfeilern und -decken, den Lochblechbalustraden, den unlackierten Handläufen aus Holz und dem grauen Linoleumboden auf eine zwar spartanische, aber dennoch interessante Weise dar. Zwar ist Kritik laut geworden, weil kein Zusammenhang zwischen Außengestalt und Innenraum bestünde, doch fügt New Metropolis der Skyline des alten Amsterdam gleichwohl ein überzeugendes Wahrzeichen hinzu und zeugt überdies von dem kontinuierlichen Interesse der Niederländer an der Architektur der Gegenwart.

Vue de loin, la forme verte massive et inattendue du New Metropolis semble jaillir du vieux port d'Amsterdam, près de la gare centrale. Construit au-dessus du tunnel iJ de l'Oosterdok (dock est, 1968), cette structure de 208 m de long et 32 m de haut offre une surface utile nette de 10 258 m². Sa couleur verte est due à son revêtement de 4 100 m² de panneaux de cuivre. À l'intérieur, 4 300 m² d'expositions interactives et une salle de cinéma de 199 places accueillent les nombreux visiteurs. Construit pour un budget de plus de 260 millions de F (expositions comprises), le bâtiment lui-même a coûté 144 millions de F. L'immense espace intérieur, presque sans séparation, a reçu une finition sommaire, mais intéressante: colonnes et plafonds en béton, garde-corps en acier perforé, rampes en bois brut, sols en linoléum gris. Critiqué parce que son apparence extérieur n'a que peu de rapport avec l'intérieur, le New Metropolis n'en est pas moins devenu l'un des monuments familiers du paysage du vieil Amsterdam, témoignage de l'intérêt permanent des Néerlandais pour l'architecture contemporaine.

Pages 154–157: Set in an otherwise traditional area near the Central railroad station, the New Metropolis Center stands out because of its copper cladding, and because of its unusual form.

Seite 154–157: Das in einem sonst traditionell bebauten Gebiet nahe dem Hauptbahnhof errichtete Wissenschaftsmuseum fällt aufgrund seiner Kupferverkleidung und seiner ungewöhnlichen Form auf.

Pages 154–157: Implanté dans un quartier traditionnel près de la Gare centrale, le New Metropolis s'en distingue par son revêtement de cuivre et sa forme inhabituelle.

Renzo Piano: New Metropolis Science & Technology Center, 1995–97 **155**

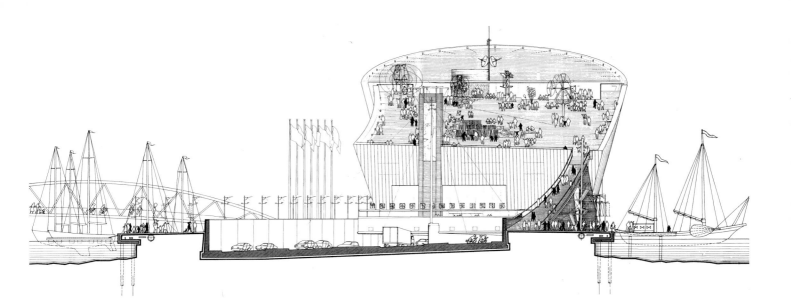

Seen in section (above), or as it is visible from the pedestrian approach paths, the museum confirms an impression of a nautically inspired form, despite the fact that its contents are unrelated to the port.

Im Schnitt (oben) oder auch in der Ansicht, die sich von den zuführenden Fußgängerwegen aus bietet, bestätigt sich der Eindruck, daß beim Entwurf des Museums auf Formen aus der Schiffahrt zurückgegriffen wurde, auch wenn die gezeigten Exponate keinen Bezug zum Hafen aufweisen.

En coupe (ci-dessus), ou vu des cheminements d'approche piétonniers, le musée confirme la nature nautique de sa forme, même si son contenu n'a aucun rapport avec le port.

Pages 160 top, 161: *The interior spaces are vast, dark, and finished in an industrial style. The exhibitions themselves are not the work of Renzo Piano.*
Page 160 bottom: *Despite its imposing mass, the entrance to the building provides a convivial area for an outdoor café.*

Seite 160 oben, 161: *Die Innenräume sind riesig und dunkel und im Stil von Industrieanlagen ausgeführt. Die Ausstellungen selbst sind nicht das Werk von Renzo Piano.*
Seite 160 unten: *Trotz seines massiven Baukörpers bietet der Eingangsbereich einen einladenden Platz für ein Café im Freien.*

Pages 160 en haut, 161: *Vastes et sombres, les espaces intérieurs ont reçu une finition de type industriel. Les expositions elles-mêmes n'ont pas été conçues par l'architecte.*
Page 160 en bas: *Malgré sa masse imposante, l'entrée du musée a permis l'aménagement d'un accueillant café en terrasse.*

Beyeler Foundation

Riehen, Switzerland, 1993–1997

Built in the Basel suburb of Riehen, this building was created to house the collection of the dealer Ernst Beyeler. It is located on the rather heavily traveled Wiesental road, which leads from Basel to the Black Forest. Piano chose to close off the Foundation on the street side with a high wall made of the same porphyry that is used on the stone walls of the building. Within, a certain modesty is immediately apparent, both in the scale of the building and in its calm facades. A small park faces the entrance, and the rear of the Foundation looks out on fields, which stretch to the neighboring German border. Within, the white walls and light wood floors seem to be the antithesis of the kind of "high-tech" appearance that Piano & Rogers gave to the Centre Pompidou twenty years earlier. An emphasis has been placed on natural lighting, and it is immediately apparent to the visitor that this is a building that was made to show works of art, no small accomplishment in itself, at a time when well-known architects often put themselves forward at the expense of the art.

Der in Riehen, einem Vorort von Basel, errichtete Bau nimmt die Sammlung des Kunsthändlers Ernst Beyeler auf. Er liegt an der stark befahrenen Wiesentalstraße, die von Basel zum Schwarzwald führt. Durch eine hohe Wand aus Porphyrstein, der auch bei den Steinwänden des Gebäudes zum Einsatz kam, schirmt Piano das Museum gegen die Straßenseite ab. Augenfällig ist eine gewisse bescheidene Zurückhaltung, sowohl in Hinblick auf die Abmessungen des Baus als auch hinsichtlich seiner ruhigen Fassaden. Dem Eingangsbereich gegenüber liegt ein kleiner Park, die Gebäuderückseite öffnet sich zu einer Felderlandschaft hin, die sich bis an die nahe Grenze zu Deutschland erstreckt. Im Innenraum erscheinen die weißen Wände und hellen Holzböden wie eine Antithese zu jenem »High-Tech-Look«, den Piano & Rogers vor rund 20 Jahren dem Centre Pompidou in Paris verliehen. Hier wurde auf die reichliche Versorgung mit Tageslicht Wert gelegt. Sofort spürt der Besucher, daß das Gebäude in erster Linie für die Präsentation von Kunstwerken entworfen wurde – keine geringe Leistung in einer Zeit, in der sich berühmte Architekten häufig auf Kosten der Kunst in den Vordergrund stellen.

Élevé à Riehen dans la banlieue de Bâle, ce bâtiment a été créé pour recevoir la collection du marchand Ernst Beyeler. Il est situé en bordure d'une route assez fréquentée qui relie Bâle à la Forêt Noire. Piano a choisi d'isoler la Fondation côté rue par un haut mur du même porphyre que les murs de pierre du bâtiment. À l'intérieur, une certaine modestie s'impose, à la fois par l'échelle du bâtiment et la sérénité des façades. Un petit parc fait face à l'entrée, et l'arrière donne sur des champs qui s'étendent jusqu'à la frontière allemande toute proche. Les murs blancs et les sols en parquet clair des galeries semblent à l'antithèse du style «high-tech» du Centre Pompidou de Piano & Rogers, édifié 20 ans plus tôt. L'attention a été portée sur l'éclairage naturel, et le visiteur comprend immédiatement que ce musée a réellement été conçu pour montrer des œuvres d'art, ce qui n'est pas une mince réussite en soi, vu que certains architectes contemporains renomés tendent souvent à se mettre en avant au détriment des œuvres.

Renzo Piano, Beyeler Foundation, Riehen, Switzerland, 1993–97.

Renzo Piano, Fondation Beyeler, Riehen, Schweiz, 1993–97.

Renzo Piano, Fondation Beyeler, Riehen, Suisse, 1993–97.

Long and low because it is set on a narrow site, but also for reasons of discretion, the Foundation boasts a majority of interior galleries with excellent, natural top lighting.

Der Bau – lang und flach wegen seiner Errichtung auf einem schmalen Grundstück, aber auch aus Gründen einer gewünschten Zurückhaltung – bietet ein Maximum an Ausstellungssälen mit ausgezeichneten Lichtverhältnissen mittels natürlichen Oberlichts.

De forme longue et basse, parce qu'elle se trouve sur un terrain étroit, mais aussi pour des raisons de discrétion, la Fondation bénéficie d'un excellent éclairage zénithal dans la majorité de ses salles.

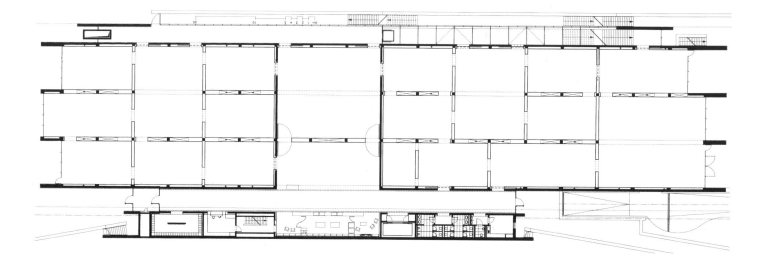

Pages 166–167: *Above left, the ramp leading to the main entrance of the building. Located to the left of this ramp, as the visitor enters, is the basin visible in the large image.*
Page 166 bottom: *A gallery looking out on the same basin, containing sculptures by Alberto Giacometti.*

Seite 166–167: *Der Besucher betritt über eine Eingangsrampe das Museum, links davon liegt das Wasserbecken.*
Seite 166 unten: *Ein Ausstellungsraum mit Blick auf das Wasserbecken zeigt Skulpturen von Alberto Giacometti.*

Pages 166–167: *À gauche de la rampe qui mène à l'entrée principale est situé un bassin, visible dans la grande photographie.*
Page 166 en bas: *Une galerie qui donne sur le même bassin contient des sculptures d'Alberto Giacometti.*

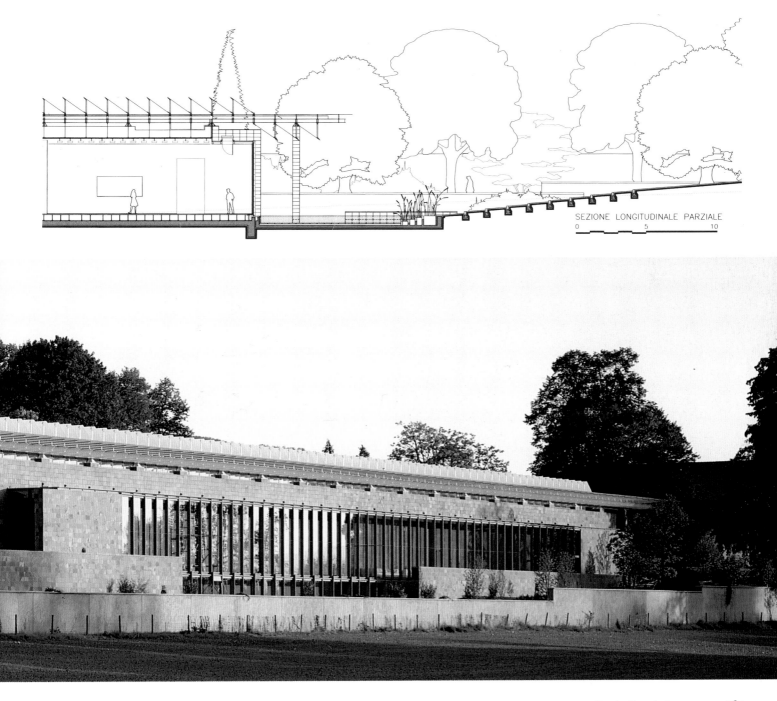

SEZIONE LONGITUDINALE PARZIALE
0   5   10

Renzo Piano: Beyeler Foundation, 1993–97 **165**

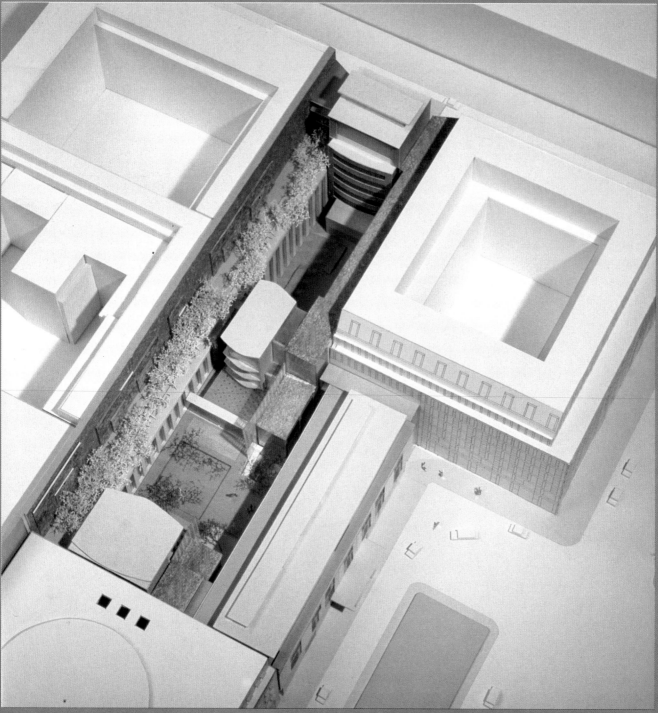

Christian de Portzamparc

Born in Casablanca, Morocco, in 1944, Christian de Portzamparc studied at the École des Beaux-Arts in Paris from 1962 to 1969. Early projects include a water tower at Marne-la-Vallée, France (1971–74), and Hautes Formes public housing, Paris, France (1975–79). He won the competition for the Cité de la Musique on the outskirts of Paris in 1984, completing the project in 1995. He was awarded the 1994 Pritzker Prize. He participated in the Euralille project with the Crédit Lyonnais Tower, France (1992–95), built over the new Lille-Europe railway station in Lille, and built housing for the Nexus World project in Fukuoka, Japan (1989–92). He also has completed an extension for the Bourdelle Museum, Paris, France (1988–92), and a housing complex in the ZAC Bercy, Paris, France (1991–94). Current work includes the LVMH Tower on 57th Street in New York, an addition to the Palais des Congrès in Paris, a tower for the Bandai toy company in Tokyo, a courthouse for Grasse in the south of France, and a new concert hall in Luxembourg.

Der 1944 in Casablanca, Marokko, geborene Christian de Portzamparc studierte von 1962–69 an der École des Beaux-Arts in Paris. Zu seinen frühen Projekten zählen ein Wasserturm in Marne-la-Vallée, Frankreich (1971–74), und die städtische Wohnanlage Hautes Formes in Paris, Frankreich (1975–79). 1984 gewann er den Wettbewerb für die Cité de la Musique am Stadtrand von Paris, die 1995 fertiggestellt werden konnte. 1994 Verleihung des Pritzker-Preises. Am Euralille-Projekt beteiligte sich Portzamparc mit einem Hochhaus für die Bank Crédit Lyonnais (1992–95), das er über dem neuen Bahnhof Lille-Europe errichtete; in Fukuoka entwarf er eine Wohnanlage für das Nexus World-Projekt, Japan (1989–92). Außerdem war er für den Erweiterungsbau des Bourdelle-Museums in Paris verantwortlich (1988–92) sowie für einen Wohnkomplex in ZAC Bercy, Paris (1991–94). Gegenwärtig arbeitet Portzamparc am LVMH-Turm in der 57. Straße in New York, an einem Anbau für das Palais des Congrès in Paris, einem Hochhaus für den Spielwarenhersteller Bandai in Tokio, einem Gerichtsgebäude im südfranzösischen Grasse und einer neuen Konzerthalle in Luxemburg.

Né à Casablanca en 1944, Christian de Portzamparc fait ses études à l'École des Beaux-Arts de Paris, de 1962 à 1969. Parmi ses premières réalisations: un château d'eau à Marne-la-Vallée (1971–74), et les H.L.M. des Hautes-Formes à Paris (1975–79). Il remporte le concours pour la Cité de la Musique à Paris (1984), dont la construction est achevée en 1995. En 1994, il reçoit le Prix Pritzker. Il participe au projet Euralille, à Lille, où il élève une tour au-dessus de la gare Lille-Europe pour le Crédit Lyonnais (1992–95), et construit un immeuble d'appartements pour Nexus World, à Fukuoka (1989–92). Il a également à son actif l'extension du Musée Bourdelle à Paris (1988–92), et un immeuble de logements de la ZAC Bercy, Paris (1991–94). Actuellement, il travaille sur le projet de la tour LVMH, 57th Street à New York, la transformation du Palais des Congrès à Paris, une tour pour la société de jouets Bandaï à Tokyo, le futur palais de justice de Grasse dans le Sud de la France, et une nouvelle salle de concert à Luxembourg.

Christian de Portzamparc, French Embassy, Berlin, Germany, 1997–2000.

Christian de Portzamparc, Französische Botschaft, Berlin, Deutschland, 1997–2000.

Christian de Portzamparc, Ambassade de France, Berlin, Allemagne, 1997–2000.

French Embassy
Berlin, Germany, 1997–2000

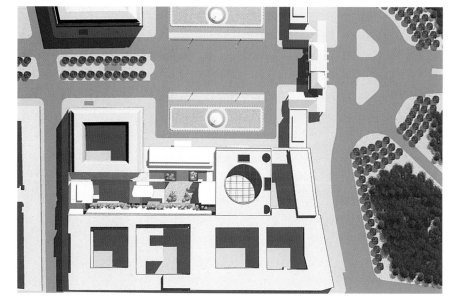

Until the time of the last war the Pariser Platz, located near the Reichstag, was one of the great squares of Berlin. Totally destroyed except for the famous Brandenburg Gate (C.G. Langhans, 1788–91), it is today being rebuilt. Christian de Portzamparc won a somewhat controversial competition against a select group of French architects including Henri Gaudin, Dominique Perrault, and Jean Nouvel with a design intended to open the interior of the difficult 4,600 square meter site to air and vegetation. His project was praised by the jury for "its facade facing Pariser Platz, perfectly embodying both the institution it hosts and the spirit of 'classical France,' the elegance and diversity of its interior spaces, its functional efficiency, the economic viability of the construction, and a stylistic/landscape-friendly design capable of epitomizing the French way of life and culture." In fact the main facade also reflects the austerity imposed by Berlin's building authorities in this highly sensitive location. The interiors of the Embassy are being designed by the architect's wife, Elisabeth de Portzamparc.

Bis zur Zeit des Zweiten Weltkriegs zählte der Pariser Platz in der Nähe des Reichstags zu den großen, weitläufigen Plätzen von Berlin. Heute wird die mit Ausnahme des Brandenburger Tors (C.G. Langhans, 1788–91) im Zweiten Weltkrieg völlig zerstörte Platzanlage neu bebaut. Gegen eine ausgewählte Gruppe französischer Architekten, darunter Henri Gaudin, Dominique Perrault und Jean Nouvel, konnte Christian de Portzamparc einen umstrittenen Wettbewerb schließlich für sich entscheiden. Sein Entwurf sieht vor, den Innenbereich des schwierigen, 4600 m² großen Grundstücks zum Himmel und zur Vegetation hin zu öffnen. Bei Portzamparc lobte die Jury vor allem »die Fassade zum Pariser Platz – eine vollkommene Darstellung sowohl der in dem Bau untergebrachten Institution als auch des Geistes des ›klassischen Frankreich‹ –, die Eleganz und Vielfalt der Innenräume, die Funktionalität und Rentabilität der Konstruktion, schließlich die stilistisch und landschaftsgärtnerisch gelungene Gestaltung, die französische Kultur und Lebensart zu verkörpern vermögen«. Tatsächlich spiegelt die Hauptfassade auch die strengen Bauauflagen der Berliner Behörden für diesen höchst bedeutsamen Ort wider. Die Innenraumausstattung gestaltet die Ehefrau des Architekten, Elisabeth de Portzamparc.

Jusqu'à la dernière guerre, la Pariser Platz, près du Reichstag, était l'une des places les plus élégantes de Berlin. Totalement détruite en 1945, à l'exception de la célèbre porte de Brandebourg (C.G. Langhans, 1788–91), elle est en cours de reconstruction. Christian de Portzamparc a remporté un concours assez contesté, face à un groupe sélectionné d'architectes français, dont Henri Gaudin, Dominique Perrault et Jean Nouvel. Son projet ouvre ce difficile terrain de 4600 m², pris entre d'autres immeubles, à la lumière et aux plantations. Il a été approuvé par le jury pour «sa façade sur la Pariser Platz, qui incarne à la perfection à la fois l'institution et l'esprit classique français, pour l'élégance et la diversité de ses espaces intérieurs, son efficacité fonctionnelle, la viabilité économique de sa construction, et un plan actuel et respectueux du site, capable de traduire le style de vie et la culture française». En fait, la façade principale reflète également l'austérité imposée par les autorités berlinoises dans ce lieu hautement sensible. Les espaces intérieurs seront aménagés par l'épouse de l'architecte, Élizabeth de Portzamparc.

Page 170: *Plan showing the insertion of the building in the Pariser Platz.*
Page 171: *The interior volumes, including the decoration, which is the responsibility of Elisabeth de Portzamparc.*

Seite 170: *Ein Lageplan, der veranschaulicht, wie sich das Gebäude in den Pariser Platz einfügt.*
Seite 171: *Die Innenräume einschließlich Innenausstattung, die der Verantwortung von Elisabeth de Portzamparc unterliegt.*

Page 170: *Plan de situation montrant l'insertion du projet dans la Pariser Platz.*
Page 171: *Les volumes intérieurs, dont la décoration a été confiée à Élisabeth de Portzamparc.*

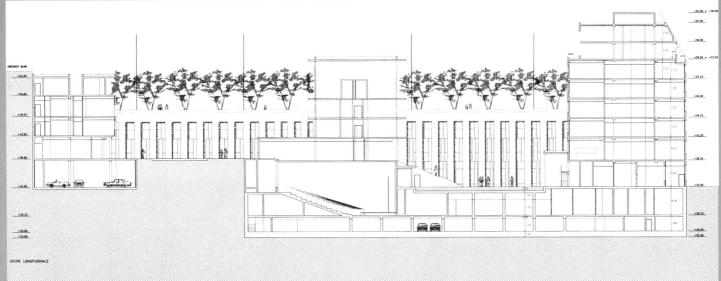

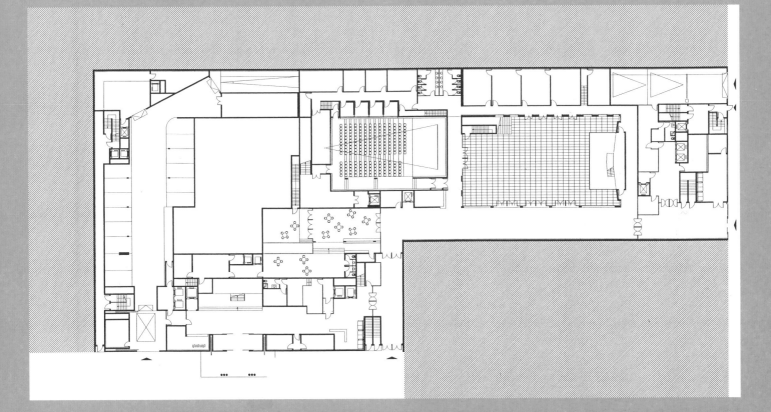

Bernard Tschumi

Although he is a resident of the United States, Bernard Tschumi has dual French/Swiss nationality. He studied in Paris at the ETH in Zurich. He has taught at the AA in London (1970–79), at the Institute for Architecture and Urban Studies in New York (1976), at Princeton (1976 and 1980), and at Columbia University in New York, where he is currently Dean of the Graduate School of Architecture, Planning and Preservation. Winner of the French Grand Prix National d'Architecture (1996), he was named Chief Architect of the Parc de la Villette in Paris in 1983. Influential in terms of theory for some time, Tschumi has built relatively little. Aside from numerous competitions in which he participated (Kansai Airport, 1988; National Library of France, 1989; Kyoto JR Railway Station, 1990), he has been responsible for the Parc de la Villette project, with its numerous small "follies," and a Glass Video Gallery in Groningen, The Netherlands (1990). Aside from the Le Fresnoy National Studio for Contemporary Arts at Tourcoing, France (1991–97), and the Lerner Student Center, Columbia University, New York (1994–99) published here, Bernard Tschumi is working on a new School of Architecture in Marne-la-Vallée, France (1994–98), and a railway station in Lausanne, Switzerland – the Interface Flon (1998–2000).

Obwohl er seinen ständigen Wohnsitz in den USA hat, besitzt Bernard Tschumi die Staatsbürgerschaft sowohl Frankreichs als auch der Schweiz. Nach dem Studium in Paris und an der ETH Zürich lehrte er an der Architectural Association in London (1970–79), am Institute for Architecture and Urban Studies in New York (1976), in Princeton, Kalifornien (1976 und 1980), sowie an der Columbia University in New York, wo er gegenwärtig das Amt des Dekans der Graduate School of Architecture, Planning and Preservation innehat. 1983 wurde Tschumi zum leitenden Architekten des Parc de la Villette in Paris ernannt, worauf er 1996 den französischen Grand Prix National d'Architecture erhielt. Tschumi übte auf dem Gebiet der Architekturtheorie jahrelang erheblichen Einfluß aus, baute aber relativ wenig. Neben der Teilnahme an mehreren Wettbewerben (Flughafen Kansai, 1988; Französische Nationalbibliothek, Paris, 1989; JR-Bahnhof in Kyoto, 1990) war er verantwortlich für den Parc de la Villette mit seinen vielen kleinen »Follies« sowie für eine Video-Galerie aus Glas in Groningen, Niederlande (1990). Zur Zeit arbeitet Tschumi außer an dem hier vorgestellten Medien- und Kulturzentrum Le Fresnoy in Tourcoing, Frankreich, (1991–97) und dem Lerner Student Center an der Columbia University, New York (1994–99) an einer neuen Hochschule für Architektur in Marne-la-Vallée, Frankreich (1994–98) und an einem Bahnhof in Lausanne, Schweiz, dem Interface Flon (1998–2000).

Bien que résidant aux États-Unis, Bernard Tschumi possède la double nationalité française et suisse. Il étudie à Paris et à l'ETH de Zurich, puis enseigne à l'AA de Londres (1970–79), à l'Institute for Architecture and Urban Studies à New York (1976), à Princeton (1976 et 1980) et à l'Université de Columbia à New York, où il est actuellement doyen de la Graduate School of Architecture, Planning and Preservation. Nommé architecte en chef du Parc de la Villette à Paris en 1983, il reçoit le Grand Prix National d'Architecture français en 1996. Théoricien influent pour un certain temps, il n'a que relativement peu construit. En dehors des nombreux concours auxquels il a participé (Aéroport de Kansai, 1988; Bibliothèque Nationale de France, 1989; Gare JR à Kyoto, 1990), il est l'auteur du projet du Parc de la Villette et de ses nombreuses petites folies, et d'une vidéo-galerie à Groningue, Pays-Bas (1990). Outre le Studio national des Arts Contemporains du Fresnoy à Tourcoing, France (1991–97), et le Lerner Student Center à l'Université de Columbia, New York (1994–99) publiés ici, il travaille sur les projets d'une nouvelle école d'architecture Marne-la-Vallée, France (1994–98), et d'une gare à Lausanne, Suisse (1998–2000).

Bernard Tschumi, Le Fresnoy National Studio for Contemporary Arts, Tourcoing, France, 1991–97.

Bernard Tschumi, Medien- und Kulturzentrum Le Fresnoy, Tourcoing, Frankreich, 1991–97.

Bernard Tschumi, Le Fresnoy, Studio national des Arts Contemporains, Tourcoing, France, 1991–97.

Le Fresnoy National Studio for Contemporary Arts

Tourcoing, France, 1991–1997

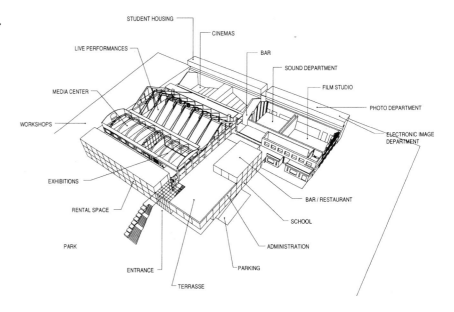

STUDENT HOUSING
CINEMAS
LIVE PERFORMANCES
BAR
SOUND DEPARTMENT
MEDIA CENTER
FILM STUDIO
PHOTO DEPARTMENT
WORKSHOPS
ELECTRONIC IMAGE DEPARTMENT
EXHIBITIONS
BAR / RESTAURANT
RENTAL SPACE
SCHOOL
PARK
ADMINISTRATION
ENTRANCE
PARKING
TERRASSE

"10,000 square meters of an international center for contemporary arts inserted into Le Fresnoy, in Tourcoing, France. A school, a film studio, a médiatheque, spectacle and exhibition halls, two cinemas, laboratories for research and production (sound, electronic image, film and video), administrative offices, housing and a bar/restaurant: this," says the architect, "is the multiple and expansive program of the new center." Rather than demolishing existing buildings, Bernard Tschumi chose to create an enormous roof over them, creating what he calls an "in-between" space, which can be used to move about the center for example. This movement through space, and the encounter that it implies between the old and the new, is at the heart of Tschumi's idea of a fractured yet very practical type of architecture. It is, as he says, "How architecture is about identifying, and ultimately, releasing potentialities hidden in a site, a program, or their social context."

»Ein Internationales Zentrum für Zeitgenössische Kunst mit 10 000 m² Gesamtfläche, eingefügt in Le Fresnoy, Tourcoing. Eine Schule, ein Filmstudio, eine Médiatheque, Räumlichkeiten für Ausstellungen und Aufführungen, zwei Kinos, Forschungs- und Produktionsstudios (für Ton, elektronisch erzeugte Bilder, Film und Video) sowie Verwaltungsbüros, Wohnungen und eine Bar bzw. ein Restaurant – das«, so der Architekt, »ist das ebenso vielfältige wie expansive Programm des neuen Zentrums.« Anstatt die existierende Bebauung einzureißen, hat sich Bernard Tschumi dafür entschieden, sie mit einem gewaltigen Dach zu überdecken und auf diese Weise das zu erzeugen, was er »Zwischenräume« nennt und die zum Beispiel dazu dienen können, sich innerhalb des Zentrums zu bewegen. Eine solche Bewegung durch den Raum und die damit verbundene Begegnung zwischen dem Alten und dem Neuen stehen im Mittelpunkt von Tschumis Idee einer zwar gebrochenen, aber gleichwohl praktischen Architektur. »Es geht darum«, so Tschumi, »wie die Architektur Möglichkeiten, die in einem Ort, einem Programm oder in deren sozialen Kontexten verborgen sind, zu identifizieren und schließlich freizulegen vermag«.

«10 000 m² de centre international d'art contemporain à insérer au Fresnoy, près de Tourcoing. Une école, un studio de cinéma, une médiathèque, des salles de spectacle et d'exposition, deux cinémas, des laboratoires de recherche et de production (son, image électronique, film et vidéo), bureaux administratifs, logements et bar-restaurant, tel était», selon l'architecte, «le programme multiple et foisonnant de ce nouveau centre.» Plutôt que de démolir les bâtiments existants, Bernard Tschumi a décidé de les recouvrir d'un énorme toit, créant ce qu'il appelle un espace «intermédiaire», qui peut permettre, par exemple, les déplacements à l'intérieur du centre. Ce mouvement dans l'espace, et les rencontres qu'il implique entre l'ancien et le nouveau, est au cœur de l'idée de Tschumi d'un type d'architecture à la fois pratique et très fracturé, une réponse au problème concernant la façon dont «l'architecture traite de l'identification et, en dernier lieu, du relâchement des potentialités cachées dans un site, un programme, ou leur contexte social.»

A drawing and photos show how the addition of an overarching roof has rendered the existing buildings viable while creating new areas, which Bernard Tschumi calls "in-between" spaces.

Die Zeichnung und die Fotos zeigen, wie das hinzugefügte, alles überragende Dach die bereits existierenden Gebäude erhalten und zugleich neue Bereiche geschaffen hat, die Bernard Tschumi als »Zwischenbereich« bezeichnet.

Dessin et photos montrant comment la création d'un toit qui recouvre l'ensemble a permis de maintenir l'utilisation des constructions existantes, tout en créant de nouvelles zones, appelées par Bernard Tschumi les espaces «intermédiaires».

The skeletal, modern roof has numerous walkways hung above the roofs of the existing buildings. It is this roof that declares the fundamentally contemporary nature of the design.

An dem skelettartigen neuen Dach hängen zahlreiche Gänge über den Dächern der bereits zuvor existierenden Gebäude. Es ist dieses Dach, das den grundsätzlich zeitgenössischen Charakter des Entwurfs ausmacht.

Suspendues à la structure squelettique du nouveau toit, de nombreuses coursives passent par-dessus les toitures des bâtiments préexistants. C'est ce toit qui affiche la nature fondamentalement contemporaine de ce projet.

Bernard Tschumi: Le Fresnoy, 1991–97 **177**

The movement of students through the space of the Art Studio is encouraged by the system of walkways. The whole is intended to heighten the perception of space, and also to encourage thought about what it means to be "contemporary."

Das Gängesystem ermuntert die Studenten dazu, den Raum des Kunstzentrums zu durchmessen. Der Entwurf soll die Raumwahrnehmung schärfen und zum Nachdenken darüber veranlassen, was »zeitgenössisch« heißt.

Les déplacements des étudiants à travers les espaces du Studio sont facilités par tout un systèmes de coursives. L'ensemble veut renforcer la perception de l'espace et encourager une réflexion sur le sens du «contemporain».

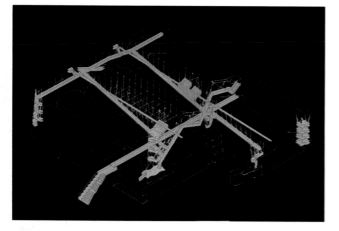

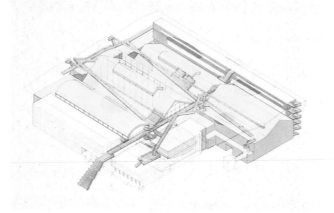

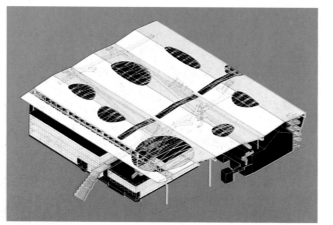

178 Bernard Tschumi: Le Fresnoy, 1991–97

Lerner Student Center, Columbia University
New York, New York, 1994–1999

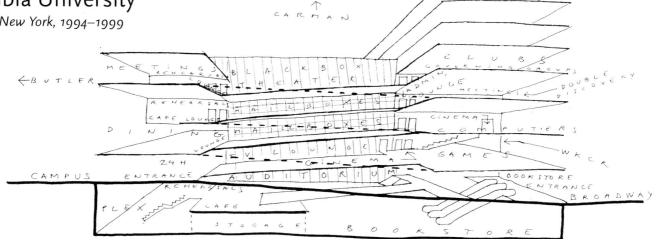

Located in upper Manhattan, on the grounds of Columbia University, where Bernard Tschumi is the Dean of the School of Architecture, this 22,500 m² student activity center "will contain a combined auditorium/assembly hall seating 1,100–1,500, dining facilities, lounges, meeting rooms, a bookstore, a radio station, student clubs and games rooms, administrative space, a black box theater, 6,000 mailboxes as well as expanded computer facilities for student use." By fitting the structure into the original 1890 McKim, Mead and White masterplan for the campus, and using materials like granite and brick, the architect intentionally looked for a design that would be harmonious with its surroundings. Taking advantage of the sloping terrain "where the campus side is half a story higher than the neighborhood (Broadway) side," Tschumi created a series of ramps connecting staggered half-floors, a dynamic solution highlighted by the use of glass ramps and walls. "During the day," according to the architect, "light filters through the suspended glass ramps. At night as light glows from the inside, figures in movement along this route will appear as in a silent shadow theater."

Das in Uptown Manhattan auf dem Gelände der Columbia-Universität – Tschumi übt dort das Amt eines Dekans der Architekturfakultät aus – errichtete, insgesamt 22 500 m² große Studentenzentrum umfaßt »ein Auditorium bzw. eine Aula für 1100–1500 Personen, Speisesäle, Salons, Begegnungsräume, eine Buchhandlung, eine Radiostation, Studentenclubs und Spielzimmer, Verwaltungsbüros, einen multi-funktionalen Raum, 6 000 Briefkästen sowie eine umfangreiche Ausstattung an Computern für die Studenten«. Indem er sich bei seinem Entwurf auf den aus dem Jahre 1890 stammenden Gesamtplan für den Campus von McKim, Mead und White stützte und zudem Materialien wie Granit oder Backstein einsetzte, versuchte Tschumi ganz bewußt den Neubau in seiner Gestaltung harmonisch in die bereits bestehende Bebauung einzufügen. Dabei machte er sich das abfallende Terrain zunutze, wobei »die Campus-Seite ein halbes Stockwerk höher liegt als die Straßenseite am Broadway«, und schuf eine Reihe von Rampen, die gegeneinander versetzte Halbstockwerke verbinden – eine dynamische Lösung, die durch die Verwendung von Glas für diese Rampen und Wände noch betont wird. »Am Tag«, so Tschumi, »strömt Licht in die aufgehängten Glasrampen. Nachts, da das Licht von innen kommt, werden die diesen Weg abschreitenden Menschen wie die Gestalten eines stummen Schattenspiels erscheinen.«

Situé dans le haut de Manhattan, sur le campus de l'Université de Columbia, où Bernard Tschumi est doyen de l'École d'architecture, ce centre pour étudiants de 22 500 m² «contiendra à la fois un auditorium de 1100 à 1500 places, un restaurant universitaire, des salles diverses, des salles de réunion, une librairie, une station de radio, des clubs d'étudiants, des salles de sport, des espaces administratifs, un petit théâtre, 6 000 boîtes aux lettres et des installations informatiques pour les étudiants». En intégrant ce bâtiment dans le plan directeur du campus dessiné par McKim, Mead et White dans les années 1890, et en faisant appel à des matériaux comme le granit et la brique, l'architecte a volontairement recherché l'harmonie avec l'environnement. Profitant de la pente du terrain («le campus est d'un demi-étage plus haut que le voisinage, côté Broadway»), Tschumi a créé une série de rampes en zig-zag qui réunissent des demi-niveaux, solution dynamique que soulignent les rampes et les murs de verre. «Pendant la journée», explique l'architecte, «la lumière filtre à travers ces rampes suspendues en verre. La nuit, la lumière émane de l'intérieur, et les figures en mouvement semblent jouer comme dans un théâtre d'ombres silencieux.»

Pages 180–183: A drawing and computer perspectives emphasize the skewed design of the internal walkways. Visible from the outside, they create an impression of vitality that is not typical of most university buildings.

Seite 180–183: Die Zeichnung und die Computersimulationen zeigen die Schrägen, die der Entwurf für die internen Gänge vorsieht. Diese von außen sichtbaren Gänge erzeugen einen Eindruck von Vitalität, der für die meisten Universitätsbauten nicht gerade typisch ist.

Pages 180–183: Dessin et perspectives par ordinateur mettent en valeur la conception en zig-zag des passerelles internes. Visibles de l'extérieur, elles donnent une impression de vitalité assez rare dans des bâtiments universitaires.

Biographies | Biographien

Mario Botta
Via Ciani 16
6904 Lugano, Switzerland
Tel : + 41 91 972 86 25
Fax : + 41 91 970 14 54

Atelier d'Architecture Chaix & Morel et Associés
16, rue des Haies
75020 Paris, France
Tel: + 33 1 43 70 69 24
Fax: + 33 1 43 70 67 65

Mario Botta

Born in Mendrisio, Switzerland (1943), Mario Botta left school at fifteen to become apprentice in a Lugano architectural office, and designed his first house the following year. After studies in Milan and Venice, he worked briefly in the entourage of Le Corbusier and Louis Kahn, and often with Luigi Snozzi. Built private houses in Cadenazzo (1970–71), Riva San Vitale (1971–73) or Ligornetto (1975–76) – all in Switzerland. Major buildings include: Cultural Center André Malraux, Chambéry, France (1982–87); Médiathèque, Villeurbanne, France (1984–88); Church San Giovanni Battista, Mogno, Switzerland (1986–98); Évry Cathedral, France (1988–95); San Francisco Museum of Modern Art, California (1989/92–95); Chapel Santa Maria degli Angeli, Monte Tamaro, Switzerland (1990–96); Museum Jean Tinguely, Basel, Switzerland (1993–96); The Synagoge and Cultural Center in Tel Aviv, Israel (1996–98), and a design for the renovation of the Presbytery of the Cathedral of Santa Maria del Fiore, Florence, Italy (1997).

Mario Botta, geboren 1943 im schweizerischen Mendrisio, verließ die Schule bereits im Alter von 15 Jahren und machte eine Lehre in einem Architekturbüro in Lugano; sein erstes Haus entwarf er im darauffolgenden Jahr. Nach Studien in Mailand und Venedig wirkte er kurzzeitig im Mitarbeiterstab von Le Corbusier und Louis Kahn und arbeitete oft mit Luigi Snozzi. Er entwarf Einfamilienhäuser wie in Cadenazzo (1970–71), Riva San Vitale (1971–73) oder in Ligornetto (1975–76) – alle in der Schweiz. Zu Bottas wichtigsten Projekten zählen: Kulturzentrum André Malraux, Chambéry, Frankreich (1982–87); Médiathèque, Villeurbanne, Frankreich (1984–88); Kirche San Giovanni Battista, Mogno, Schweiz (1986–98); Kathedrale von Évry, Frankreich (1988–95); Museum of Modern Art, San Francisco, Kalifornien (1989/92–95); Kapelle Santa Maria degli Angeli, Monte Tamaro, Schweiz (1990–96); Jean Tinguely-Museum, Basel, Schweiz (1993–96); die Synagoge mit jüdischem Kulturzentrum in Tel Aviv, Israel (1996–98) sowie Entwurf für die Neugestaltung des Presbyteriums der Kirche Santa Maria del Fiore in Florenz, Italien (1997).

Né en 1943 à Mendrisio (Suisse), Mario Botta quitte l'école à 15 ans pour commencer son apprentissage dans une agence d'architecture de Lugano. Il dessine sa première maison l'année suivante. Après des études à Milan et Venise, il travaille brièvement dans l'entourage de Le Corbusier et de Louis Kahn et souvent avec Luigi Snozzi. Il construit des maisons individuelles comme à Cadenazzo (1970–71), Riva San Vitale (1971–73) ou Ligornetto (1975–76) – toutes situées en Suisse. Parmi ses principales réalisations: Maison de la culture André Malraux à Chambéry, France (1982–87); Médiathèque de Villeurbannes, France (1984–88); église San Giovanni Battista, Mogno, Suisse (1986–98); cathédrale d'Évry, France (1988–95); Musée d'art moderne de San Francisco, Californie (1989/92–95); Chapelle Santa Maria degli Angeli, Mont Tamaro, Suisse (1990–96); Musée Jean Tinguely, Bâle, Suisse (1993–96); synagogue et centre culturel juif à Tel Aviv, Israël (1996–98); projet de rénovation du presbytère de la cathédrale de Santa Maria del Fiore, Florence, Italie (1997).

Chaix & Morel

Philippe Chaix and Jean-Paul Morel were both born in 1949, and have been associates since 1983. Chaix attended the École des Beaux-Arts, Paris (UP6, DPLG, 1972), while Morel received his degree in Nancy, France (École UP1, DPLG, 1976). Their built work includes: the Zénith, Parc de la Villette, Paris (1984); two other Zénith concert halls in Montpellier (1986) and Orléans (1996); the École des Ponts et Chaussées et des Sciences Géographiques, Marne-la-Vallée (1990–96); Archeological Museum, Saint-Romain-en-Gal (1994–96); and the Avancée, Renault Technocenter, Guyancourt (1995–97) – all in France. Current work includes a soccer stadium in Amiens (1995–98); and the European Center of Federal Express at Roissy near Paris (1998–99) – both in France.

Philippe Chaix und Jean-Paul Morel, beide 1949 geboren, haben seit 1983 eine Bürogemeinschaft. Chaix besuchte die École des Beaux-Arts in Paris (UP6, DPLG, 1972), während Morel 1976 an der École UP1 in Nancy, Frankreich, graduierte (DPLG). Zu ihren realisierten Projekten zählen: Zénith, Parc de la Villette, Paris (1984); zwei weitere Zénith-Konzerthallen in Montpellier (1986) und Orléans (1996); École des Ponts et Chaussées et des Sciences Géographiques, Marne-la-Vallée (1990–96); Archäologisches Museum, Saint-Romain-en-Gal (1994–96); und das Avancée, Technologiezentrum von Renault, Guyancourt (1995–97) – alle in Frankreich. Laufende Projekte sind unter anderem ein Fußballstadion in Amiens (1995–98) und die Europazentrale von Federal Express in Roissy nahe Paris (1998–99) – beide ebenfalls in Frankreich.

Associés depuis 1983, Philippe Chaix et Jean-Paul Morel sont tous deux nés en 1949. Chaix étudie à l'École des Beaux-Arts de Paris (UP6), dont il sort diplômé (DPLG) en 1972, tandis que Morel est diplômé (DPLG) de l'École UP1 de Nancy, France, en 1976. Parmi leurs réalisations: le Zénith du Parc de la Villette à Paris (1984); deux autres salles Zénith pour Montpellier (1986) et Orléans (1996); l'École des Ponts et Chaussées et des Sciences Géographiques, Marne-la-Vallée (1990–96); le Musée archéologique de Saint-Romain-en-Gal (1994–96); et L'Avancée pour le Technocentre Renault, Guyancourt (1995–97) – toutes situées en France. Ils travaillent actuellement sur un stade de football à Amiens, France (1995–98), et le Centre européen de Federal Express, à l'aéroport de Roissy, France (1998–99).

David Chipperfield Architects
1A Cobham Mews, Agar Grove
London NW1 9SB, Great Britain
Tel: + 44 171 267 9422
Fax: + 44 171 267 9347

Jo Coenen & Co
St. Servaaskloster 28
6211 TE Maastricht, The Netherlands
Tel: + 31 43 351 18 00
Fax: + 31 43 351 00 02

EEA Erick van Egeraat associated architects
Calandstraat 23
3016 CA Rotterdam, The Netherlands
Tel : + 31 10 436 9686
Fax: + 31 10 436 9573

David Chipperfield

Born in London 1953, David Chipperfield obtained his Diploma in Architecture from the Architectural Association (London, 1977). Worked in offices of Norman Foster and Richard Rogers, before establishing David Chipperfield Architects (London, 1984). Built work includes: Private Museum in Japan (1987); Design Store in Kyoto, Japan (1989); River & Rowing Museum, Henley-on-Thames, Great Britain (1989/96–97); Matsumoto Corporation Headquarters, Okayama, Japan (1990); Plant Gallery and Central Hall of the Natural History Museum, London (1993); Wagamama Restaurant, London (1996); Office Building in Düsseldorf, Germany (1997); Cornerhouse Cinema, Manchester, Great Britain (1997); Joseph Menswear shop, London (1997); Circus Restaurant, London (1997). Current work includes: the headquarters building for the Landeszentralbank, Gera, Germany; the Grassimuseum, Leipzig, Germany; the Neues Museum, Berlin, Germany; Shore Club Hotel, Miami, USA; two hotels in New York, USA; private house in Spain; house in Martha's Vineyard, USA.

Geboren 1953 in London, erhielt David Chipperfield sein Architektur-Diplom an der Architectural Association in London (1977). Tätigkeit in den Büros von Norman Foster und Richard Rogers, 1984 Gründung des Büros David Chipperfield Architects in London. Realisierte unter anderem: Privatmuseum in Japan (1987); Design Store in Kyoto, Japan (1989); River & Rowing Museum, Henley-on-Thames, Großbritannien (1989/96–97); Hauptzentrale für Matsumoto, Okayama, Japan (1990); Pflanzengalerie und zentrale Haupthalle des Natural History Museum, London (1993); Wagamama Restaurant, London (1996); Bürogebäude in Düsseldorf, Deutschland (1997); Cornerhouse Cinema, Manchester, Großbritannien (1997); Joseph Menswear shop, London (1997); Circus Restaurant, London (1997). Laufende Projekte: Landeszentralbank in Gera, Deutschland; das Grassimuseum in Leipzig, Deutschland; Neues Museum, Berlin; Shore Club Hotel, Miami, USA; zwei Hotels in New York, USA; Privathaus in Spanien sowie in Martha's Vineyard, USA.

Né à Londres en 1953, David Chipperfield est diplômé de l'Architectural Association (AA, Londres, 1977). Il travaille dans les agences de Norman Foster et de Richard Rogers, avant de fonder David Chipperfield Architects à Londres en 1984. Parmi ses réalisations: Musée privé au Japon (1987); Design Store in Kyoto, Japon (1989); River & Rowing Museum, Henley-on-Thames, Grande-Bretagne (1989/96–97); siège social de Matsumoto, Okayama, Japon (1990); galerie des plantes et hall central du Natural History Museum, Londres (1993); Wagamama Restaurant, Londres (1996); un immeuble de bureaux à Düsseldorf, Allemagne (1997); Cinéma Cornerhouse, Manchester, Grande-Bretagne (1997); Joseph Menswear shop, Londres (1997); Circus Restaurant, Londres (1997). Parmi ses réalisations récentes: la Landeszentralbank de Gera, Allemagne; le Grassimuseum de Leipzig, Allemagne; la reconstruction du Neues Museum, Berlin, Allemagne; l'hôtel Shore Club, Miami, États-Unis; deux hôtels à New York, États-Unis; une résidence privée en Espagne et sur Martha's Vineyard aux États-Unis.

Jo Coenen

Born in 1949 in Heerlen, The Netherlands, Jo Coenen graduated from the Eindhoven University of Technology in 1975. Between 1976 and 1979 he lectured both in Eindhoven and in Maastricht, and worked with Luigi Snozzi, James Stirling, and Aldo van Eyck. He opened his own office in 1979, and built his first important project, a library and exhibition gallery in Heerlen, The Netherlands (1983–86). Other built works include the Chamber of Commerce, Maastricht, The Netherlands (1988–91); offices for the Haans Company, Tilburg, The Netherlands (1989–91); and the Netherlands Architecture Institute, Rotterdam (1993). He also designed a Library for the Delft University of Technology, The Netherlands (1992), an arts college, ballet school and city concert hall for Tilburg, The Netherlands (1992–96), and a masterplan for Treptow, Berlin, Germany (1993). More recent work includes a police station in Sittard (1997), and an apartment building in Rijswijkseplein area of the Hague (1997) – both in The Netherlands.

Der 1949 in Heerlen, Niederlande, geborene Jo Coenen erhielt 1975 sein Diplom an der Technischen Universität Eindhoven. Zwischen 1976 und 1979 lehrte er in Eindhoven und in Maastricht (Niederlande) – und arbeitete in den Büros von Luigi Snozzi, James Stirling und Aldo van Eyck. Nach Gründung eines eigenen Büros im Jahre 1979 baute er als sein erstes wichtiges Projekt eine Bibliothek samt Ausstellungsfläche in Heerlen, Niederlande (1983–86). Andere realisierte Bauten sind die Handelskammer in Maastricht (1988–91); Büros für die Firma Haans in Tilburg (1989–91) und das Niederländische Architektur-Institut in Rotterdam (1993), alle in den Niederlanden. Außerdem entwarf er eine Bibliothek für die TU in Delft, Niederlande (1992), eine Kunsthochschule, eine Ballettschule und eine Konzerthalle für Tilburg, Niederlande (1992–96) sowie einen Gesamtplan für Berlin-Treptow (1993). Zu Coenens jüngsten Arbeiten zählen eine Polizeiwache in Sittard (1997) und ein Apartmenthaus im Stadtteil in Rijswijkseplein von Den Haag (1997) – beide in den Niederlanden.

Né en 1949 à Heerlen (Pays-Bas), Jo Coenen est diplômé de l'Université de Technologie d'Eindhoven en 1975. De 1976 à 1979, il enseigne à Eindhoven et Maastricht, et travaille pour Luigi Snozzi, James Stirling et Aldo van Eyck. Il ouvre son agence en 1979, et réalise son premier projet important, une bibliothèque et une galerie d'exposition à Heerlen (1983–86). Parmi ses réalisations: la Chambre de Commerce de Maastricht, Pays-Bas (1988–91); les bureaux de la société Haans, à Tilburg, Pays-Bas (1989–91); l'Institut néerlandais d'architecture (NAI), à Rotterdam (1993). Il a également conçu une bibliothèque pour l'Université de Technologie de Delft, Pays-Bas (1992), un collège d'enseignement artistique et une salle de concert à Tilburg, Pays-Bas (1992–96), ainsi qu'un plan directeur pour Treptow, Berlin, Allemagne (1993). Réalisations plus récentes: un poste de police à Sittard, Pays-Bas (1997) et un immeuble d'appartements dans le quartier du Rijswijkseplein à la Haye, Pays-Bas (1997).

Erick van Egeraat

Born in 1936 in Amsterdam, Erick van Egeraat attended the Technical University Delft Department of Architecture, from which he graduated in 1984. Professional practice since 1981. Co-founder of Mecanoo architects in Delft (1983). Founder of EEA Erick van Egeraat associated architects (1995). Recent and current work includes: Nature and Science Museum, Rotterdam, The Netherlands (1989–95); Faculty building of the Faculties of Physics and Astronomy, University of Leiden, The Netherlands (1993–97); Extension ING Bank & NNH Head Offices, Budapest, Hungary (1993–97); Housing Sternstrasse, Dresden, Germany (1994); School for Fashion and Graphic Industry, Utrecht, The Netherlands (1994–97); reconstruction of the Grote Markt square east, Groningen, The Netherlands (1995–98); restaurant and luxury apartments in Rotterdam, The Netherlands (1995–99); Crawford Municipal Art Gallery, Cork, Ireland (1996–98); Royal Netherlands Embassy and Embassy housing, New Delhi, India (1997–2002); Photographer's Gallery, London (1998–2001); and theatres for the Royal Shakespeare Company, Stratford-upon-Avon, Great Britain (1998–2004).

Geboren 1936 in Amsterdam, besuchte Erick van Egeraat die Technische Universität in Delft, deren Diplom er 1984 erlangte. Tätigkeit als Architekt seit 1981. 1983 Mitbegründer des Büros Mecanoo in Delft. Gründung des Büros EEA Erick van Egeraat associated architects im Jahre 1995. Wichtige Projekte: Naturkunde- und Wissenschaftsmuseum in Rotterdam, Niederlande (1989–95); Gebäude der Fakultät für Physik und Astronomie der Universität Leiden, Niederlande (1993–97); Erweiterung der ING Bank und Hauptzentrale von NNH in Budapest, Ungarn (1993–97); Wohnanlage Sternstraße in Dresden, Deutschland (1994); Fachtechnisches Gymnasium in Utrecht, Niederlande (1994–97); Rekonstruktion des Grote Markt (Ost) in Groningen, Niederlande (1995–98); Restaurant und Luxusappartments in Rotterdam, Niederlande (1995–99); Crawford Municipial Art Gallery in Cork, Irland (1996–98); Royal Netherlands Embassy and Embassy Housing, New Delhi, Indien (1997–2002); Photographer's Gallery, London (1998–2001); Theater für die Royal Shakespeare Company, Stratford-upon-Avon, Großbritannien (1998–2004).

Né en 1936 à Amsterdam, Erick van Egeraat suit les cours du département d'architecture de l'Université Technique de Delft, dont il sort diplômé en 1984, tout en exerçant une activité professionelle depuis 1981. Cofondateur de Mecanoo Architects à Delft (1983). Fondateur d'EEA Erick van Egeraat associated architects (1995). Réalisations: Musée de la Nature et de la Science, Rotterdam, Pays-Bas (1989–95); bâtiment pour les facultés de physique et d'astronomie de l'Université de Leyde, Pays-Bas (1993–97); extension de l'ING Bank et siège social de NNH, Budapest, Hongrie (1993–97); immeuble d'appartements, Sternstrasse, Dresde, Allemagne (1994); École de mode et de graphique industrielle, Utrecht, Pays-Bas (1994–97); reconstruction de la place Grote Markt secteur est de Groningue, Pays-Bas (1995–98); restaurant et appartements de luxe à Rotterdam, Pays-Bas (1995–99); Municipal Art Gallery de Crawford, Cork, Irlande (1996–98); l'ambassade royale des Pays-Bas et ses appartements de fonction, New Delhi, Inde (1997–2002); Photographer's Gallery, Londres (1998–2001); théâtres pour la Royal Shakespeare Company, Stratford-upon-Avon, Grande-Bretagne (1998–2004).

Foster and Partners
Riverside Three, 22 Hester Road
London SW11 4AN, Great Britain
Tel: + 44 171 738 0455
Fax: + 44 171 738 1107

Norman Foster

Born in Manchester, 1935, Norman Foster studied
Architecture and City Planning at Manchester University
(1961). Awarded Henry Fellowship to Yale University,
where he received M. Arch. degree, and met Richard
Rogers with whom he created Team 4. Royal Gold
Medal for Architecture (1983); knighted in 1990;
American Institute of Architects Gold Medal for
Architecture (1994). Sir Norman Foster has notably
built: IBM Pilot Head Office, Cosham, Great Britain
(1970–71); Sainsbury Centre for Visual Arts and
Crescent Wing, University of East Anglia, Norwich,
Great Britain (1976–77; 1989–91); Hongkong and
Shanghai Banking Corporation Headquarters, Hong
Kong (1981–86); London's Third Airport, Stansted,
Great Britain (1987–91); University of Cambridge,
Faculty of Law, Cambridge, Great Britain (1993–95);
Commerzbank Headquarters, Frankfurt am Main,
Germany (1994–97). Airport at Chek Lap Kok, Hong
Kong (1995–98); Current projects include: New German
Parliament, Reichstag, Berlin, Germany (1995–99);
British Museum Redevelopment, London (1997–2000).

Norman Foster wurde 1935 in Manchester geboren und
studierte Architektur und Städteplanung an der University of Manchester. Nach seiner Abschlußprüfung
(1961) erhielt er ein Stipendium (Henry Fellowship) für
die Yale University, wo er 1963 seinen Master's Degree
in Architektur erlangte und Richard Rogers kennenlernte, mit dem er das Team 4 gründete. 1983 erhielt
Foster die Royal Gold Medal for Architecture, 1990
wurde er in den Adelsstand erhoben. Im Jahre 1994
bekam er die Gold Medal for Architecture des AIA. Zu
seinen herausragenden Bauten gehören das IBM Pilot
Head Office, Cosham, Großbritannien (1970–71); das
Sainsbury Centre for Visual Arts and Crescent Wing der
University of East Anglia in Norwich, Großbritannien
(1976–77; 89–91); das Gebäude der Hongkong und
Shanghai Bank in Hongkong (1981–86); der Terminal
des Stansted Airport, London (1987–91); die Faculty of
Law der Universität Cambridge, Großbritannien
(1993–95), die Hauptverwaltung der Commerzbank in
Frankfurt am Main (1994–97) und der Chek Lap Kok-
Flughafen in Hongkong (1995–98). Zur Zeit arbeitet
sein Büro u.a. an der Fertigstellung des Deutschen
Bundestags im Reichstag in Berlin (1995–99) und am
Umbau des British Museum in London (1997–2000).

Né à Manchester en 1935, il étudie l'architecture et
l'urbanisme à l'Université de Manchester, dont il est
diplômé en 1961. Il bénéficie d'un Henry Fellowship
pour l'Université de Yale, où il passe son M. Arch. et
rencontre Richard Rogers avec lequel il fonde Team 4.
Médaille royale d'or pour l'architecture (1983); anobli en
1990; médaille d'or de l'American Institute of Architects
pour l'architecture (1994). Sir Norman Foster a
construit en particulier: les bureaux pilotes d'IBM,
Cosham, Grande-Bretagne (1970–71); le Sainsbury
Centre for Visual Arts et la Crescent Wing, Université
d'East Anglia, Norwich, Grande-Bretagne (1976–77,
1989–91); le siège social de la Hongkong and Shanghai
Banking Corporation, Hong Kong (1981–86); le
troisième aéroport de Londres, Standsted (1987–91); la
faculté de droit de l'Université de Cambridge, Grande-
Bretagne (1993–95); le siège social de la Commerzbank,
Francfort-sur-le-Main, Allemagne (1994–97). L'aéroport
de Chek Lap Kok, Hong Kong (1995–98); Projets
actuels: nouveau parlement allemand, Reichstag,
Berlin, Allemagne (1995–99); redéploiement du British
Museum, Londres (1997–2000).

Thomas Herzog + Partner, Hanns J. Schrade
Imhofstrasse 3a
80805 Munich, Germany
Tel: + 49 89 360 57 0
Fax: + 49 89 360 57 139

Søren Robert Lund Architects
St. Kongensgade 110E,1
1264 Copenhagen, Denmark
Tel: + 45 33 91 01 00
Fax: + 45 33 91 45 10

Penkhues Architekten
Brandaustrasse 10
34127 Kassel, Germany
Tel: + 49 561 9 83 52 10
Fax: + 49 561 8 41 50

Thomas Herzog

Born in 1941 in Munich. Diploma, Technical University Munich, 1965; Doctorate, University of Rome „La Sapienza" (1972). Opened office (1972); created partnership with Hanns Jörg Schrade (1994). Notable buildings: Houses in Regensburg (1978–79) and Munich (1981–83), both in Germany; Solar House Module, Sulmona, Italy (1983–85); Conference and Exhibition Hall, Linz, Austria (1988–93); Production Halls and Central Energy Plant for Wilkhahn, Eimbeckhausen, Germany (1989–92); and Hall 26, Deutsche Messe, Hanover, Germany (1994–96). 1971–72 Rome Prize; 1981 Mies-van-der-Rohe Prize; 1993 Gold Medal, Bund Deutscher Architekten (BDA); 1996 August Perret Prize of the UIA; 1998 La grande médaille d'or of the french Academy of Architects.

Geboren 1941 in München. Diplom an der TU München 1965. 1972 Promotion an der Universität La Sapienza in Rom. Im gleichen Jahr Gründung eines eigenen Architekturbüros. Seit 1994 Bürogemeinschaft mit Hanns Jörg Schrade. Wichtige Bauten: Wohnhäuser in Regensburg (1978–79) und München (1981–83); solarbetriebenes Hausmodul, Sulmona, Italien (1983–85); Kongreß- und Ausstellungshalle, Linz, Österreich (1988–93); Fertigungshallen und Energieversorgungszentrale für die Firma Wilkhahn, Eimbeckhausen, Deutschland (1989–92); Halle 26 der Deutschen Messe, Hannover, Deutschland (1994–96). 1971–72 Prix de Rome; 1981 Mies-van-der-Rohe Preis; 1993 Goldmedaille des Bundes Deutscher Architekten (BDA); 1996 August-Perret-Preis des Weltverbandes der Architekten UIA; 1998 La grande médaille d'or der französischen Akademie für Architektur.

Né en 1941 à Munich. Diplômé de l'Université technique de Munich (1965). Docteur de l'Université de Rome, La Sapienza (1972). Ouvre son agence la même année à Munich. S'associe à Hans Jörg Schrade (1994). Principales réalisations: Résidences privées à Ratisbonne (1978–79) et à Munich (1981–83); module de maison solaire, Sulmona, Italie (1983–85); hall de conférence et d'exposition, Linz, Autriche (1988–93); halls de production et centrale d'énergie pour Wilkhahn, Eimbeckhausen, Allemagne (1989–92); Hall 26 de la Deutsche Messe, Hanovre, Allemagne (1994–96). Prix de Rome en 1971–72; Prix Mies van der Rohe en 1981; médaille d'or du Bund Deutscher Architekten (BDA) en 1993; Prix Auguste Perret de l'UIA en 1996; grande médaille d'or de l'académie d'architecture française en 1998.

Søren Robert Lund

Born in Copenhagen, Denmark, 1962. Attended Royal Academy of Fine Arts, Copenhagen, Denmark (1982–89). Established own architectural office in Copenhagen, 1991. Recent and current work includes: Arken Museum of Modern Art, Copenhagen, Denmark (1988–96); Main lobby of a mall, Lyngby, Denmark (with Busk Design, 1991); the entrance area of Skagen Museum with the same partner (1991); Brick House, Allerød, Denmark (1996–97); Asia House, Copenhagen, Denmark (1996–97); Printing Factory, Slagelse, Denmark (phase one to be completed in 1999); global shop concept for a shoemaker (1999). Exhibition designs and competitions: Competition for the library in Alexandria, Egypt (Special Merit Award, 1989); Competition organized by the Aga Khan, city center of Samarkand, Uzbekistan (1991), Exhibition for Stockholm Cultural Capital 1998 (Stockholm, Sweden).

Geboren 1962 in Kopenhagen, Dänemark. Studium an der Königlichen Akademie der Schönen Künste in Kopenhagen, Dänemark (1982–89), dort 1991 Gründung eines eigenen Architekturbüros. Wichtige Projekte: Arken-Museum für Moderne Kunst, Kopenhagen, Dänemark (1988–96); Lobby eines Einkaufszentrums in Lyngby (Dänemark, gemeinsam mit Busk Design, 1991); Eingangszone des Skagen-Museums (ebenfalls mit Busk-Design, 1991); Backsteinhaus, Allerød, Dänemark (1996–97); Asia House, Kopenhagen, Dänemark (1996–97); Druckerei, Slagelse, Dänemark (Bauphase 1 bis 1999); Konzept für weltweite Geschäftsfilialen eines Schuhherstellers (1999). Ausstellungsentwürfe und Wettbewerbe: Wettbewerb für die Bibliothek in Alexandria, Ägypten (1989, Spezialpreis); Ideenwettbewerb, organisiert von der Aga Khan-Stiftung, für das Stadtzentrum von Samarkand (Usbekistan, 1991), Ausstellung für die Stadt Stockholm als Europäische Kulturhauptstadt 1998.

Né à Copenhague en 1962; études à l'Académie royale des Beaux-Arts de Copenhague (1982–89). Il fonde son agence en 1991. Parmi ses travaux récents ou en cours: Musée d'art moderne de l'Arken, Copenhague, Danemark (1988–96); hall principal d'un centre commercial à Lyngby (Danemark), avec Busk Design (1991); espace d'entrée du Musée de Skagen avec le même associé (1991); maison en briques, Allerød, Danemark (1996–97); Asia House, Copenhague, Danemark (1996–97); imprimerie à Slagelse, Danemark (première phase achevée en 1999); concept de boutiques globales pour un fabricant de chaussures. Conception d'expositions et concours: concours pour la bibliothèque d'Alexandrie, Égypte (1989), concours d'idées organisé par l'Aga Khan (1991) pour le centre de Samarkand (Ouzbékistan); exposition pour «Stockholm capitale culturelle de l'Europe» (1998).

Berthold Penkhues

Born in Schloss Holte, Westphalia, Germany (1955). Studied architecture and urban planning, University of Kassel, Germany (1976–84). Worked for firm of Josef Paul Kleihues (1980). DAAD scholarship, California fellowship (1984). UCLA Graduate School of Architecture and Urban Planning (California, M. Arch., 1984–86). Visiting critic, Southern California Institute of Architecture, Santa Monica. Worked in office Frank O. Gehry, Santa Monica, California (1986–89). Founded own firm in Kassel (1989). Since 1994 professor at the Polytechnik of Brunswick, Germany. Aside from the Korbach Museum, he participated in the competition for a hotel and city hall design in Kassel (1992); built a villa in Kassel (1993–98) and a fire station in Kaufungen (1995) – all in Germany. Won first prize in a competition for the Federal Labor Relations Court, Erfurt, Germany (1995) two first prizes in a design competition for town houses on Sternstrasse in Kassel, Germany (1997); and first prize for the design of a fire station in Kaarst, Germany (1998).

Geboren 1955 in Schloß Holte, Westfalen, Deutschland. Studium der Architektur und Stadtplanung an der Universität Kassel, Deutschland (1976–84). Tätigkeit im Büro von Josef Paul Kleihues (1980). Stipendium des DAAD, Fellowship in Kalifornien (1984). UCLA Graduate School of Architecture and Urban Planning, Kalifornien (1984–86, M. Arch.). Gastkritiker am Southern California Institute of Architecture in Santa Monica. Tätigkeit im Büro von Frank O. Gehry in Santa Monica, Kalifornien (1986–89). 1989 Gründung eines eigenen Büros in Kassel. Seit 1994 lehrt er an der Technischen Universität Braunschweig, Deutschland. Neben dem Museum in Korbach beteiligte er sich an einem Wettbewerb für ein Hotel mit Kongresszentrum in Kassel (1992), baute ein Villa in Kassel (1993–98) und einen Feuerwehrstützpunkt in Kaufungen, Deutschland (1995). Er gewann einen ersten Preis im Wettbewerb für das Bundesarbeitsgericht in Erfurt (1995) und zwei weitere erste Preise im Entwurfswettbewerb für Stadthäuser in der Kasseler Sternstraße (1997), sowie einen ersten Preis für den Entwuf der neuen Feuerwache in Kaarst bei Düsseldorf (1998).

Né à Schloss Holte en Westphalie, Allemagne (1955). Études d'architecture et d'urbanisme, Université de Cassel, Allemagne (1976–84). Travaille pour l'agence de Josef Paul Kleihues (1980). Bourse californienne DAAD. UCLA Graduate School of Architecture and Urban Planning (M. Arch.,1984–86). Critique invité au Southern California Institute of Architecture, à Santa Monica. Travaille pour Frank O. Gehry à Santa Monica, Californie (1986–89). Fonde son agence à Cassel, Allemagne (1989). Depuis 1994, il enseigne à l'université technique de Brunswick, Allemagne. Réalisations: Musée historique de Korbach, Allemagne (1995–97); concours pour un hôtel et un centre de congrès pour Cassel (1992); villa à Cassel (1993–98) et une caserne de pompiers à Kaufungen (1995) – toutes situées en Allemagne. Premier prix au concours de la Cour fédérale des relations du travail, Erfurt, Allemagne (1995); premiers prix du concours de conception de résidences urbaines à Cassel, Allemagne (1997) ainsi que le premier prix pour une poste d'incendie à Kaarst, Allemagne (1998).

Dominique Perrault Architecte
26, rue Bruneseau
75629 Paris cedex 13, France
Tel: + 33 1 44 06 00 00
Fax: + 33 1 44 06 00 99

Dominique Perrault

Dominique Perrault was born in 1953 in Clermont-Ferrand, France. He received his diploma as an architect from the École des Beaux-Arts UP 6 in Paris in 1978. He received a further degree in urbanism at the École nationale des Ponts et Chaussées, Paris, in 1979. He created his own firm in 1981 in Paris. Recent and current work includes the Engineering School (ESIEE) in Marne-la-Vallée, France (1984–87); the Hôtel industriel Jean-Baptiste Berlier, Paris (1986–90); Hôtel du département de la Meuse, Bar-le-Duc, France (1988–94); Bibliothèque Nationale de France, Paris (1989–97); a large-scale study of the urbanism of Bordeaux, France (1992–2000), and the Velodrome and Olympic Swimming Pool in Berlin, Germany (1993–98).

Dominique Perrault wurde 1953 in Clermont-Ferrand, Frankreich, geboren und erhielt 1978 sein Architektur-diplom von der École des Beaux-Arts UP 6 in Paris. 1979 erhielt er ein weiteres Diplom im Städtebau an der Pariser École nationale des Ponts et Chaussées. 1981 gründete er ein eigenes Büro in Paris. Zu seinen Arbeiten zählen die Ingenieurschule (ESIEE) in Marne-la-Vallée, Frankreich (1984–87), das Hôtel industriel Jean-Baptiste Berlier, Paris (1986–90), das Hôtel du département de la Meuse, Bar-le-Duc, Frankreich (1988–94), die Bibliothèque Nationale de France, Paris (1989–97), eine großangelegte städteplanerische Studie für Bordeaux, Frankreich (1992–2000) sowie die Rad- und Schwimmsporthallen in Berlin (1993–98).

Né en 1953 à Clermont-Ferrand (France), Dominique Perrault est diplômé en architecture de l'UP6 de l'École des Beaux Arts de Paris en 1978, et d'urbanisme de l'École nationale des Ponts et Chaussées (1979). Il crée son agence à Paris en 1981. Parmi ses travaux récents ou actuels: École d'Ingénieurs (ESIEE), Marne-la Vallée, France (1984-87); Hôtel industriel Jean-Baptiste Berlier, Paris (1986–90); Hôtel du département de la Meuse, Bar-le-Duc, France (1988–94); Bibliothèque Nationale de France, Paris (1989–97); projet d'urbanisme pour Bordeaux, France (1992–2000), vélodrome et piscine olympique, Berlin, Allemagne (1993–98).

Renzo Piano Building Workshop
34, rue des Archives
75004 Paris, France
Tel: + 33 1 44 61 49 00
Fax: + 33 1 42 78 01 98

Christian de Portzamparc
1, rue de l'Aude
75014 Paris, France
Tel: + 33 1 40 64 80 00
Fax: + 33 1 43 27 74 79

Bernard Tschumi Architects
227 West 17th Street
New York, NY 10011, USA
Tel: + 1 212 807 6340
Fax: + 1 212 242 3693

Renzo Piano

Born in 1937 in Genoa, Italy. Studied at University of Florence, and at Polytechnic Institute, Milan (1964). Formed own practice (Studio Piano) in 1965, then associated with Richard Rogers (Piano & Rogers, 1971–78). Completed Pompidou Center in Paris in 1977. From 1978 to 1980, Piano worked with Peter Rice (Piano & Rice Associates). Received RIBA Gold Medal, 1989. Created Renzo Piano Building Workshop in 1981 in Genoa and Paris. Built work includes: Menil Collection Museum, Houston, Texas (1981–86); San Nicola stadium, Bari, Italy (1987–90); extension for the IRCAM, Paris, and renovation of Lingotto complex Turin (both 1989); Kansai International Airport Terminal, Osaka, Japan (1988–94); Mercedes-Benz Center, Stuttgart, Germany (1992–96). Recent work includes: Cité Internationale de Lyon, Lyon, France (1985–96); Jean-Marie Tjibaou Cultural Center, New Caledonia (1994–98); and projects of the Potsdamer Platz in Berlin, Germany as well as the New Metropolis Science Center and Beyeler Foundation published here.

Geboren 1937 in Genua, Italien. Studium an der Universität Florenz und am Polytechnikum in Mailand (1964). Gründete 1965 ein eigenes Büro (Studio Piano), dann eine Bürogemeinschaft mit Richard Rogers (Piano & Rogers, 1971–78). 1977 Fertigstellung des Centre Pompidou in Paris. Von 1978–80 Zusammenarbeit mit Peter Rice (Piano & Rice Associates). 1989 wurde Piano die Goldmedaille des RIBA verliehen. 1981 Gründung des Renzo Piano Building Workshop in Genua und Paris. Zu seinen realisierten Projekten zählen: Menil Collection, Houston, Texas (1981–86); San Nicola-Stadion, Bari, Italien (1987–90); Erweiterung des IRCAM-Instituts in Paris und Umbau der Lingotto-Fabrik in Turin (beide 1989); Terminalgebäude des Flughafens Kansai, Osaka, Japan (1988–94); Mercedes-Benz Center, Stuttgart, Deutschland (1992–96). Zu Pianos jüngsten Arbeiten gehören: Cité Internationale de Lyon, Lyon, Frankreich (1985–96); Kulturzentrum Jean-Marie Tjibaou, Neukaledonien (1994–98); Projekte am Potsdamer Platz in Berlin sowie das hier vorgestellte Wissenschaftsmuseum New Metropolis und die Fondation Beyeler.

Né en 1937, à Gênes, Italie. Études à l'Université de Florence et au Politecnico de Milan (1964). Il crée sa propre agence, Studio Piano, en 1965, avant de s'associer à Richard Rogers (Piano & Rogers, 1971–78). Ensemble, ils construisent le Centre Pompidou, Paris (1971–77). De 1978 à 1980, Piano travaille avec Peter Rice (Piano & Rice Associates). Médaille d'or de la RIBA (1989). Crée Renzo Piano Building Workshop en 1981, à Gênes et à Paris. Parmi ses réalisations: Menil Collection Museum, Houston, Texas (1981–86); Stade San Nicola, Bari, Italie (1987–90); extension de l'IRCAM, Paris (1989); rénovation de l'usine du Lingotto, Turin, Italie (1989); terminal de l'aéroport international de Kansai, Osaka, Japon (1988–94); Centre Mercedes-Benz, Stuttgart, Allemagne (1992–96); la Cité Internationale, Lyon, France (1985–96); le Centre culturel Jean-Marie Tjibaou, Nouvelle Calédonie (1994–98); et des projets près de la Postdamer Platz (Berlin, Allemagne), ainsi que le New Metropolis et la Fondation Beyeler publiés dans ce livre.

Christian de Portzamparc

Born in Casablanca, Morocco, 1944. Studied at the École des Beaux-Arts, Paris (1962–69). Built projects include: Water tower, Marne-la-Vallée, France (1971–74); Hautes Formes public housing, Paris (1975–79); Cité de la Musique, Paris (1985–95); Extension for the Bourdelle Museum, Paris (1988–92); Housing, Nexus World, Fukuoka, Japan (1989–92); a Housing complex, ZAC Bercy, Paris (1991–94); Crédit Lyonnais Tower, Euralille, Lille, Frankreich (1992–95) built over the new Lille-Europe railway station in Lille. He was awarded the 1994 Pritzker Prize. Current work includes the LVMH Tower on 57th Street in New York, an addition to the Palais des Congrès in Paris, a tower for the Bandai toy company in Tokyo, a courthouse for Grasse in the south of France, and a new concert hall in Luxembourg, as well as the French Embassy in Berlin published here.

Geboren 1944 in Casablanca, Marokko. Studium an der École des Beaux-Arts in Paris (1962–69). Zu seinen realisierten Projekten gehören: Wasserturm in Marne-la-Vallée, Frankreich (1971–74); städtische Wohnanlage Hautes Formes in Paris (1975–79); Cité de la Musique, Paris (1985–95); Erweiterung des Bourdelle-Museums in Paris (1988–92); Wohnanlage für das Nexus World-Projekt, Fukuoka, Japan (1989–92); Wohnkomplex in der ZAC Bercy, Paris (1991–94), und ein Hochhaus für die Bank Crédit Lyonnais, Euralille, Lille, Frankreich (1992–95) über dem neuen Bahnhof Lille-Europe. Im Jahre 1994 wurde ihm der Pritzker-Preis verliehen. Zur Zeit arbeitet Portzamparc am LVMH-Hochhaus in der 57. Straße in New York, an einem Anbau zum Palais des Congrès in Paris, einem Hochhaus für den Spielwaren-hersteller Bandai in Tokio, einem Gerichtsgebäude im südfranzösischen Grasse, einer neuen Konzerthalle in Luxemburg sowie an dem hier vorgestellten Neubau der französischen Botschaft in Berlin, Deutschland.

Né à Casablanca au Maroc en 1944. Études à l'École des Beaux-Arts de Paris (1962–69). Parmi ses réalisations: château d'eau, Marne-la Vallée, France (1971–74); H.L.M. des Hautes-Formes, Paris (1975–79); Cité de la Musique, Paris (1985–95); extension du Musée Bourdelle, Paris (1988–92); immeuble d'appartements pour Nexus World, Fukuoka, Japon (1989–92); immeuble de logements ZAC Bercy, Paris (1991–94); tour du Crédit Lyonnais, Euralille, Lille, France (1992–95), édifiée au-dessus de la nouvelle gare Lille-Europe. Il a reçu le prix Pritzker en 1994. Projets actuels: tour LVMH, 57th Street à New York; transformation du Palais des Congrès à Paris; tour pour la société de jouets Bandaï à Tokyo; futur palais de justice de Grasse dans le Sud de la France; salle de concert à Luxembourg; ambassade de France à Berlin en Allemagne, publiée ici.

Bernard Tschumi

Born Lausanne, Switzerland, 1944. Studied in Paris and at Federal Institute of Technology (ETH), Zurich, Switzerland. Taught at the Architectural Association, London (1970–79), and at Princeton, New Jersey (1976–80). Dean, Graduate School of Architecture, Planning and Preservation, Columbia University, New York since 1984. Opened office, Bernard Tschumi Architects (Paris, New York), 1981. Major projects include: Parc de la Villette, Paris (1982–95); Second prize in the Kansai International Airport Competition, Japan (1988); Video Gallery, Groningen, The Netherlands (1990); Le Fresnoy National Studio for Contemporary Arts, Tourcoing, Frankreich (1991–97); Lerner Student Center, Columbia University, New York (1994–98); School of Architecture, Marne-la-Vallée, Frankreich (1994–99); and a railroad station in Lausanne, Switzerland, the Interface Flon (1998–2000).

Geboren 1944 in Lausanne. Studium in Paris und an der ETH Zürich. Lehrtätigkeit an der Architectural Association in London (1970–79) und in Princeton, New Jersey (1976–80). Seit 1984 Dekan der Graduate School of Architecture, Planning and Preservation der Columbia University in New York. 1981 Gründung des Büros Bernard Tschumi Architects mit Niederlassungen in Paris und New York. Wichtige Bauten und Projekte: Parc de la Villette, Paris (1982–95); Zweiter Preis im Wettbewerb für den Internationalen Flughafen Kansai, Japan (1988); Video-Galerie in Groningen, Niederlande (1990); Medien- und Kulturzentrum Le Fresnoy, Tourcoing, Frankreich (1991–97); Lerner Student Center, Columbia University, New York (1994–99); Hochschule für Architektur, Marne-la-Vallée, Frankreich (1994–98); Bahnhof Interface Flon in Lausanne, Schweiz (1998–2000).

Né à Lausanne (Suisse) en 1944. Études à Paris et à l'Institut Fédéral de Technologie (ETH) à Zurich. A enseigné à l'Architectural Association, Londres (1970–79), et à Princeton (1976–80). Doyen de la Graduate School of Architecture, Planning and Preservation, Université de Columbia, New York, depuis 1984. Ouvre son agence, Bernard Tschumi Architects (Paris, New York), en 1981. Principales réalisations: Parc de la Villette, Paris (1982–95); second prix au concours pour l'aéroport international de Kansai, Japon (1988); vidéo-galerie, Groningue, Pays-Bas (1990); Le Fresnoy, Studio national des Arts Contemporain, Tourcoing, France (1991–97); Lerner Student Center, Université de Columbia, New York (1994–99); école d'architecture, Marne-la-Vallée, France (1994–98); gare de chemin de fer Interface Flon, Lausanne, Suisse (1998–2000).

Bibliography | Bibliographie

Ambassade de France à Berlin. Ministère des Affaires Etrangères, Paris, 1997.

Barreneche, Raul: "It Takes a Village," *Architecture,* October 1997.

Buchanan, Peter: "Ship Shape," *Architecture,* September 1997.

Buchanan, Peter: *Renzo Piano Building Workshop, Complete Works, Volume Three.* Phaidon Press, London, 1997.

Johnson, Philip, and Mark Wigley: *Deconstructivist Architecture.* The Museum of Modern Art, New York, 1988.

Le Dantec, Jean-Pierre: *Christian de Portzamparc.* Éditions du Regard, Paris, 1995.

Oxenaar, Aart: *Jo Coenen.* Uitgeverij 010 Publishers, Rotterdam, 1994.

Dominique Perrault. Artemis, Zurich, 1994.

Pizzi, Emilio (editor): *Botta. The Complete Works, Volume 3, 1900–97.* Birkhäuser, Basel.

Rambert, Francis: "Berlin: Portzamparc sur la Pariser Platz," *Le Figaro,* May 29, 1997.

Riley, Terence: *Light Construction.* The Museum of Modern Art, New York, 1995.

Steele, James: *Architecture Today.* Phaidon Press, London, 1997.

Sudjic, Deyan: *Erick van Egeraat, Six Ideas About Architecture.* Birkhäuser, Basel, 1997.

Tschumi, Bernard: *Architecture In/Of Motion.* NAI Publishers, Rotterdam, 1997.

Woortman, Arthur: "Form, Function, Location – Renzo Piano, New Metropolis in Amsterdam," *Archis,* 1997.

Zumthor, Peter: *Three Concepts.* Architektur-galerie Luzern, Birkhäuser, Basel, 1997.

Index

Credits | Fotonachweis | Crédits photographiques

l. = left | links | à gauche
r. = right | rechts | à droite
t. = top | oben | en haut
c. = center | Mitte | center
b. = bottom | unten | en bas

2	© Bernard Tschumi Architects
7–13	© Photo: Christian Richters
14	© Photo: Ralph Richter/Architekturphoto
17	© Photo: Dieter Leistner/ARCHITEKTON
18	© Photo: Marco D'Anna
21	© Photo: Richard Bryant/Arcaid
22	© Photo: Christian Richters
25/26	© Photo: Friedrich Busam/Architekturphoto
28/31	© Bernard Tschumi Architects
32/35	© Photo: Christian Richters
37	© Photo: Klemens Ortmeyer/ Architekturphoto
38	© Photo: Ralph Richter/Architekturphoto
41/42	© Photo: Christian Richters
45	© Photo: Eric Morency
46/49	© Christian de Portzamparc
51	© Photo: Dieter Leistner/ARCHITEKTON
52–53	© Photo: Christian Richters
54–61	© Photo: Marco D'Anna
60 b.	© Mario Botta
61 t.	© Mario Botta
62	© Photo: Christian Richters
63	© Photo: Mario Pignata Monti
64/65 t.	© Chaix & Morel et Associés
65 b.	© Photo: Christian Richters
66–75	© Photo: Christian Richters
76	© Chaix & Morel et Associés
77–81	© Photo: Christian Richters
82	© Photo: Richard Bryant/Arcaid
83	© Photo: Morley von Sternberg
84	© David Chipperfield Architects
85/86	© Photo: Richard Bryant/Arcaid
87 t.	© David Chipperfield Architects
87 b.	© Photo: Richard Bryant/Arcaid
88/89	© Photo: Richard Bryant/Arcaid
88 c.	© David Chipperfield Architects
90	© Photo: Christian Richters
91	© Photo: Clea Betlem
92/93 t.	© Jo Coenen & Co
93 b.	© Photo: Christian Richters
94 l.	© Photo: Christian Richters
94 t.r.	© Photo: Christian Richters
94 b.r.	© Jo Coenen & Co
95–99	© Photo: Christian Richters
100	© EEA Rotterdam
101–105	© Photo: Christian Richters
106	© Photo: Ralph Richter/Architekturphoto
107	© Photo: Richard Davies
108	© Foster and Partners
109	© Photo: Ralph Richter/Architekturphoto
110 l.	© Foster and Partners
110–115	© Photo: Ralph Richter/Architekturphoto
116	© Photo: Dieter Leistner/ARCHITEKTON
117	© Photo: Peter Bonfig
118	© Herzog + Partner
119–123	© Photo: Dieter Leistner/ARCHITEKTON
124	© Photo: Friedrich Busam/Architekturphoto
125	© Photo: Christian Lund
126	© Søren Robert Lund Architects
127–133	© Photo: Friedrich Busam/Architekturphoto
132 t.l.	© Søren Robert Lund Architects
132 b.r.	© Søren Robert Lund Architects
133	© Photo: Friedrich Busam/Architekturphoto
134	© Photo: Klemens Ortmeyer/ Architekturphoto
135/137 t.	© Penkhues Architekten
137–141	© Photo: Klemens Ortmeyer/ Architekturphoto
142	© Photo: Christian Richters
143	© Photo: Georges Fessy
145–147	© Photo: Christian Richters
148 t.	© Dominique Perrault
148 b.	© Photo: Perrault Projects S.A.
149	© Photo: Christian Richters
150–151 t.	© Dominique Perrault
150–151 b.	© Photo: Christian Richters
152	© Photo: Ralph Richter/Architekturphoto
153	© Photo: Stefano Goldberg
154	© Renzo Piano Building Workshop
155 t.	© Photo: Christian Richters
155 b.–158	© Photo: Ralph Richter/Architekturphoto
159 t.	© Renzo Piano Building Workshop
159	© Photo: Christian Richters
160/161	© Photo: Ralph Richter/Architekturphoto
162	© Photo: Christian Richters
164–165 t.	© Renzo Piano Building Workshop
166 b.	© VG Bild-Kunst, Bonn 1998 (Alberto Giacometti: sculptures)
164/165 b.	© Photo: Christian Richters
166/167	© Photo: Michel Denancé/Archipress
168	© Christian de Portzamparc
169	© Photo: Francesca Mantouani
170–171	© Christian de Portzamparc
172	© Photo: Christian Richters
173	© Photo: Jean Strongin
174	© Bernard Tschumi Architects
175–177	© Photo: Christian Richters
178 l.	© Bernard Tschumi Architects
178–179	© Photo: Christian Richters
180	© Bernard Tschumi Architects
181	© Bernard Tschumi/Gruzen Samton
182–183	© Bernard Tschumi Architects